Actuarial and Financial Risks in Life Insurance, Pensions and Household Finance

Special Issue Editor

Luca Regis

MDPI • Basel • Beijing • Wuhan • Barcelona • Belgrade

Special Issue Editor
Luca Regis
University of Siena
Siena

Editorial Office
MDPI AG
St. Alban-Anlage 66
Basel, Switzerland

This edition is a reprint of the Special Issue published online in the open access journal *Risks* (ISSN 2227-9091) from 2016–2017 (available at: http://www.mdpi.com/journal/risks/special_issues/household_finance).

For citation purposes, cite each article independently as indicated on the article page online and as indicated below:

Lastname, F.M.; Lastname, F.M. Article title. *Journal Name*. **Year**. Article number, page range.

First Edition 2018

ISBN 978-3-03842-730-8 (Pbk)
ISBN 978-3-03842-729-2 (PDF)

Table of Contents

About the Special Issue Editor v

Luca Regis
Special Issue Actuarial and Financial Risks in Life Insurance, Pensions and Household Finance
doi: 10.3390/risks5040063 1

Kevin Dowd, David Blake and Andrew J. G. Cairns
The Myth of Methuselah and the Uncertainty of Death: The Mortality Fan Charts
doi: 10.3390/risks4030021 3

Gabriella Piscopo and Marina Resta
Applying Spectral Biclustering to Mortality Data
doi: 10.3390/risks5020024 10

Carlo Maccheroni and Samuel Nocito
Backtesting the Lee–Carter and the Cairns–Blake–Dowd Stochastic Mortality Models on Italian Death Rates
doi: 10.3390/risks5030034 23

Pierre Devolder and Sébastien de Valeriola
Minimum Protection in DC Funding Pension Plans and Margrabe Options
doi: 10.3390/risks5010005 46

Catherine Donnelly
A Discussion of a Risk-Sharing Pension Plan
doi: 10.3390/risks5010012 60

Thomas G. Koch
The Shifting Shape of Risk:
Endogenous Market Failure for Insurance
doi: 10.3390/risks5010009 80

Pierre Devolder and Adrien Lebègue
Compositions of Conditional Risk Measures and Solvency Capital
doi: 10.3390/risks4040049 93

Yuguang Fan , Philip S. Griffin, Ross Maller, Alex Szimayer and Tiandong Wang
The Effects of Largest Claim and Excess of Loss Reinsurance on a Company's Ruin Time and Valuation
doi: 10.3390/risks5010003 114

Jan Natolski and Ralf Werner
Mathematical Analysis of Replication by Cash Flow Matching
doi: 10.3390/risks5010013 141

About the Special Issue Editor

Luca Regis, Assistant Professor at the Department of Economics and Statistics of the University of Siena, has research interests that lie at the interface between financial and actuarial mathematics, and include corporate finance as well. In particular, he has recently been focusing on the modeling and management of longevity risk and on the capital and ownership structure choices of business groups.

risks

MDPI

Editorial

Special Issue "Actuarial and Financial Risks in Life Insurance, Pensions and Household Finance"

Luca Regis

Department of Economics and Statistics, University of Siena, Siena 53100, Italy; luca.regis@unisi.it

Received: 16 October 2017; Accepted: 28 November 2017; Published: 5 December 2017

The aim of the Special Issue is to address some of the main challenges individuals and companies face in managing financial and actuarial risks, when dealing with their investment/retirement or business-related decisions. We have received a large number of submissions, and ultimately published the nine high quality contributions that compose this issue. The papers address a variety of important issues, ranging from mortality modeling to risk management.

The paper by Kevin Dowd, David Blake and Andrew Cairns (Dowd et al. 2016), introduces mortality fan charts as a novel instrument to visualize the most likely forecasts of human mortality rates, together with their uncertainty. Their application to UK mortality data suggests that there are clear limits to mortality improvements: living as long as Methusalah, who according to the Bible reached the age of 969, is pure utopia.

Pierre Devolder and Adrièn Lebegue (Devolder and Lebègue 2016), in their contribution, study compositions of time-consistent dynamic risk measures, a crucial issue insurance companies have to tackle when computing their economic capital.

Yuguang Fan, Philip S. Griffin, Ross Maller, Alexander Szimayer and Tiandong Wang (Fan et al. 2017) carry out an extensive simulation-based study of the effects of two reinsurance policies, namely the Largest Claim and the Excess of Loss, on the ruin probability, ruin time and value of an insurance company under the classical compound Poisson risk model. Their exercise should help guide insurers in the design of their most appropriate reinsurance strategy.

The contribution by Pierre Devolder and Sébastien de Valeriola (Devolder and de Valeriola 2017) examines the two options that a new Belgian law offers to employers about the types of guarantees that the pension plans they offer to their employers should embed. Two different methodologies compare the alternatives. The paper highlights that the reform will most likely have the effect of changing the investment choices of pension plan funding vehicles.

Thomas Koch (Koch 2017) addresses theoretically the issue of adverse selection in insurance markets, and applies the theoretical framework to better understand the equilibrium in the market for insurance against medical risks in the U.S. The paper suggests that changes in insurance prices were the most important determinant of the changes in the demand for medical insurance.

The article by Catherine Donnelly (Donnelly 2017) deals with risk-sharing pension plans, that adjust the investment strategy and benefits to stabilize the funding ratio. The paper compares the theoretical performance of this type of plan vis-à-vis defined contribution plans, comparing the degrees of stability of the benefits provided to plan members.

The paper by Jan Natolski and Ralf Werner (Natolski and Werner 2017) gives a proper mathematical formulation to the replicating portfolio approach that insurance companies commonly utilize to compute risk capital under the Solvency II framework.

Gabriella Piscopo and Marina Resta (Piscopo and Resta 2017) propose an application of spectral bi-clustering to human mortality datasets. This technique can be a useful tool to guide mortality model selection, because, for instance, it may help identify the presence of cohort effects.

Finally, the paper by Carlo Maccheroni and Samuel Nocito (Maccheroni and Nocito 2017) provides a backtesting analysis of the performance of the two most known stochastic mortality models, the Lee-Carter and the Cairns-Blake and Dowd models, to Italian male and female mortality rates. The paper identifies when the use of one of the two models should be preferable.

All the papers went through the refereeing process subject to the high standard of Risks.

I am deeply thankful to all the referees who collaborated. Their contribution was invaluable. I would also like to express my gratitude to the editor of Risks, Mogens Steffensen, to the Assistant Editors, Shelly Liu and Jamie Li, and to MDPI for their support in the editorial process.

Finally, I would like to thank all of the authors who contributed; it is thanks to their excellent articles that I am particularly proud of the quality of this Special Issue.

Conflicts of Interest: The author declares no conflict of interest.

References

Devolder, Pierre, and Sébastien de Valeriola. 2017. Minimum Protection in DC Funding Pension Plans and Margrabe Options. *Risks* 5: 5. Available online: http://www.mdpi.com/2227-9091/5/1/5 (accessed on 1 December 2017). [CrossRef]

Devolder, Pierre, and Adrien Lebègue. 2016. Compositions of Conditional Risk Measures and Solvency Capital. *Risks* 4: 49. Available online: http://www.mdpi.com/2227-9091/4/4/49 (accessed on 1 December 2017). [CrossRef]

Donnelly, Catherine. 2017. A Discussion of a Risk-Sharing Pension Plan. *Risks* 5: 12. Available online: http://www.mdpi.com/2227-9091/5/1/12 (accessed on 1 December 2017). [CrossRef]

Dowd, Kevin, David Blake, and Andrew J. G. Cairns. 2016. The Myth of Methuselah and the Uncertainty of Death: The Mortality Fan Charts. *Risks* 4: 21. Available online: http://www.mdpi.com/2227-9091/4/3/21 (accessed on 1 December 2017). [CrossRef]

Fan, Yuguang, Philip S. Griffin, Ross Maller, Alexander Szimayer, and Tiandong Wang. 2017. The Effects of Largest Claim and Excess of Loss Reinsurance on a Company's Ruin Time and Valuation. *Risks* 5: 3. Available online: http://www.mdpi.com/2227-9091/5/1/3 (accessed on 1 December 2017). [CrossRef]

Koch, Thomas G. 2017. The Shifting Shape of Risk: Endogenous Market Failure for Insurance. *Risks* 5: 9. Available online: http://www.mdpi.com/2227-9091/5/1/9 (accessed on 1 December 2017). [CrossRef]

Maccheroni, Carlo, and Samuel Nocito. 2017. Backtesting the Lee-Carter and the Cairns-Blake-Dowd Stochastic Mortality Models on Italian Death Rates. *Risks* 5: 34. Available online: http://www.mdpi.com/2227-9091/5/3/34 (accessed on 1 December 2017). [CrossRef]

Natolski, Jan, and Ralf Werner. 2017. Mathematical Analysis of Replication by Cash Flow Matching. *Risks* 5: 13. Available online: http://www.mdpi.com/2227-9091/5/1/13 (accessed on 1 December 2017). [CrossRef]

Piscopo, Gabriella, and Marina Resta. 2017. Applying Spectral Biclustering to Mortality Data. *Risks* 5: 24. Available online: http://www.mdpi.com/2227-9091/5/2/24 (accessed on 1 December 2017). [CrossRef]

risks

MDPI

Article

The Myth of Methuselah and the Uncertainty of Death: The Mortality Fan Charts

Kevin Dowd [1,*], David Blake [2] and Andrew J. G. Cairns [3]

1 Durham University Business School, Millhill Lane, Durham DH1 3LB, UK
2 Pensions Institute, Cass Business School, 106 Bunhill Row, London EC1Y 8TZ, UK; d.blake@city.ac.uk
3 Actuarial Mathematics and Statistics, School of Mathematical and Computer Sciences, Heriot-Watt University, Edinburgh EH14 4AS, UK; a.j.g.cairns@hw.ac.uk
* Correspondence: kevin.dowd@outlook.com

Academic Editor: Luca Regis
Received: 11 May 2016; Accepted: 22 June 2016; Published: 4 July 2016

Abstract: This paper uses mortality fan charts to illustrate prospective future male mortality. These fan charts show both the most likely path of male mortality and the bands of uncertainty surrounding that path. The fan charts are based on a model of male mortality that is known to provide a good fit to UK mortality data. The fan charts suggest that there are clear limits to longevity—that future mortality rates are very uncertain and tend to become more uncertain the further ahead the forecast—and that forecasts of future mortality uncertainty must also take account of uncertainty in the parameters of the underlying mortality model.

Keywords: mortality; fan charts; longevity risk; parameter risk

1. Introduction

As every schoolchild knows, the oldest living man was Methuselah, the grandfather of Noah. Genesis tells us that he survived to the ripe old age of 969 years [1] and died in the same year as the Great Flood. The Sumerian literature goes even further: the Epic of Gilgamesh states that Utnapishtim, the Sumerian equivalent of Noah, was actually granted immortality as a gift from the gods. [2] By any comparison, the current generation of men living on this planet are weaklings, with only a few living to the measly age of 120.

Yet evidence has been growing over the last quarter century that the longevity of men in developed countries has been improving considerably. Demographers such as Vaupel et al. [1], Tuljapurkar et al. [2], Oeppen and Vaupel [3], and Tuljapurkar [4], argue that there is no natural upper limit to the length of human life and that we could be well on the way to living as long as Methuselah. The approach that these demographers use is based on an extrapolation of recent mortality trends. This approach has inevitably come in for criticism because it ignores factors relating to lifestyle and the environment that might influence future mortality trends. On the other hand, another group of demographers (e.g., Olshansky et al. [5–7], Mizuno et al. [8], and Loladze [9]) have suggested that future life expectancy might level off or even decline due to factors such as obesity and decreased food-derived health benefits associated with higher levels of atmospheric CO_2. But even demographers (e.g., de Grey [10]) critical of the extrapolative forecasting approach adopted by Vaupel still accept the possibility that scientific advances and the socio-political responses to them might lead to substantial increases in life expectancy over the next century.

1 Book of Genesis 5:27: 'And all the days of Methuselah were nine hundred sixty and nine years: and he died.'
2 Sandars ([11], p. 107).

This debate within the demography profession clearly indicates that there is considerable uncertainty about future trends in mortality. In this article we seek to contribute further to this debate by providing some new mortality projections based on a calibrated mortality model that is known to provide good fit to recent mortality data (Cairns et al. [12]). The calibrations are based on the mortality rates of UK males aged 65 and older. The actual projections take the form of mortality fan charts – these are charts showing some central projection (such as the median, mode or mean) of the forecasted mortality rate, surrounded by bounds showing the probabilities that future mortality will lie within specified ranges. Fan charts are ideal for showing not only the most likely future outcomes, but also the degree of quantitative uncertainty surrounding future mortality rates, and have been used with considerable success by the Bank of England in its efforts to promote public debate on UK monetary policy. [3]

2. Mortality Fan Charts

Figure 1 shows the mortality fan chart forecasts for males who were 65 years old in 2002. The fan charts are projected out to a horizon of 100 years, i.e., to 2102. The fan chart in the upper panel of the Figure assumes estimated parameters to be known, while that in the lower panel makes allowance for possible uncertainty in the parameters of the mortality model. For each fan chart, the highest and lowest bounds mark the 90% prediction interval over the forecast horizon (i.e., they suggest that we can be 90% confident that future mortality on any given date will lie between these bounds), the second highest and second lowest bounds mark the 80% prediction interval, and so forth, and the darkest bounds in the central regions of the fan charts represent the most likely mortality outcomes as predicted by the model. [4]

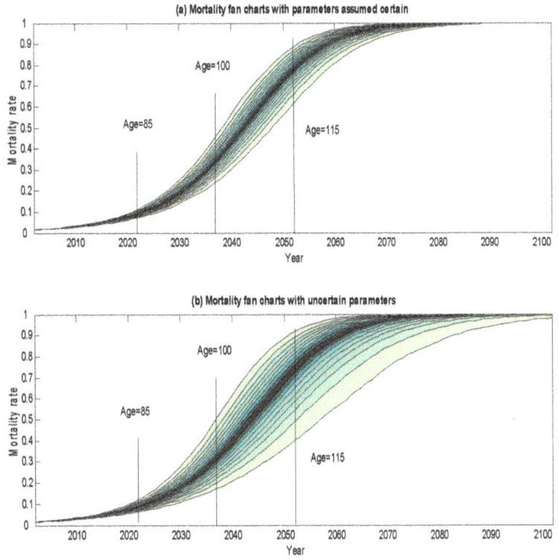

Figure 1. Mortality Fan Charts for Cohorts of Males Currently Aged 65 Years Old. Notes: The chart shows the central 10% prediction interval with the heaviest shading, surrounded by the 20%, 30%, . . . , 90% prediction intervals with progressively lighter shading. Estimated using 10,000 Monte Carlo simulation trials with the mortality model of Cairns et al. [12] calibrated on Government Actuary's Department (GAD) data over the period 1982–2002.

---

3 The first inflation fan chart was published by the Bank of England in 1996 (Bank of England [13]), and inflation fan charts have been published in each of the Bank's quarterly *Inflation Reports* ever since. Some longevity fan charts were published in King [14] and further mortality-related fan charts are shown in Blake et al. [15], Dowd et al. [16] and Li et al. [17].

4 Details of the calculations underlying the mortality fan charts are given in the Appendix A.

Both fan charts have an initial mortality rate of about 2% per annum, but mortality is projected to rise over the horizon period as the cohort ages and approach 1 for extreme old ages. At first sight, the mortality rates for very old ages might appear to be rather low and suggest that a small number of men might reach grand old ages of well over 115. However, the mortality rates in the Figure need to be interpreted against the likely survival probabilities implied by the model, and some illustrative survival probabilities are presented in Table 1. These show, for example, that a man aged 65 in 2002 has about a 2% probability of reaching 100, a 0.2% probability of reaching 105, and an almost negligible probability of reaching 110. Furthermore, even if he reaches 100, his probability of reaching 115 is negligible. This means that the post-115 mortality rates in the Figure are essentially conjectural, as almost no-one will reach those ages. According to these results, the probability of anyone getting to grand old ages like 130 is essentially zero: sadly, Methusalah is a myth.

Table 1. Projected Survival Probabilities.

	Probability Assuming:	
Survival to Age	**Parameters Certain**	**Parameters Uncertain**
Survival Probabilities for Males Aged 65 in 2002 (%)		
70	90.77	90.78
75	78.42	78.49
80	62.52	62.75
85	43.61	44.19
90	24.34	25.25
95	9.33	10.23
100	1.92	2.37
105	0.15	0.23
110	0.00	0.01
Survival Probabilities for Males Aged 65 in 2002, Conditional on Reaching 85 (%)		
90	55.81	57.13
95	21.39	23.16
100	4.40	5.37
105	0.34	0.52
110	0.01	0.01
115	0.00	0.00
Survival Probabilities for Males Aged 65 in 2002, Conditional on Reaching 100 (%)		
105	7.66	9.64
110	0.13	0.25
115	0.00	0.00

Notes: Projected survival probabilities are calculated as the median projections using the model and parameter values in the notes to Figure 1. All probabilities are rounded to two decimal places.

The widths of the fan chart intervals in Figure 1 show that our mortality projections are very uncertain, and over the range of empirically plausible ages this uncertainty increases as the forecast horizon gets longer.

A comparison of the two fan charts also shows that the fan chart that takes account of parameter uncertainty is much wider than the one that assumes parameters to be known with certainty [5]—and, since we do not actually know the true values of the parameters, we would suggest the parameter-uncertainty estimates are likely to be more reliable. As a rough order of magnitude, the gap between the lowermost and uppermost bounds of the parameter uncertainty fan chart is close to twice that of its parameter certainty counterpart. If we take this gap as a rough indicator of our uncertainty about future mortality, we can therefore say that taking account of parameter uncertainty leads our

[5] The principal reason for this increased width is uncertainty in the underlying trend rather than in the volatility of mortality rates. As the time horizon increases, uncertainty in the trend dominates all other sources of risk in influencing the width of the lower side fan chart.

estimates of mortality uncertainty to nearly double. We can also see that parameter uncertainty has a very skewed effect on the fan chart prediction intervals, and pushes the lower bounds down very considerably whilst pushing the upper bounds up only slightly. Thus, taking account of parameter uncertainty significantly decreases the projected mortality rates of the 'luckier' members of the cohort, namely those who live longer than implied by the cohort's generational life table.

To give some indication of the quantitative magnitudes involved, the more reliable parameter-uncertain (i.e., lower) fan chart suggests that we can be 90% confident that the mortality rate of survivors from this cohort will lie (roughly) between 6% and 11% by the time they reach 85, will lie (roughly) between 17% and 53% by the time they reach 100, and will lie (roughly) between 40% and 90% for any who reach 115.

Figure 2 gives the comparable fan charts for the cohort of males aged 75 in 2002. As we would expect, these fan charts start out from a higher base mortality rate (of about 4% per annum) and involve higher mortality rate projections than for the 65-year olds. The broad shapes of the fan charts are similar to those of the earlier fan charts, and we again find that the fan charts are quite broad and (except for implausibly extreme old ages) tend to widen as the horizon lengthens. As before, we also find that the parameter-uncertain fan chart has nearly twice the dispersion of the parameter-certain fan chart, and that the impact of parameter uncertainty is to push the lower bounds well down and to push the upper bounds only slightly up.

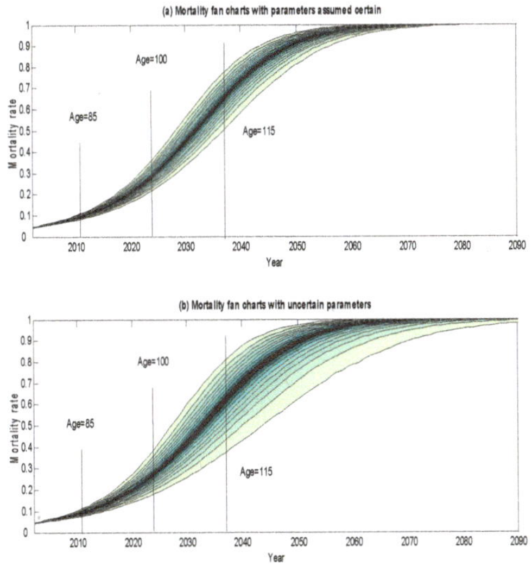

Figure 2. Mortality Fan Charts for Cohorts of Males Currently Aged 75 Years Old. Notes: As per Figure 1.

To illustrate the quantitative magnitudes, the parameter-uncertain fan chart suggests that we can be 90% confident that the mortality rate of survivors from this cohort will lie (roughly) between 8% and 13% by the time they reach 85, will lie (roughly) between 23% and 48% by the time they reach 100, and will lie (roughly) between 49% and 92% for any who reach 115.

Figure 3 gives the fan charts for males aged 85 in 2002. These are also in line with what we would expect: the fan charts start at a higher base mortality rate (about 12%), involve higher mortality projections and indicate considerable uncertainty which rises with the horizon period for any plausible ages. As before, parameter uncertainty makes the fan charts nearly twice as wide and pushes the lower bounds considerably downwards whilst pushing the upper bounds only slightly up. In this case, we can be approximately 90% confident that the mortality rate for survivors of this cohort who reach 100 will lie between 27% and 48%, and that the mortality rate of any who reach 115 will lie between 53% and 89%.

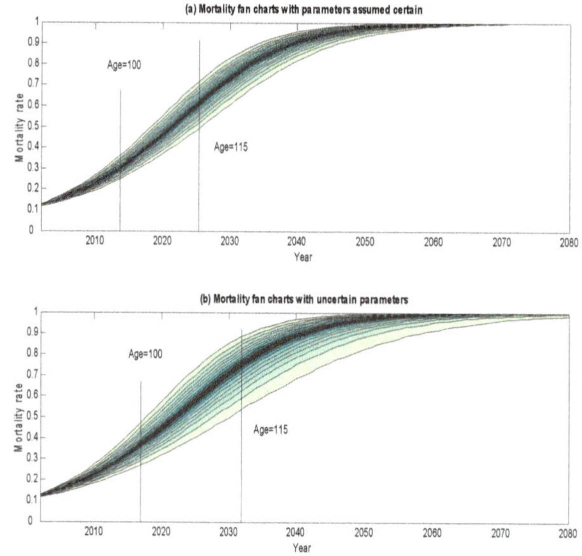

Figure 3. Mortality Fan Charts for Cohorts of Males Currently Aged 85 Years Old. Notes: As per Figure 1.

Finally, Figure 4 shows the 90% prediction bounds for all three cohorts derived from the parameter-uncertain fan charts of the previous three Figures. The bounds for the older cohorts are higher and tend to be wider than those for younger cohorts. To illustrate numerically, it takes a horizon of about 25 years before the width of the prediction bounds of the youngest cohort widens to 10%, but it takes about 15 years for the middle cohort and only 10 for the oldest one. The Figure also shows how the bounds become very wide as we go 30 to 40 years out, and then start to narrow again for extreme old ages. Leaving aside extreme ages, we can conclude that mortality rates are very uncertain, and become even more uncertain for older cohorts.

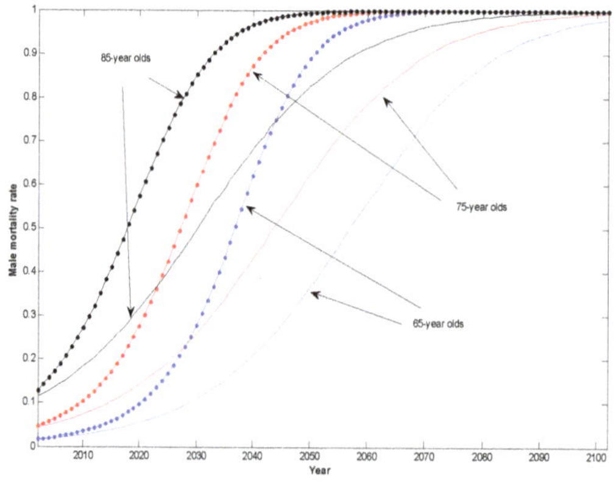

Figure 4. 90% Prediction Bounds for Male Mortality Rates. Notes: As per the uncertain-parameter fan chart in Figure 1.

3. Conclusions

The mortality fan charts presented here are a useful way of forecasting future mortality rates. They also quantify the uncertainty in our mortality projections and provide an intuitively revealing way of visually representing that uncertainty: put simply, the wider the fan charts, the more uncertainty there is. They are also quantitatively plausible, in so far as they are based on an underlying mortality model that is known to provide a good fit to the data, and because these data reflect recent mortality improvements.

Our fan charts suggest three main findings. First and foremost, despite recent mortality improvements, the fan chart projections suggest that no-one will live to the very extreme old ages that have sometimes been suggested in the more 'optimistic' literature on likely future longevity. According to these results, the idea that anyone will live to the ages reported for any of the unnaturally long-lived Patriarchs in Genesis—let alone Methusalah—is a pipe dream. Second, the fan charts clearly show that future mortality rates are highly uncertain and become more uncertain as the forecast horizon increases. They also show that future mortality rates for older cohorts are more uncertain than those for younger cohorts, other things being equal. Mortality rates are difficult to predict, especially for older cohorts, and this is so even though the mortality model provides a close fit to recent historical data: one is reminded of the old quip that forecasting is a difficult business, especially forecasting the future. Finally, the fan charts show that allowing for parameter uncertainty has a very major impact in widening the dispersion of estimated fan charts: as a rough rule of thumb, we found that allowing for uncertain parameters nearly doubles the dispersion of our fan charts. Failing to allow for parameter uncertainty therefore leads to fan chart forecasts that are far too narrow and that have lower bounds with a significant upwards bias. If we wish to reliably forecast the uncertainty in future mortality, we must therefore take account of the uncertainty in our parameter estimates as well. [6]

These findings have obvious and disturbing implications for those providing services to the elderly such as health and long-term care or pensions. If people are living longer than previously anticipated, then provision needs to be made for more services for the elderly and pensioners will be drawing pensions for longer than expected. Someone then has to bear the resulting higher costs. In addition, since future mortality is very uncertain, the fan charts also suggest that the healthcare system, pension funds, life companies and, indeed, the state itself, are all heavily exposed to longevity risk, and their exposure to this risk needs to be managed.

Author Contributions: KD and AJGC wrote the underlying software; all authors contributed to writing the paper.

Conflicts of Interest: The authors declare no conflict of interest.

Appendix A Mortality Model

The mortality fan charts discussed in this paper are based on an underlying mortality model set out by Cairns et al. [12]. Let $q(t, x)$ be the realized mortality rate in year $t + 1$ (that is, from time t to time $t + 1$) of a cohort aged x at time 0. We assume that $q(t, x)$ is governed by the following two-factor Perks stochastic process:

$$q(t,x) = \frac{\exp\left[A_1(t+1) + A_2(t+1)(t+x)\right]}{1+\exp\left[A_1(t+1) + A_2(t+1)(t+x)\right]} \tag{A1}$$

where $A_1(t + 1)$ and $A_2(t + 1)$ are themselves stochastic processes that are measurable at time $t + 1$ (see Perks [18], Benjamin and Pollard [19]). Now let $A(t) = (A_1(t), A_2(t))$ and assume that $A(t)$ is a random walk with drift:

$$A(t+1) = A(t) + \mu + CZ(t+1) \tag{A2}$$

[6] Of course, in interpreting the fan chart forecasts, we also need to be on our guard against possible biases in the model. (1) The mortality forecasts have a possible upward bias, in so far as they do not take account of future improvements to medical science (e.g., miracle cures of major illnesses) that we cannot predict; (2) On the other hand, the forecasts have a possible downward bias in that they ignore important factors such as the impact of obesity that threaten to increase future mortality but have not yet fed through into the mortality data on which our model is calibrated. Readers who have strong views on these issues might wish to take them into account in interpreting the fan charts.

where μ is a constant 2 × 1 vector of drift parameters, C is a constant 2 × 2 lower triangular Choleski square root matrix of the covariance matrix V, and $Z(t)$ is a 2 × 1 vector of independent standard normal variables. Cairns et al. (2006) show that this model provides a good fit to UK Government Actuary's Department (GAD) data for English and Welsh males over 1961–2002. For each set of parameter values, we simulated 10,000 paths of $A_1(t+1)$ and $A_2(t+1)$, and then used these in Equation (A1) to obtain 10,000 simulated paths of $q(t, x)$ over a chosen horizon. For each given t, the quantiles of $q(t, x)$ were then obtained from the relevant order statistics of our 'sample' of $q(t, x)$ values. These quantiles give us the bounds of the fan chart intervals.

References

1. Vaupel, J.; Carey, J.; Christensen, K.; Johnson, T.; Yashin, A.; Holm, V.; Iachine, I.; Kannisto, V.; Khazaeli, A.; Liedo, P.; et al. Biodemographic Trajectories of Longevity. *Science* **1998**, *280*, 855–860. [CrossRef] [PubMed]
2. Tuljapurkar, S.; Li, N.; Boe, C. A Universal Pattern of Mortality Decline in the G7 Countries. *Nature* **2000**, *405*, 789–792. [CrossRef] [PubMed]
3. Oeppen, J.; Vaupel, J.W. Broken Limits of Life Expectancy. *Science* **2002**, *296*, 1029–1031. [CrossRef] [PubMed]
4. Tuljapurkar, S. Future Mortality: A Bumpy Road to Shangri-La? *Sci. Aging Knowl. Environ.* **2005**, *2005*. [CrossRef] [PubMed]
5. Olshansky, S.J.; Carnes, B.A.; Cassel, C. In Search of Methuselah: Estimating the Upper Limits to Human Longevity. *Science* **1990**, *250*, 634–640. [CrossRef] [PubMed]
6. Olshansky, S.J.; Carnes, B.A.; Désesquelles, A. Prospects for Human Longevity. *Science* **2001**, *291*, 1491–1492. [CrossRef] [PubMed]
7. Olshansky, S.J.; Passaro, D.; Hershow, R.; Layden, J.; Carnes, B.A.; Brody, J.; Hayflick, L.; Butler, R.N.; Allison, D.B.; Ludwig, D.S. A Potential Decline in Life Expectancy in the United States in the 21st Century. *N. Engl. J. Med.* **2005**, *352*, 1103–1110. [CrossRef] [PubMed]
8. Mizuno, T.; Shu, I.-W.; Makimura, H.; Mobbs, C. Obesity Over the Life Course. *Sci. Aging Knowl. Environ.* **2004**, *2004*. [CrossRef]
9. Loladze, I. Rising Atmospheric CO_2 and Human Nutrition: Toward Globally Imbalanced Plant Stoichiometry? *Trends Ecol. Evolut.* **2002**, *17*, 457–461. [CrossRef]
10. De Grey, A.D.N.J. Extrapolaholics Anonymous: Why Demographers' Rejections of a Huge Rise in Cohort Life Expectancy in This Century are Overconfident. *Ann. N. Y. Acad. Sci.* **2006**, *1067*, 83–93. [CrossRef] [PubMed]
11. Sandars, N.K. *The Epic of Gilgamesh: An English Version with an Introduction*, 3rd ed.; Penguin: Harmondsworth, Middlesex, UK, 1972.
12. Cairns, A.J.G.; Blake, D.; Dowd, K. A Two-Factor Model for Stochastic Mortality with Parameter Uncertainty: Theory and Calibration. *J. Risk Insur.* **2006**, *73*, 687–718. [CrossRef]
13. Bank of England. *Inflation Report*; Bank of England: London, UK, 1996.
14. King, M.A. *What Fates Impose: Facing up to Uncertainty?*; The British Academy: London, UK, 2004.
15. Blake, D.; Cairns, A.J.G.; Dowd, K. Longevity Risk and the Grim Reaper's Toxic Tail: The Survivor Fan Charts. *Insur. Math. Econ.* **2008**, *42*, 1062–1066. [CrossRef]
16. Dowd, K.; Blake, D.; Cairns, A.J.G. Facing up to Uncertain Life Expectancy: The Longevity Fan Charts. *Demography* **2010**, *47*, 67–78. [CrossRef] [PubMed]
17. Li, J.S.H.; Ng, A.C.Y.; Chan, W.S. Stochastic Life Table Forecasting: A Time-Simultaneous Fan Chart Application. *Math. Comput. Simul.* **2013**, *93*, 98–107. [CrossRef]
18. Perks, W. On Some Experiments in the Graduation of Mortality Statistics. *J. Inst. Actuar.* **1932**, *63*, 12–57.
19. Benjamin, B.; Pollard, J.H. *The Analysis of Mortality and Other Actuarial Statistics*, 3rd ed.; Institute of Actuaries: London, UK, 1993.

risks

MDPI

Article

Applying Spectral Biclustering to Mortality Data

Gabriella Piscopo * and Marina Resta

DIEC, University of Genova, 16126 Genova, Italy; resta@economia.unige.it
* Correspondence: piscopo@economia.unige.it; Tel.: +39-010-2095008

Academic Editor: Luca Regis
Received: 6 October 2016; Accepted: 29 March 2017; Published: 4 April 2017

Abstract: We apply spectral biclustering to mortality datasets in order to capture three relevant aspects: the period, the age and the cohort effects, as their knowledge is a key factor in understanding actuarial liabilities of private life insurance companies, pension funds as well as national pension systems. While standard techniques generally fail to capture the cohort effect, on the contrary, biclustering methods seem particularly suitable for this aim. We run an exploratory analysis on the mortality data of Italy, with ages representing genes, and years as conditions: by comparison between conventional hierarchical clustering and spectral biclustering, we observe that the latter offers more meaningful results.

Keywords: mortality data; biclustering; cohort effect

---

1. Introduction

During the last decade, the analysis of mortality datasets has been deepened by actuaries and statisticians. The growing attention devoted to mortality investigation is due to the financial impact on actuarial liabilities of private life insurance companies, pension funds and national pension systems: as a matter of fact, monthly pension payments are generally based on remaining life expectancy at retirement; the accurate modeling and projection of mortality rates and life expectancy are therefore of growing interest to researchers. In this respect, it makes sense to monitor how much longevity improvements are sizeable: it has been noted that, in the past century survival, probabilities have increased for each age group, even though with some undeniable differences.

As mortality forecasts have become increasingly important, various parametric models have been proposed to describe mortality patterns and produce predictions: in the actuarial literature and practice, the well-known Lee-Carter (LC) model [1] extrapolates the trends of mortality and describes the secular change in longevity as a function of three determinants: the overall time trend, the age component, and the extent of change over time by age. Let us introduce the matrix M = {log $m_{x,t}$} of log-mortality data for the age x at time t in more detail: x is an integer number in the range [0, 120], and t an integer representing the year of observation (to make an example: $m_{58,2001}$ is the log-mortality rate recorded in 2001 for individuals 58 years old), so that M has 121 rows and a number of columns depending on the overall number of years for which log-mortality data are available. The model seeks to summarize an age-period surface of log–mortality rates in terms of the vectors **a** and **b** along the age dimension, and **k** along the time dimension: $\log m_{x,t} = a_x + b_x k_t + \varepsilon_{x,t}$, for every $x \in [0, 120]$, and for every t, with restrictions such that the "b"s are normalized to sum to one, the "k"s sum to zero, and the "a"s are average log rates. The vector **a** can be interpreted as an average age profile, tracking mortality changes over time; the vector **b** determines how much each age group changes when k_t changes. Finally, the error term $\varepsilon_{x,t}$ reflects age-period effects eventually not captured by the model. In the basic model, the fit to historical data is made through the Singular Value Decomposition (SVD) [2] of M, and then the time-varying parameter is modeled and forecasted as an ARIMA process using standard Box-Jenkins methodology.

As per [3], the diffusion of the LC model is mainly due to its capability to generate realistic life expectancy forecasts; moreover, many developments of the LC method have been suggested (see [4,5]). Furthermore, in the last decade, several authors have proposed approaches to mortality fitting based on smoothing procedures [6,7]; finally, [8] shows a version of the Lee–Carter methodology, the so-called Functional Demographic Model, based on the combination of smoothing techniques and functional data analysis.

More recently, authors have focused attention on mortality patterns of particular generations: increased focus on the size of pension-scheme deficits, in fact, led actuaries to know more about the possible trends in future life span [9]: to such aim, some studies compare the relative influence of both the year of birth and the year of observation, and [10] introduced a variation on the LC model in order to capture the so-called cohort effect, which occurs when a particular generation exhibits patterns of mortality improvements different to those of previous generations. The LC can model the age-period effects; nevertheless, it does not consider the cohort effects, as the analysis of UK data confirms [11]. As a matter of fact, the LC age-period model does not always fit empirical data well (see, for example, [12]), while incorporating the cohort effect into the model sensitively improves the results of the fitting, as well as the comprehension of the mortality evolution. Finally, in the most recent years, a different approach is being experimented to consider the instances and issues highlighted in previous rows; it is based on clustering techniques that are employed to improve the estimation of mortality rates and the cohort effect [13]; in addition, a few number of contributions applied fuzzy logic techniques in mortality projection [14,15]. In particular, [15] applied fuzzy logic to mortality datasets of different countries, capturing the main time effect of the Lee-Carter model for each country.

With respect to the cited literature, our work fits into different research streams, as it extends the application of biclustering techniques, already widely employed to classify gene expression matrices, to the problem of exploring mortality patterns, and it has contact points with the actuarial research strand focused on pattern recognition towards the path already opened by [13]. While, in general, the aim of clustering in genomics is to find gene similarities across all given conditions, in the mortality context, we may assume that the genes are represented by ages and the conditions by years. In the physical world, as with mortality datasets, however, a group of genes often shows similar behavior across just some of the conditions and different properties when looking at others; in these cases, the simple clustering approach is unsuitable for describing the specific patterns in the data. To overcome this limitation, biclustering approaches have been introduced to capture specific patterns in the data even if genes behave similarly over just a subset of conditions ([16–18], see also: [19] for a survey). Considering this, as well as the peculiar structure of mortality datasets, we follow the recent actuarial literature on pattern recognition and enhance the clustering approach with the novel introduction of biclustering to analyze mortality data.

In practice, while clusters correspond to disjoint strips in the data matrix, biclusters correspond to arbitrary subsets of rows and columns. To this extent, the notion of bicluster gives rise to a more flexible computational framework. A bicluster can be defined as a submatrix spanned by a set of genes and a set of samples or equivalently, in our case, as the corresponding age and year subsets. Given a mortality matrix, we can therefore characterize the features it embodies by a collection of biclusters, each representing a different type of joint behaviour of a set of ages in a corresponding set of years, without any a priori constraints on the organization of biclusters. The biclustering problem consists then in finding a set of significant biclusters in the data matrix.

Keeping in mind what was stated in previous rows, using biclustering on mortality data should make it possible to identify structural changes in the mortality trend, avoiding the estimation of terms specifically designed to incorporate cohort effects, but rather letting the features of data emerge from the analysis in quite a natural and intuitive way, as we will explain in the section of the paper devoted to describe the methodology. This, in turn, might help to develop more tailored models of mortality forecasting, providing a possibility to compare cohort effects among different countries or groups.

The paper is organized as follows: Section 2 briefly recalls the notions of biclustering and spectral biclustering; Section 3 applies spectral biclustering on a mortality dataset: some numerical results and comments are presented; and final remarks are offered in Section 4.

2. Methodological Aspects of Spectral Biclustering

2.1. Biclustering

The goal of clustering is to partition the elements into sets (clusters), while trying to both optimize groups homogeneity (i.e., elements of a cluster should be highly similar to each other), and group separation, which is to say: elements from different clusters should have low similarity to each other. Clustering may be a very powerful tool to automatically detect relevant sub–groups when one does not have prior knowledge about the hidden structure of these data. However, an important issue related to clustering techniques was firstly investigated in the past decade while identifying local patterns in gene expression data: it was highlighted that cluster analysis makes several a priori assumptions [16] that may not be perfectly adequate in all circumstances. As a matter of fact, clustering can be applied to either genes or samples, implicitly directing the analysis to a peculiar aspect of the system under study; in addition, clustering algorithms usually seek a disjoint cover of the set of elements, requiring that no gene or sample belongs to more than one cluster.

The notion of bicluster then gave rise to a more flexible computational framework. Given a gene expression matrix, we can characterize the biological phenomena that it embodies by a collection of biclusters, each representing a different type of joint behavior of a set of genes in a corresponding set of samples. Moreover, as clustering can be separately applied to either the rows or the columns of the data matrix; biclustering, on the other hand, performs clustering in these two dimensions simultaneously. This, in turn, means that while clustering derives a global model, biclustering produces a local model [19]: likewise, in genomics, this aspect is of importance within the mortality context because of the interest of actuaries for age-specific mortality patterns.

As already mentioned in Section 1, in fact, scholars are intended to capture three relevant aspects: the period, the age and the cohort effects, as their knowledge is a key factor in understanding actuarial liabilities of private life insurance companies, pension funds and national pension systems.

2.2. Spectral Biclustering

Following the work of [16], biclustering has quickly become popular in analyzing gene expression data and various biclustering algorithms have been proposed [17–26]. Since each algorithm focuses on identification of different bicluster patterns, it is a very challenging task to thoroughly evaluate these algorithms.

The rationale inside the spectral biclustering method [27] is that checkerboard structures may emerge in matrices of expression data once they have been properly arranged using a linear algebra approach, by means of the Singular Value Decomposition (SVD). Using SVD, the data matrix D of dimensions $N \times M$ can be decomposed as $D = U\Lambda V^T$, where Λ is a diagonal matrix with decreasing non-negative entries, and U and V are orthonormal column matrices with dimensions $N \times min(N,M)$ and $M \times min(N,M)$, respectively. If the data matrix has a block diagonal structure (with all elements outside the blocks equal to zero), then each block can be associated with a bicluster. Specifically, if the data matrix is of the form:

$$D = \begin{bmatrix} D_1 & 0 & \dots & 0 \\ 0 & D_2 & \dots & 0 \\ \vdots & \vdots & \ddots & \vdots \\ 0 & 0 & \dots & D_k \end{bmatrix} \quad (1)$$

where D_i ($i = 1, \dots, k$) are arbitrary matrices, then, for each D_i, there will be a singular vector pair (u_i, v_i) such that a nonzero component of u_i corresponds to rows occupied by D_i, and a nonzero component of v_i corresponds to columns occupied by D_i.

In a less idealized case, when the elements outside the diagonal blocks are not necessarily zeros but the diagonal blocks still contain dominating values, the SVD can reveal the biclusters as dominating components in the singular vector pairs.

Box 1 illustrates the algorithmic details of the procedure, as reported in [27].

Box 1. Spectral biclustering: the algorithm.

U: conditions; V: genes
$D_{N\times M}$: gene expression matrix.
Compute $R = \mathrm{diag}(D\cdot\mathbf{1}_M)$ and $C = \mathrm{diag}(\mathbf{1}_M{}^T D)$
Compute SVD of $R^{-1/2}\, D\, C^{-1/2}$
Discard the pair of eigenvectors corresponding to the largest eigenvalue
For each pair of eigenvectors u,v of $R^{-1}DC^{-1}D^T$ and $C^{-1}D^TR^{-1}D$ with the same eigenvalue do:
    Apply K-means to check the fit of u and v to stepwise vectors
    Report the block structure for the p couples u, v with the best stepwise fit.

In our case, the choice of the biclustering method was suggested by the analogies existing between spectral biclustering and the Singular Value Decomposition on which the Lee–Carter method [1]—LCm—is based.

Furthermore, the starting point of the introduction of biclustering method in mortality context is to design a clustering approach suitable for the kind of data we are working on. Most biclustering algorithms, in fact, are apt to binary data only, and, therefore, they are not appropriate for mortality rates. Instead, spectral biclustering appears suitable for death rates matrix because it finds the checkerboard structure in data through the extraction of significant eigenvectors using the SVD associated to some normalization steps; this approach is also in line with the most used approach for fitting mortality data, the LCm, based on the SVD of the mortality matrix. Moreover, the normalization step reduces the effects of random differences in experimental conditions and levels of genes, and it is useful to highlight biclusters, if a structure exists. Finally, as a common practice in biclustering analysis is transforming the data by taking logarithms, we believe the log-normalization is appropriate in a mortality context because two or more ages are experiencing the same evolution if their mortality profiles are constantly proportional, and the log-transformation is not affected by an additive constant.

3. Discussion Case

The structural description of mortality table constitutes the base to understand mortality patterns and to derive an opportune mortality model to fit and project historical data; our research aims to identify every demographic feature in mortality data, capturing both the so-called period and age effects: the former is related to the evolution of life expectancy during the years, the latter to the differences of mortality across ages. Recently, demographers and actuaries have focused their attention on a third effect, the so-called cohort effect, looking for generations that show particular mortality patterns. Without an ex-ante investigation of the structure of data, the demographical models are often worsened with cohort parameters to capture generational effect, while the interaction of age–time effects in the data structure could be misunderstood and, for example, wrongly attributed to the cohort effect. For this reason, a preliminary investigation of data becomes useful to design a parsimonious mortality model.

While the microarray technology is a central tool in biological studies, it is an unexplored field in demographic context, where the identification of individuals with similar mortality patterns represents a key step in the analysis of life tables. However, traditional clustering algorithms, like the hierarchical one, organize the mortality matrix into submatrices assuming that all genes behave similarly in groups of conditions, but it would be unreasonable in the mortality context.

The biclustering methods are useful to find meaningful checkerboard patterns in matrices where data represent marker genes expressed under a particular set of conditions; they permit simultaneously clustering genes and conditions. In the mortality datasets, the genes are represented by ages and the conditions by years: we observe how the mortality for individuals aged differently has changed under different conditions, i.e., as time changes.

The aim of biclustering is therefore to highlight groups of mortality rates in which ages are clustered together if they exhibit similar patterns across years and, likewise, years are clustered together if they include ages whose mortality has shown a similar evolution. In this way, it is possible to discover homogeneous submatrices that are relevant for understanding mortality evolution in social and actuarial studies.

3.1. *Demographical Settings and Notational Conventions*

In the context of mortality data, demographers and actuaries work on life tables. A life table is a finite decreasing sequence $l_0, l_1, \dots, l\omega$ where l_x refers to an integer age x and represents the estimated number of people alive at x in a given population composed by l_0 individuals aged 0 at inception; note that ω commonly indicates the so-called extreme age, representing the age at which it occurs: $l\omega = 0$: for sake of convenience, we can assume $\omega = 120$. A cohort table is obtained if the sequence l_0, $l_1, \dots, l\omega$ is the longitudinal observation of the actual numbers of individuals alive at ages 1, 2, . . . , ω out of a given initial cohort of l_0 newborns. If we consider an existing population and observe the frequency of death at different ages in a given period, for example, one year, then we obtain the period table. Finally, $M = \{\log m_{ij}\}$ is usually employed to denote the matrix of death rates of a particular population, where the data are organized in rows by age, and in columns by years, so that $m_{i,j}$ is the mortality rate at the age i ($i = 0, \dots, \omega$) in the year j.

3.2. *Empirical Results*

In our case study, we considered the death rates of the whole (male and female) Italian population; the data were downloaded from the Human Mortality Database [1] (HMD). The genes are represented by ages collected between 40 and 60, and the conditions by the years between 1950 and 2006. We focus on the ages in the range [40, 60] because those ages are the most important in pensions and actuarial product design.

We applied to data both the hierarchical Euclidean clustering (whose algorithm is provided in Appendix A, at the end of the paper) and the spectral biclustering, already explained in Box 1 of Section 2, and visualized the results through heatmaps.

The first step of our analysis consists in grouping the data through a Euclidean hierarchical cluster method; we applied the algorithm to the columns and rows of death rates matrix separately, and Figures 1 and 2 show the corresponding heat maps.

Clustering performs data in one dimension at a time, so each gene in a given gene cluster is defined using all the conditions, and, similarly, each condition in a condition cluster is characterized by the activity of all the genes that belong to it. From a graphical point of view, this produces vertical regions that appear in Figures 1 and 2, where the period effect and the age effect become visible: moving from yellow regions to red regions, the mortality decreases during years and increases across ages. We also highlight the presence of the cohort effect, as some generations have experienced specific mortality patterns differently from others. If the cohort effect is present, a kind of "ladder" appears in the heatmap: genes aged x in t, $x + 1$ in $t + 1$, and so on are grouped in the same cluster and are represented with the same color shade in the heatmap.

---

1 http://www.mortality.org.

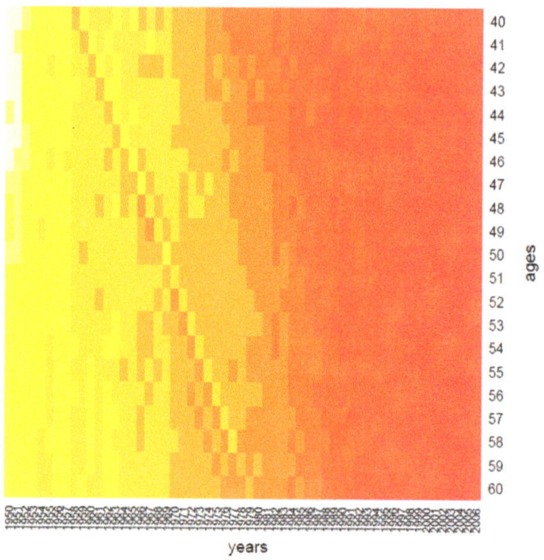

Figure 1. Clustering: the period effect.

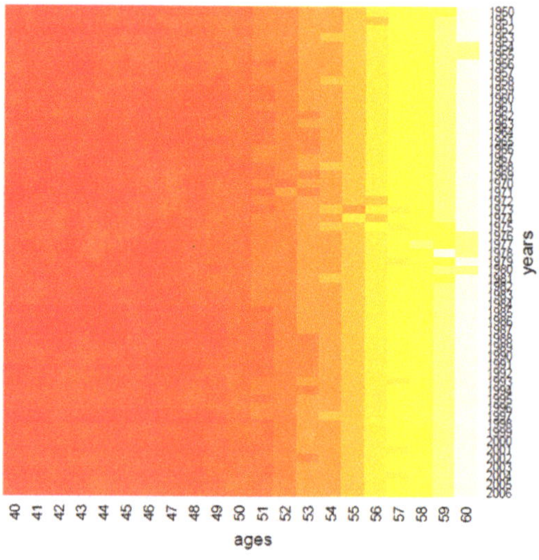

Figure 2. Clustering: the age effect.

In more detail, in Figure 1, we may observe a diagonal line, corresponding to the individuals aged 40 in 1958, i.e., the generation born in 1918; such graphical evidence suggests that this group has experienced a particular reduction in mortality during the years.

However, it is not reasonable that groups of genes behave similarly under all conditions; it could occur, for example, that group of ages show similar features just during some years, and they cluster differently during other years. To capture this detailed structure, we introduce the biclustering as a useful tool to find meaningful checkerboard patterns.

In the second step of our application, we have therefore randomly applied the spectral biclustering algorithm to the matrix of mortality rates, normalized through the log-transformation, thus obtaining 20 clusters: main results are visually summarized in Figures 3–7. Above all, the heat map of Figure 3 shows not only vertical regions, but also rectangular areas produced by the interaction between age and period effects.

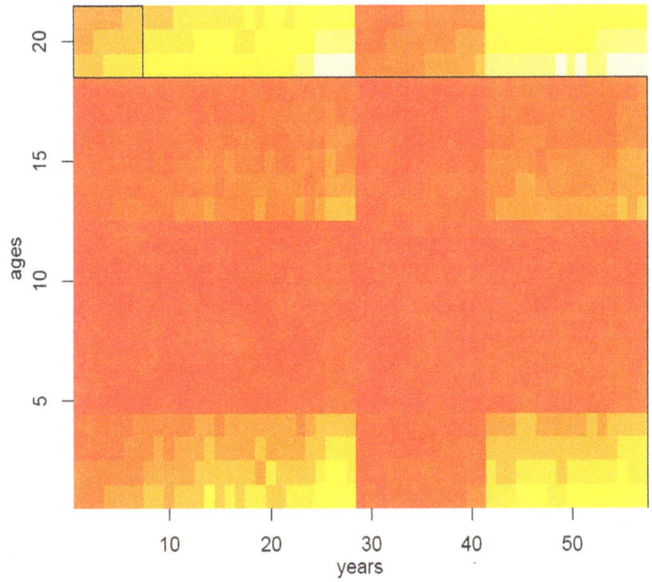

Figure 3. Biclustering on the mortality dataset.

Moreover, Figures 4 and 5 highlight the composition of each bicluster, summarized in Table 1: four groups of ages (40–47, 48–53, 54–57, 58–60) are defined, each of them characterized by significant patterns across particular years. For example, the first bicluster contains ages 58–60 during the years 1987–1993; the same ages act differently during the years 1970–1986 and are grouped in the second bicluster, and so on.

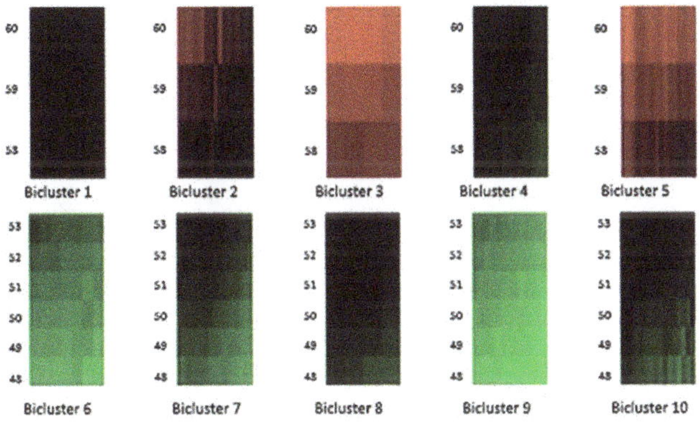

Figure 4. Biclusters 1–10.

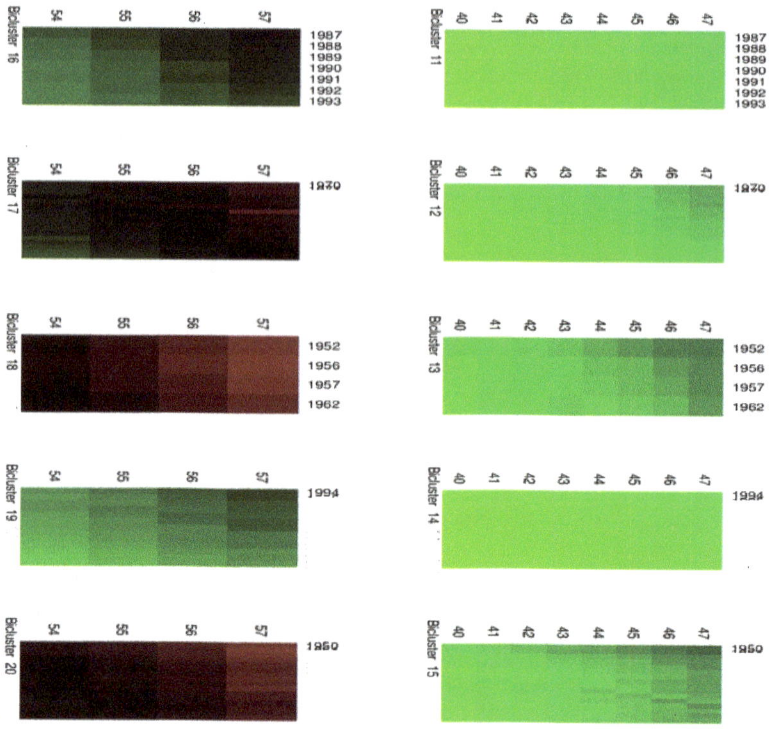

Figure 5. Biclusters 11–20.

Table 1. The composition of biclusters.

Cluster	Age	Years
1	58–60	1987–1993
2	58–60	1970–1986
3	58–60	1952, 1956, 1957, 1962
4	58–60	1994–2006
5	58–60	1950–1969 except for 1952, 1956, 1957, 1962
6	48–53	1987–1993
7	48–53	1970–1986
8	48–53	1952, 1956, 1957, 1962
9	48–53	1994–2006
10	48–53	1950–1969 except for 1952, 1956, 1957, 1962
11	40–47	1987–1993
12	40–47	1970–1986
13	40–47	1952, 1956, 1957, 1962
14	40–47	1994–2006
15	40–47	1950–1969 except for 1952, 1956, 1957, 1962
16	54–57	1987–1993
17	54–57	1970–1986
18	54–57	1952, 1956, 1957, 1962
19	54–57	1994–2006
20	54–57	1950–1969 except for 1952, 1956, 1957, 1962

In order to provide the reader with additional interpretative keys, in Figures 6 and 7, we show parallel coordinate graphs for mortality levels.

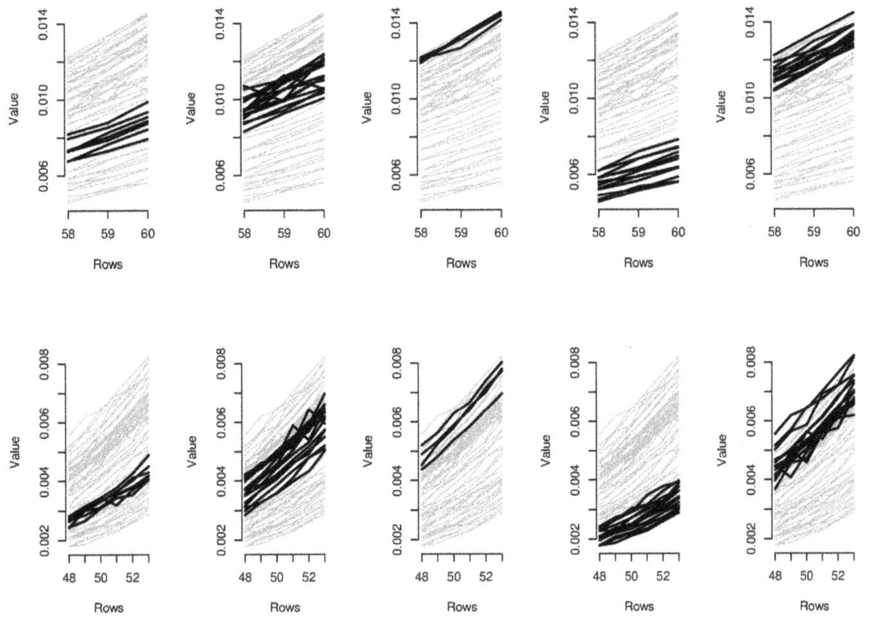

Figure 6. Parallel coordinate graphs for biclusters 1–10.

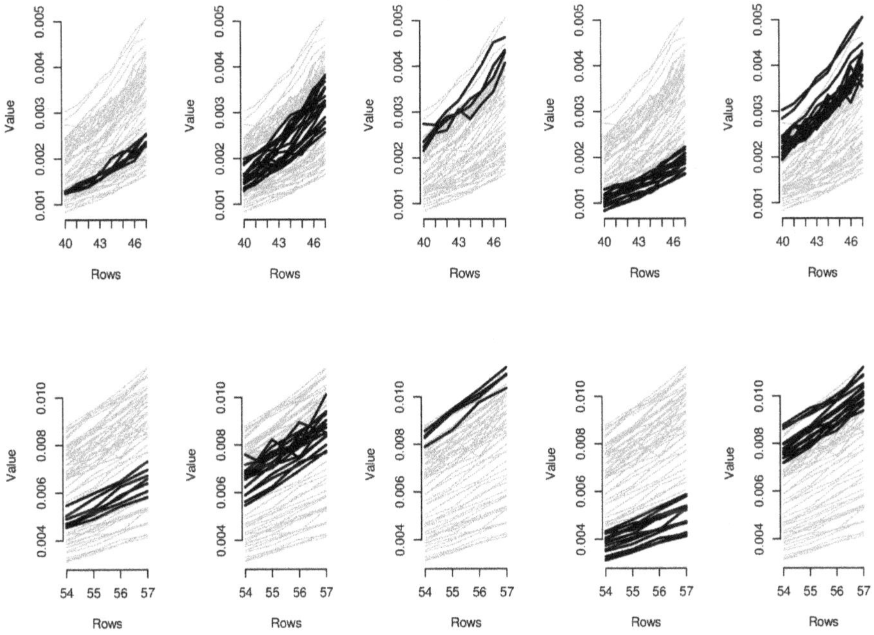

Figure 7. Parallel coordinate graphs for biclusters 11–20.

Let us take a look, for instance, at the first two clusters including the levels of mortality between the ages 58 and 60 during the years 1987–1993 and 1987–1993. In the parallel coordinate graphs, the light gray lines represent the mortality for each year of the whole dataset, while the bold lines represent the level of mortality for each year included in the bicluster. By a mutual comparison of the lines in the first two boxes of Figure 7, we can note that the mortality between the ages 58–60 moving from the period 1970–1986 to the period 1987–1993 has sensitively decreased. In particular, we can note the effect of the reduction of mortality trend during the period 1950–2006, looking in sequence at box 5-2-1-4 of Figure 7. The years included in the third bicluster represent an exception to the general trend, probably due to accidental deviations in the mortality trend. In the actuarial practice, it is well known that the demographic risk can be split into two components: the insurance risk and the longevity risk. The former arises from accidental deviations of the number of deaths from its expected trend, while the latter derives from systematic improvements in the mortality trend. It is possible to improve mortality forecasts removing the accidental deviations from the dataset on which the fitting and forecasts are implemented and the bicluster method can be useful to this scope.

Similar considerations can be easily extended to the other biclusters; for instance, as it is clear from biclusters 4-9-14-19, in Figures 6 and 7, all ages have experimented a reduction from the mortality trend during the last two decays.

We also checked the statistical significance and the stability of the applied biclustering technique. To this aim, F-statistics are calculated from the two-way ANOVA mode with the row and column effect; low p-values denote non-random selection of columns for a given bicluster. We have calculated the F-statistics for each cluster and have obtained p-values of almost zero for both row and column effects. Table 2 shows the p-values of the F-statistics corresponding to the row and column effects.

Moreover, for each cluster, Constant and Additive Variances are calculated, as one can see in Table 3. They represent measures of how a bicluster is coherent, following [19], and return the corresponding variance of genes or conditions as the average of the sum of Euclidean distances between all rows and columns of the bicluster. The lower the values returned, the more constant or coherent the bicluster is. If the value returned is near 0, the bicluster is ideally constant or coherent. Usually, a value above 1–1.5 is enough to determine if the bicluster is not constant or coherent.

Table 2. The p-values of the F-statistics from the two-way ANOVA.

Cluster	Row Effect	Column Effect
1	9.457631e-19	3.080849e-12
2	2.154947e-22	1.920493e-09
3	1.539265e-20	2.823244e-16
4	7.044707e-17	3.358952e-11
5	7.679044e-32	3.538135e-17
6	3.098577e-31	1.597127e-19
7	1.830569e-77	1.243124e-42
8	1.646694e-63	1.872372e-38
9	1.909664e-37	1.459496e-07
10	4.317890e-57	3.326384e-28
11	8.420389e-19	1.149809e-07
12	1.218959e-22	4.788635e-08
13	3.097022e-23	6.420247e-18
14	5.204899e-20	1.365834e-14
15	1.877757e-30	5.348786e-11
16	1.244019e-15	7.830883e-10
17	7.935750e-44	6.552596e-30
18	2.060731e-33	5.490419e-24
19	3.489601e-17	4.602981e-06
20	3.741736e-37	9.304545e-23

Table 3. Constant and additive variance.

Cluster	Constant Variance	Additive Variance
1	0.0008312501	0.0001943193
2	0.0010608750	0.0007238702
3	0.0008112594	0.0002344328
4	0.0008110202	0.0002252854
5	0.0009152584	0.0003184399
6	0.0006558884	0.0002591269
7	0.0011777088	0.0004089964
8	0.0010524882	0.0001846966
9	0.0006908077	0.0001800295
10	0.0012443249	0.0005012390
11	0.0004307733	0.0001486275
12	0.0008466223	0.0002278785
13	0.0007208565	0.0002152609
14	0.0004183225	0.0001126892
15	0.0009253514	0.0004143284
16	0.0007953189	0.0002157055
17	0.0010980629	0.0006934491
18	0.0009243758	0.0002063028
19	0.0007612718	0.0002334575
20	0.0010023427	0.0003085179

4. Conclusions

In this paper, we discussed the use of biclustering techniques to discover patterns in mortality data tables. This approach can be motivated by the attention devoted to mortality investigations: the accurate modeling and projection of mortality rates and life expectancy, in fact, are of growing interest to researchers because of their impact on actuarial liabilities of private life insurance companies, pension funds and national pension systems; in this respect, it makes sense to monitor the extent to which the longevity improvements is meaningful.

Our work therefore nests in at least two research strands. The first research vein deals with biclustering: to the best of our knowledge, this is a first-time application, with spectral biclustering applied to a classification problem where the role of genes is played by individuals' ages, and the time to represent condition. Furthermore, we show that using spectral biclustering instead of standard clustering techniques presents several advantages, as in this way it is possible to capture demographical effects that are generally disregarded by other techniques. An example in such sense is offered by the so-called cohort effect that occurs when it is possible to identify generations exhibiting particular mortality patterns and where condition is represented by time: without proper ex ante investigations of the mortality data structure, the demographical models are often worsened with cohort parameters to capture generational effect, while the interaction of age–time effect in the data structure could be misunderstood and, for example, wrongly attributed to the cohort effect. In this respect, a preliminary investigation of data with biclustering methods becomes useful to design a parsimonious mortality model.

However, as biclustering algorithms are mostly apt to binary data, they are not always appropriate to deal with mortality rates. Nevertheless, the spectral biclustering appears suitable for a death rates matrix because it finds the checkerboard structure in data through the extraction of significant eigenvectors using the SVD associated with some normalization steps; this approach is also in line with the most used approach for fitting mortality data.

In our case study, we applied spectral biclustering to the death rates of the whole (male and female) Italian population, with genes represented by ages collected between 40 and 60, and the conditions by the years between 1950 and 2006. We applied both the hierarchical clustering and the spectral biclustering, and visualized the results through heat maps. By visual comparison of the results, we highlighted that the spectral biclustering was able both to capture effects lost in the case of standard clustering, and to correctly address the significance of existing patterns, as testified by the analysis of biclusters' coherence.

However, we are aware that the scope of the clusterization and biclusterization technique is not to explain why certain patterns occur, but to identify patterns in the data. They are unsupervised learning methods: the results of clustering algorithms are data driven, and, for this reason, they explain better the underlying structure of the data. This represents an advantage, but also a drawback: without a possibility to tell the system what to do like in other supervised methods, it is often difficult to explain clustering results. Every method has advantages and drawbacks, and the choice of a particular one depends on the scope of the research. The biclusterization we have proposed could be useful for a preliminary investigation of the mortality dataset, before implementing a stochastic model for the mortality projections. In fact, the widely used stochastic mortality models, like the Lee–Carter model, are based on time series extrapolation, and the results are influenced by the historical series considered and the estimation window. Projections change considerably according to the age and years considered, and the biclusters could represent important preliminary information about how data have to be included in the projections.

We can therefore conclude that biclustering can offer a useful technique to run exploratory analysis of mortality datasets, as a prelude to the construction of an efficient and parsimonious model of mortality. Steps for future works include the possibility to fit some well-known mortality models separately on different biclusters and verify the potential improvements in the fitting with an opportune analysis of the residuals. The biclustering approach can also offer useful preliminary information for the segmentation of the pension and insurance market.

Acknowledgments: The authors would like to thank the reviewers for insightful comments and suggestions, which led to a much improved manuscript.

Author Contributions: Gabriella Piscopo and Marina Resta conceived and designed the paper; Marina Resta illustrated the algorithms; Gabriella Piscopo developed the application.

Conflicts of Interest: The authors declare no conflict of interest.

Appendix A. The Euclidean Hierarchical Clustering Method

We assume to have a set of N items to be clustered, and an N $\times$ N distance matrix whose components are calculated by evaluating the Euclidean distance between each couple of item. Then, the basic process of hierarchical clustering (as defined by [28]) works as follows:

1. Assigning each item to a cluster, so that if you have N items, you now have N clusters, each containing just one item. The distances between the clusters are assumed to be the same as the distances (similarities) between the items they contain.
2. Find the closest (i.e., the most similar) pair of clusters and merge them into a single cluster, hence reducing by one the original number of clusters, as defined in 1.
3. Compute the distances between the new cluster and each of the old clusters.
4. Repeat steps 2 and 3 until the items are clustered into the desired number k of clusters.

References

1. Lee, D.; Carter, L. Modeling and Forecasting U.S. Mortality. *J. Am. Stat. Assoc.* **1992**, *87*, 659–671. [CrossRef]
2. Golub, G.; Van Loan, C. *Matrix Computations*, 3rd ed.; Johns Hopkins University Press: Baltimore MD, USA, 1996.
3. Booth, H.; Hyndman, R.; Tickle, L. Lee-Carter mortality forecasting: A multi-country comparison of variants and extensions. *Demogr. Res.* **2006**, *15*, 289–310. [CrossRef]
4. Booth, H.; Maindonald, J.; Smith, L. Applying Lee-Carter under conditions of variable mortality decline. *Popul. Stud.* **2002**, *56*, 325–336. [CrossRef] [PubMed]
5. Butt, Z.; Haberman, S.; Verrall, R.; Wass, V. Calculating compensation for loss of earnings: Estimating and using work life expectancy. *J. R. Stat. Soc. Ser. A* **2008**, *171*, 763–805. [CrossRef]

6. Delwarde, A.; Denuit, M.; Eilers, P. Smoothing the Lee-Carter and Poisson log-bilinear models for mortality forecasting. A penalized loglikelihood approach. *Stat. Model.* **2007**, *7*, 29–48. [CrossRef]
7. Currie, I.; Durban, M.; Eilers, P. Smoothing and forecasting mortality rates. *Stat. Model.* **2004**, *4*, 279–298. [CrossRef]
8. Hyndman, R.; Ullah, S. Robust forecasting of mortality and fertility rates: A functional data approach. *Comput. Stat. Data Anal.* **2007**, *51*, 4942–4956. [CrossRef]
9. Richards, S. Understanding Pensioner Longevity. *The Actuary Magazine*, 26–27 May 2007.
10. Renshaw, A.; Haberman, S. A cohort-based extension to the Lee-Carter model for mortality reduction factors. *Insur. Math. Econ.* **2006**, *38*, 556–570. [CrossRef]
11. Willets, R. The cohort effect: Insights and explanations. *Br. Actuar. J.* **2004**, *10*, 833–877. [CrossRef]
12. Renshaw, A.; Haberman, S. *Lee-Carter Mortality Forecasting Incorporating Bivariate Time Series*; Actuarial Research Paper 153; Faculty of Actuarial Science Insurance, City University London: London, UK, 2003.
13. Leong, Y.; Yu, J. A Spatial Cluster Modification of the Lee-Carter Model. In Proceedings of the Longevity Risks 8, Cass Business School, London, UK, 7–8 September 2012.
14. Skiadas, C.; Skiadas, C. A Modeling Approach to Life Table Data Sets. In *Recent Advances in Stochastic Modeling and Data Analysis*; World Scientific: Singapore, Singapore, 2007; pp. 350–359.
15. Hatzopoulos, P.; Haberman, S. Common mortality modelling and coherent forecasts. An empirical analysis of worldwide mortality data. *Insur. Math. Econ.* **2013**, *52*, 320–337. [CrossRef]
16. Cheng, Y.; Church, G. Biclustering of expression data. In Proceedings of the International Conference on Intelligent Systems for Molecular Biology, San Diego, CA, USA, 19–23 August 2000; Volume 8, pp. 93–103.
17. Ihmels, J.; Friedlander, G.; Bergmann, S.; Sarig, O.; Ziv, Y. Revealing Modular Organization in the Yeast Transcriptional Network. *Nat. Genet.* **2002**, *31*, 370–377. [CrossRef] [PubMed]
18. Murali, T.; Kasif, S. Extracting conserved gene expression motifs from gene expression data. In Proceedings of the Pacific Symposium on Biocomputing, Kauai, HI, USA, 3–7 January 2003; Volume 8, pp. 77–88.
19. Madeira, S.; Oliveira, A. Biclustering algorithms for biological data analysis: A survey. *IEEE/ACM Trans. Comput. Biol. Bioinform.* **2004**, *1*, 24–45. [CrossRef] [PubMed]
20. Segal, E.; Taskar, B.; Gasch, A.; Friedman, N.; Koller, D. Rich probabilistic models for gene expression. *Bioinformatics* **2001**, *17*, S243–S252. [CrossRef] [PubMed]
21. Tanay, A.; Sharan, R.; Shamir, R. Discovering statistically significant biclusters in gene expression data. *Bioinformatics* **2002**, *18*, 136–144. [CrossRef]
22. Wang, H.; Wang, W.; Yang, J.; Yu, P. Clustering by Pattern Similarity in Large Data Sets. In Proceedings of the 2002 ACM SIGMOD International Conference on Management of Data, Madison, WI, USA, 3–6 June 2002; pp. 394–405.
23. Jiang, D.; Pei, J.; Zhang, A. DHC: A density-based hierarchical clustering method for time series gene expression data. In Proceedings of the IEEE International Symposium on Bioinformatics and Bioengineering, Bethesda, MD, USA, 12 March 2003; pp. 393–400.
24. Liu, J.; Wang, W. Op-cluster: Clustering by tendency in high dimensional space. In Proceedings of the IEEE International Conference on Data Mining, Melbourne, FL, USA, 22 November 2003; p. 187.
25. Gu, J.; Liu, J. Bayesian biclustering of gene expression data. *BMC Genom.* **2008**, *9*, S4. [CrossRef] [PubMed]
26. Li, G.; Ma, Q.; Tang, H.; Paterson, A.; Xu, Y. QUBIC: A qualitative biclustering algorithm for analyses of gene expression data. *Nucleic Acids Res.* **2009**, *37*, e1015. [CrossRef] [PubMed]
27. Kluger, Y.; Basri, R.; Chang, J.; Gerstein, M. Spectral biclustering of microarray data: Coclustering genes and conditions. *Genome Res.* **2003**, *13*, 703–716. [CrossRef] [PubMed]
28. Johnson, S.C. Hierarchical clustering schemes. *Psychometrika* **1967**, *3*, 241–254. [CrossRef]

risks

MDPI

Article

Backtesting the Lee–Carter and the Cairns–Blake–Dowd Stochastic Mortality Models on Italian Death Rates

Carlo Maccheroni [1,2,*] **and Samuel Nocito** [2,*]

[1] Dondena Centre for Research on Social Dynamics, Bocconi University, 20100 Milano, Italy
[2] University of Turin, 10124 Torino, Italy
* Correspondence: carlo.maccheroni@unito.it (C.M.); samuel.nocito@unito.it (S.N.)

Academic Editor: Luca Regis
Received: 23 December 2016; Accepted: 27 June 2017; Published: 4 July 2017

Abstract: This work proposes a backtesting analysis that compares the Lee–Carter and the Cairns–Blake–Dowd mortality models, employing Italian data. The mortality data come from the Italian National Statistics Institute (ISTAT) database and span the period 1975–2014, over which we computed back-projections evaluating the performances of the models compared with real data. We propose three different backtest approaches, evaluating the goodness of short-run forecast versus medium-length ones. We find that neither model was able to capture the improving shock on mortality observed for the male population on the analysed period. Moreover, the results suggest that CBD forecasts are reliable prevalently for ages above 75, and that LC forecasts are basically more accurate for this data.

Keywords: lee-carter model; cairns-blake-dowd model; backtesting; mortality forecast

---

1. Introduction

Dowd et al. (2010a) performed a backtesting analysis on seven different stochastic mortality models with results showing that the models performed adequately by most backtests. The analysis was applied to English and Welsh male mortality data. We decided to perform a backtesting investigation using Italian mortality data. The decision was motivated by the study of the historical mortality trend, observed on the forty-past-years horizon for both the male and female populations. The gap between genders deeply decreased over the considered horizon with steep improvements in male mortality. Thus, the first aim of this paper is to scrutinize the forecast proposed by the models for both sexes, which have experienced different mortality evolutions. Moreover, in the last three decades, mortality projections have been widely used by Italian policy-makers for making decisions about public pension reforms. The study of *mortality risk*, intended as the uncertainty in future mortality rates as well as *longevity risk* for the long-term trend in mortality rates (Cairns et al. 2006), played a central role for both public and private annuity providers. For these reasons, among all the principal stochastic mortality models[1], we chose to compare Lee–Carter (LC) and the Cairns–Blake–Dowd (CBD) ones. In particular, the Italian National Statistics Institute (ISTAT) adopted the original formulation of the LC model to forecast mortality over the projection horizon 2007–2051 (Istat 2008) now updated[2] over the horizon 2011–2065. The National Association of Insurance Companies (ANIA) uses those projections as demographic basis for annuity

---

[1] Refer to Cairns et al. (2009) for a detailed list and quantitative comparison of the principal stochastic mortality models.
[2] ISTAT population projections 2011–2065: http://demo.istat.it/uniprev2011/note.html.

computations (ANIA 2014). Therefore, we chose to compare the original formulation of the LC model to the original CBD since they also represent the two most used parametric families of mortality models.

On the one hand, the Lee–Carter model has sparked a deep methodological revolution in the field of demographic forecast, particularly in mortality. The mortality model has been used together with a similar fertility model and deterministic migration assumptions to generate stochastic forecasts about the population and its components. These stochastic population forecasts, in turn, have been used as the key component of stochastic projections of the finances of the US Social Security system. The stochastic forecast avoids some of the problems inherent to using the classic scenario method for representing forecast uncertainty (Lee 2000). Then, in concurrence with the main demographic applications, the LC model suggested:

- an important research front on problems related to the parameter estimations (Booth et al. 2006), with many applications also in the actuarial and economics literature (Loisel and Serant 2007); and
- extension of the forecasting analysis with disaggregated projections on demographic subsets to maintain consistency at the aggregate level (Lee and Miller 2001; Li and Lee 2005; Li 2010).

On the other hand, the Cairns–Blake–Dowd model, even if more recent in its formulation than the LC model, has played an important role in forecasting mortality at higher ages (i.e., ages starting at 60 and over). The mortality model made great contributions for pension funds, life-insurance companies and private annuity providers in general. It is mainly used for pricing longevity bonds as suggested also by the authors in the first formulation of the model (Cairns et al. 2006).

The second aim of this work is to analyse the medium-length forecast with respect to the short term, observing potential differences in the parameter estimations (Mavros et al. 2014)[3] accordingly with changes in the starting point of the database. Chan et al. (2014) have also studied the new-data-invariant property on the quality of the CBD mortality index. For this purpose, we introduced a new backtesting approach named the jumping fixed-length horizon, which makes short-run projections of five years, "jumping forward" in the historical database by five-year-steps.

Considerations of the backtesting results do not imply a conclusive evaluation of the models, since we perform the analysis exclusively for the range of ages 57 to 90. The choice for the interval of ages was motivated by the fact that, in Italy, Ragioneria dello Stato computes the so-called transformation coefficients for pension annuities, starting from age 57. Moreover, since the CBD model is recommended as a good predictor of mortality at higher ages, we chose this interval of ages to make a more prudent and accurate comparison between the models. Furthermore, we decided to take into consideration only death probabilities $q_{x,t}$ among all of the other possible biometric functions.

We used[4] death probabilities $q_{x,t}$ provided by ISTAT spanning the period 1975–2014. Then, over the designated horizon of historical data, we select the "lookback" and the "lookforward" windows[5], respectively, for the parameter estimation and forecast. In particular, the length of the forecast window will be different for each of the three backtesting approaches proposed by the work:

- *fixed horizon backtests*: lookback and lookforward windows of 20 years;
- *jumping fixed-length horizon backtests*: lookback window of 20 years and lookforward window of 5 years (short-term projections); and
- *rolling fixed-length horizon backtests*: lookback window of fixed-length (20 years) and a contracting lookforward window from 20 to 2 years of projections.

The paper is organized as follows. Section 2 briefly presents the models and the adopted terminology, Section 3 shows the historical Italian mortality data, and Section 4 and subsections explain methodology and the backtesting results obtained by the different approaches. Section 5 provides conclusions.

---

3 Particularly for the case of Cairns–Blake–Dowd model.
4 Data downloaded on June 2016. Source: http://demo.istat.it/tvm2016/index.php?lingua=eng.
5 For the sake of simplicity, we decided to adopt the same terminology used by Dowd et al. (2010a).

2. Model Specifications

2.1. The Lee–Carter Model

We took into consideration the original formulation of Lee and Carter (1992), represented by the following model equation:

$$m_{x,t} = e^{\alpha_x+\beta_x k_t+\varepsilon_{x,t}}, \tag{1}$$

where $m_{x,t}$ is the central rate of mortality at age x and at time t, and it is given by the formula:

$$m_{x,t} = \frac{d_{x,t}}{L_{x,t}},$$

with[6] $d_{x,t}$ representing the number of deaths that occurred between x and $x+1$, and $L_{x,t}$ called the age units living in x, which is simply the average number of individuals alive between x and $x+1$.

For simplicity, the model was implemented by adopting its logarithm transformation:

$$\ln m_{x,t} = \alpha_x + \beta_x k_t + \varepsilon_{x,t},$$

with the following parameter interpretations:

- k_t is the time index representing the level of mortality at time t;
- α_x represents the average trend of mortality on the time horizon at age x;
- β_x represents a measure of the sensitivity in movement from the parameter k_t. In particular, β_x describes the relative speed of mortality changes, at each age, when k_t changes; and
- $\varepsilon_{x,t}$ is the homoskedastic error term, which incorporates historical trends not considered by the model. It is assumed to be $\varepsilon_{x,t} \sim \mathcal{N}(0, \sigma_\varepsilon^2)$.

Appendix A illustrates the method adopted for the estimation and projection of the parameters.

2.2. The Cairns–Blake–Dowd Model

We considered the original formulation of the model provided by Cairns et al. (2006) with the following model equation:

$$\ln\left[\frac{q_{x,t}}{p_{x,t}}\right] = k_t^{(1)} + k_t^{(2)}(x-\bar{x}) + \varepsilon_{x,t}, \tag{2}$$

where

- $k_t^{(1)}$ and $k_t^{(2)}$ are two stochastic processes and represent the two time indexes of the model;
- $q_{x,t}$ and $p_{x,t}$ represent, respectively, the death and the survival probability, at time t for an individual aged x;
- $\ln\left[\frac{q_{x,t}}{p_{x,t}}\right] = \ln(\phi_x) = logit\ q_{x,t}$ is the *logit* transformation of $q_{x,t}$, with ϕ_x representing the mortality odds;
- $\bar{x}$ is the mean age of the considered interval of ages; and
- $\varepsilon_{x,t}$ is the error term that encloses the historical trend that the model does not express. All of the error terms are i.i.d following the Normal distribution with mean 0 and variance σ_ε^2.

The model is fully identified, so it does not require additional constraints.

Moreover, the time index $k_t^{(1)}$ is the intercept of the model. It affects every age in the same way, and it represents the level of mortality at time t. More precisely, if it declines over time, it means that

6 The variables $d_{x,t}$ and $L_{x,t}$ are the common biometric functions as described in the life tables.

the mortality rate has been decreasing over time at all ages. The time index $k_t^{(2)}$ represents the slope of the model: every age is differently affected by this parameter. For instance, if during the fitting period, the mortality improvements have been greater at lower ages than at higher ages, the slope period term $k_t^{(2)}$ would be increasing over time. In such a case, the plot of the logit of death probabilities against age would become steeper as it shifts downwards over time (Pitacco et al. 2009).

Appendix B illustrates the estimation and projection methods involved.

3. Case Study: Italian Mortality Data from 1975 to 2014

The application of the presented models requires the use of the death probabilities time series for extrapolating mortality forecast. As already mentioned, we use data provided by ISTAT because these data are commonly used by private insurance companies and public pension providers. The range of ages is $57 \leq x \leq 90$. In particular, we chose the upper limit for taking into consideration the ISTAT graduation method of ending the life table (Istat 2001). The calculation of the probabilities of dying for ages over 95 is performed by extrapolating the $q_{x,t}$ graduated values following the Thatcher et al. (1998) model[7]:

$$q_{x,t} = \frac{\vartheta e^{\gamma x}}{1 + \vartheta e^{\gamma x}}; \qquad x \geq 95. \tag{3}$$

This kind of graduation could affect the backtesting results, comparing realized data with forecasts obtained by applying the LC (1) and the CBD (2) models, since they offer a different mortality pattern at old ages. For the ages from 5 to 94, ISTAT uses a moving average of crude rates with the length of seven values. Moreover, we selected the time period from 1975 to 2014 because, from in the mid-seventies in Italy, the successful fight against cardiovascular diseases began. More recently, efforts against tumors, which are still the main cause of death, have been launched. These successes have contributed to an extraordinary acceleration of growth in life expectancy, especially at higher ages: e.g., from 1975 to 2014, life expectancy at 60 years has seen an average increase of about four hours each day, both for men and women. In the male case, this phenomena extraordinarily occurred. Previously, life expectancy at birth had registered the first significant increase due to the control of infant and child mortality, while during the years under review, it has also benefited from the control of adult age mortality.

Currently, the probability of reaching an old age for a young adult is really high: for a 30 year old, the probability of reaching the age of 60 is almost 94% for males and 96.4% for females. However, it remains difficult to reach the threshold of 90 years, especially for men. Table 1 accurately shows[8] how this probability changed starting from age 50. Moreover, it shows how the difference in probability between genders became greater as the age increased.

This process is known as the rectangularization and shift forward of the survival curves. Its measure can be derived from the entropy of a life table (Equation (4)). It was introduced by Keyfitz and Caswell (2005) and it is referred to in this paper as ${}^tH_{K,\xi}$ with ξ the age by which the survival curve is built, and t the year of the period life table at which the entropy is computed (in our case $t = 1975, 1976, \ldots 2014$). Then,

$${}^tH_{K,\xi} = -\frac{\sum_j (\ln l_j) l_j}{\sum_j l_j}, \tag{4}$$

7 In Equation (3) ϑ and γ are parameters that need to be estimated. In general, those parameters are estimated by applying Ordinary Least Squares (OLS) on the logit transformation of Equation (3).

8 Even though the backtesting analysis will be focused on the interval of ages 57–90, here we decided to provide information also on ages lower than $x = 57$. In this way, we are able to present a more accurate Italian demographic scenario for the period observed.

where l_j is the probability of surviving from age[9] ξ ($\xi = 0, 1, ..., w$; l_ξ=1 $\forall$ ξ) to age j ($j = \xi + 1, \xi + 2, \ldots w$). The entropy index becomes smaller whenever the survivorship curve l_j moves towards a rectangular form; in this limit case, ${}^tH_{K,\xi} = 0$.

Table 1. Proportion of persons aged 30 and expected to be alive at selected ages.

Italian Period Life Tables									
Ages	1975	1980	1985	1990	1995	2000	2005	2010	2014
Male									
50	0.9438	0.9483	0.9554	0.9583	0.9591	0.9662	0.9722	0.9755	0.9777
60	0.8406	0.8487	0.8646	0.8839	0.8951	0.90962	0.9242	0.9324	0.9376
70	0.6292	0.6409	0.6691	0.7081	0.7351	0.7732	0.8060	0.8257	0.8385
80	0.3014	0.3161	0.3539	0.4029	0.4406	0.4936	0.5434	0.5912	0.6188
90	0.0464	0.0527	0.0682	0.0954	0.1170	0.1396	0.1648	0.1996	0.2250
95	0.0080	0.0096	0.0140	0.0235	0.0318	0.0401	0.0491	0.0595	0.0743
Female									
50	0.9703	0.9739	0.9769	0.9785	0.9796	0.9822	0.9850	0.9865	0.9871
60	0.9194	0.9290	0.9364	0.9427	0.9473	0.9525	0.9585	0.9620	0.9639
70	0.8009	0.8168	0.8337	0.8546	0.8681	0.8828	0.8972	0.9053	0.9087
80	0.5070	0.5403	0.5814	0.6249	0.6576	0.69561	0.7322	0.7540	0.7674
90	0.1154	0.1433	0.1629	0.2141	0.2547	0.2860	0.3297	0.3653	0.3878
95	0.0226	0.0326	0.0380	0.0626	0.0830	0.1030	0.1259	0.1420	0.1654

Figure 1 shows how the trend of the rectangularization process has changed according to ages (i.e., from $\xi = 50$ to $\xi = 65, 75$). Regarding women, this process was already in place before 1975. In particular, starting from ages 50 and 65, it is continued with a substantially linear continuity. In the case of men, the rectangularization process begins to escalate smoothly after 1984. However, the following trend shows a deep reduction of mortality, from which is derived an attenuation of the inequality between sexes even though it has not disappeared. In Figure 1, ${}^tH_{k,\xi}$ shows that the mortality improvement in the elderly population has taken place at different rates over time, particularly with a faster steep decline for both sexes after 1993.

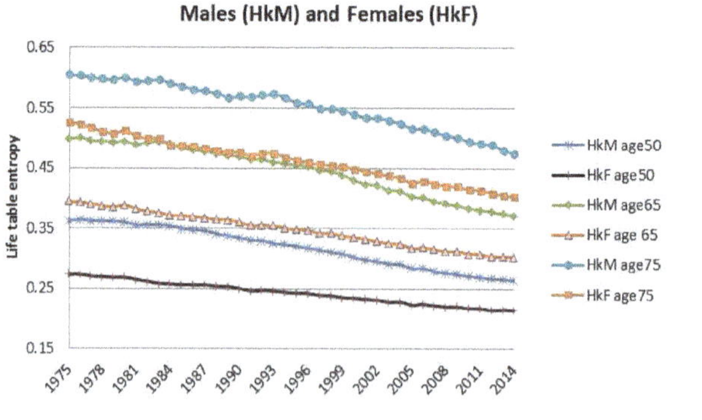

Figure 1. Italian life tables 1975–2014: males and females entropy (${}^tH_{K,\xi}$).

The differentiation of the pace in reducing mortality of both sexes starting from adult age up to those who are old is confirmed by the results of the Kullback and Leibler (1951) divergence:

9 The starting point for the final age interval is denoted by w.

$$^{t}D_{KL,\xi}(h_z, g_z) = \sum_{z=0}^{w-\xi} h_z \ln\left(\frac{h_z}{g_z}\right), \quad (5)$$

where h_z and g_z are the probability distributions of the "time until death" random variable Z_ξ for a person aged ξ, respectively, for males and females. Equation (5) measures the "difference" between these two probability distributions, which, in our case, is taken as the reference model g_z. The choice is motived not only by the fact that mortality is significantly lower for women than for men, but also because the continuous decline of female mortality in the reporting period occurred much more regularly (Maccheroni 2014). The divergence in mortality between genders mortality has different characteristics depending on the considered age group.

Figure 2 shows that the divergence in mortality between sexes presents different characteristics, depending on the observed age. In particular, until 1981, the divergence gradually increased on the full range of ages. At a later time, differentials in mortality between sexes decrease whenever x is lower than 60, while they progressively increase at higher ages. These diverging trends make the application of the models interesting, especially for the comparison of results. Needless to say, the mortality forecast will be more accurate for women than men because women experienced a death risk reduction process with greater regularity than men.

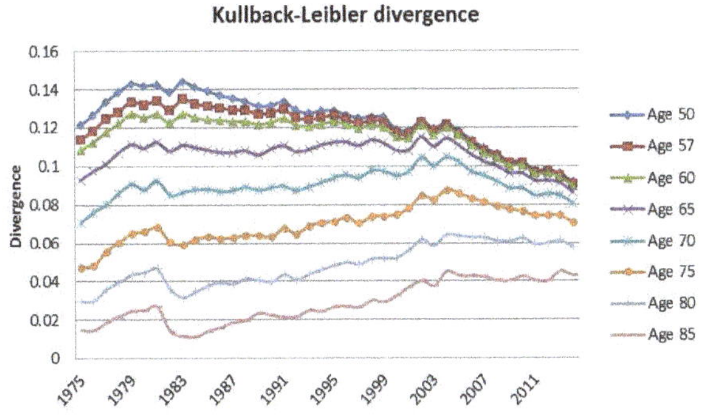

Figure 2. Kullback–Leibler divergence with respect to Z_ξ at selected ages.

4. Backtesting Analysis

In this section, we introduce the three different backtesting frameworks, and we present the related forecast results.

- The *fixed horizon backtest* uses a fixed twenty-year historical "lookback" interval, $1975 \leq t \leq 1994$, and a fixed "lookforward" horizon, $1995 \leq t \leq 2014$ (20 years).
- The *jumping fixed-length horizon backtests* make short run projections of five years[10] and keep fixed the length of the "lookback" horizon (20 years), but make jumps of five years ahead to cover the "lookforward" interval, $1995 \leq t \leq 2014$. This analysis is divided into four groups of estimations and forecast, described in Table 2.
- Finally, the *rolling fixed-length horizon backtests* keep fixed the length of the "lookback" horizon (i.e., 20 years) and let it roll ahead year by year. The projections are made over the remaining horizon, keeping fixed the last year of the projection at $t = 2014$. This analysis is divided into nineteen groups of estimations and forecast, described in Table 3.

10 We made a forecast of each year in the short-run projection window (5 years).

Table 2. Jumping fixed-length horizon backtests data horizon.

Lookback Horizon	Lookforward Horizon
1975–1994	1995–1999
1980–1999	2000–2004
1985–2004	2005–2009
1990–2009	2010–2014

Table 3. Rolling fixed-length horizon backtests data horizon.

Lookback	Lookforward	Lookback	Lookforward
1975–1994	1995–2014 (20)	1985–2004	2005-2014 (10)
1976–1995	1996–2014 (19)	1986–2005	2006–2014 (9)
1977–1996	1997–2014 (18)	1987–2006	2007–2014 (8)
1978–1997	1998–2014 (17)	1988–2007	2008–2014 (7)
1979–1998	1999–2014 (16)	1989–2008	2009–2014 (6)
1980–1999	2000–2014 (15)	1990–2009	2010–2014 (5)
1981–2000	2001–2014 (14)	1991–2010	2011–2014 (4)
1982–2001	2002–2014 (13)	1992–2011	2012–2014 (3)
1983–2002	2003–2014 (12)	1993–2012	2013–2014 (2)
1984–2003	2004–2014 (11)		

The numbers in parentheses show the length of the "lookforward" horizon. Moreover, they indicate the position of the year 2014 over the related projection interval. This will be particularly useful for the analysis of results that will be presented in Section 4.3.

Before going in depth about the backtesting analysis, we check for the estimation quality of the models over the historical "lookback" interval, $1975 \leq t \leq 1994$. For this purpose, we use the index Λ_x^2, a form of R^2 that particularly fits our case (Draper and Smith 2014), described as follows:

$$\Lambda_x^2 = 1 - \frac{\frac{1}{n}\sum_t (q_{x,t}^O - q_{x,t}^{ft})^2 - \left[\frac{1}{n}\sum_t (q_{x,t}^O - q_{x,t}^{ft})\right]^2}{\frac{1}{n}\sum_t (q_{x,t}^O)^2 - \left[\frac{1}{n}\sum_t (q_{x,t}^O)\right]^2},$$

where $q_{x,t}^{ft}$ is the fitted value for the $q_{x,t}$ and n is the total number of considered years (i.e., $n = 20$). The index provides the proportion of the temporal variance explained by the model for all $57 \leq x \leq 90$. Figure 3 shows that both models fit the observed data generally well. Particularly in the case of males, the share of the "explained variance" at any age is always greater than 88%, while, for females, in the case of LC, it falls to 85% at $x = 63$. However, such a decrease takes place within a very limited age range between 61 and 65 years.

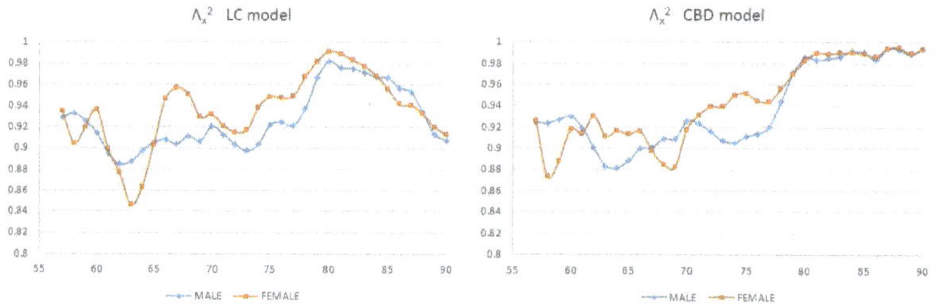

Figure 3. Proportion of temporal variance explained by the models: 1975–1994.

More specifically, by the analysis of the "explained variance" for both models, we see that the irregular path of the curves may be influenced by a cohort effect before the age $x = 80$. This effect is diagonally observable on the graphs in Figure 4 for those individuals aged 57–59 in 1975 and 76–78 in 1994, respectively. These are the generations born during the First World War (1915-1918) who, in the course of their lives, have experienced higher mortality at the same ages than the previous and next cohorts (Maccheroni 2016). For ages older than $x = 75$, the differences between the models are sharply evident. In particular, LC overestimates $q^O_{x,t}$ and CBD underestimates (Figure 4).

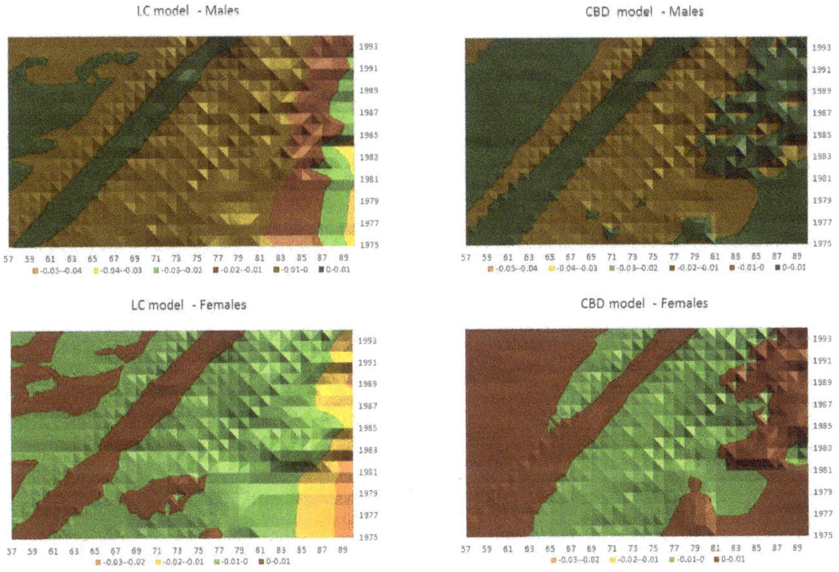

Figure 4. Residuals $(q^O_{x,t} - q^P_{x,t})$ by age x: 1975–1994.

Analysis of the projection results that will be presented in the next section shows that the described cohort effect has an impact on the forecast quality of the models in two ways.

- Both models slightly suffer the cohort effect for both populations over the projection horizon (1995–2014) for the same cohort aged 77–79 in 1995 that is no longer observed from 2006. In particular, both models show an underestimated forecast for such birth cohorts on both sexes with observed values above the upper limit of the confidence interval for some ages of the cohort. This occurred particularly for males.
- The observed male $q_{x,t}$ for individuals aged 57–59 in 1995 and 76–78 in 2014, respectively, are often under the lower extreme of the forecast confidence interval. It seems that models have replicated the cohort effect over an homologous cohort in 1995, but since the male mortality evolution has changed consistently from 1975–1994 to 1995–2014, the two homologous cohorts (i.e., 57–59 in 1975 and 57–59 in 1995) showed different trends that lead to forecast errors. This scenario does not occur for females, since women experienced a more ordinary mortality evolution. Therefore, the homologous cohorts are similar, so the bias is not observable.

For these reasons, the results obtained with the three backtesting approaches need to be evaluated, taking into consideration the analysed cohort effect and its related impact on the forecast. In particular, forecasts seem to suffer the cohort effect as long as the data used for the estimation of the parameters take into account years from 1975 to 1985. After 1985, the cohort effect is small compared to the overall sample; therefore, projections do not suffer greatly from it.

4.1. Fixed Horizon Backtest (1995–2014)

The first backtesting analysis takes into account a forecast horizon that is demographically considered a medium-term projection horizon. The comparisons proposed are among the most likely values of $q^P_{x,t}$ prediction, which is the projected central value derived by the model on which we constructed the 95% confidence interval and those observed $q^O_{x,t}$; comparisons between the central value and extremes of the confidence interval occur only for the ages 65 and 85. These are the ages that in the demographic literature mark the entrance in the range of so-called "young-old" and "oldest-old". Unfortunately, due to space limitations, it was not possible to present the comparison to the age of 75, which divides the old from the "young-old" (Vaupel 2010).

The $q^O_{x,t}$ can present a strong temporal variability due to the observed cohort effect and to the so-called "period effect", which is the time condition that affects mortality via a variety of factors. Among these, the best known is the climatic effect that can, for instance, cause a rise in mortality at old ages during a very hot summer (e.g., an episode occurred in Italy in 2003), or epidemiological effects that arise from flu in winter in low-mortality countries. Needless to say, the impact of those factors is stronger on the most vulnerable people. For this reason, a rise in mortality due to those factors is generally followed by a decrease in mortality, since those who remained alive have a lower frailty level. These mortality shocks can affect short-term forecasts rather than medium-term ones, since the latter are usually more capable of capturing changes in environmental and socio-economic conditions and people's lifestyles.

From an applicative point of view, particularly focused on the insurance and social security sector, we were interested in analysing the performance of the models on assessing the risk of death at various ages. It is from this point of view that we are going to develop our analysis. For this purpose, we make a brief assessment of forecast errors that was performed using as an index the Root Mean Squared Errors (RMSE), defined as follows:

$$RMSE = \sqrt{MSE},$$

with

$$MSE = \frac{1}{v}\sum_{x}\sum_{t}(q^O_{x,t} - q^P_{x,t})^2,$$

where the mean squared errors (MSE) are equal to the sum of squared errors adjusted for the residual degrees of freedom v. Moreover, $q^O_{x,t}$ and $q^P_{x,t}$ are, respectively, the death probabilities observed and forecast (projected). We use the root of the adjusted SSE to take into account the difference in the number of free parameters between the models. Table 4 shows $RMSE$ for the first and the second backtesting approach that will be presented in the following section. Moreover, it takes into account exclusively the central value of the confidence interval as the most relevant for pension policy-makers and annuity providers (Whitehouse 2007).

Table 4 shows how the LC model proposes a more accurate forecast with respect to the CBD model for the period 1995–2014 for females; it is more difficult to judge the models' performances for males given the small difference between the RMSE results. These predictions are produced on the extrapolated parameters k_t (Appendix Equations (A7) and (A9)), but the result is made more flexible by the stochastic component of the models that allows building of the forecast confidence interval. One cause of error can arise from the fact that the central value of the projection may be shifted with respect to the observed data, even though it does not differ from the observed trend recorded over the projection horizon. Figure 5 provides a graphic explanation of the phenomenon. In particular, for individuals aged 65, the male forecasts 1995–2014 are above the mortality trend observed for the same period, with divergent paths for the LC model. In the female case (age 65), only the CBD model shows divergences. However, these deviations may be instead very low, as in the case of the LC model for females aged 65, or in the case of both models for both sexes aged 85 (Figure 5). Moreover, the bias due to the continuing fluctuations of the risk of death over time has to be taken in consideration.

The confidence interval provided by the two models takes into account this stochastic component of mortality (Figures 7 and 9), although this may occur with different levels of precision (Figure 10).

Figures 6 and 8 show the overall error dynamic highlighted by the ratio between the projected $q^P_{x,t}$ and the observed $q^O_{x,t}$.

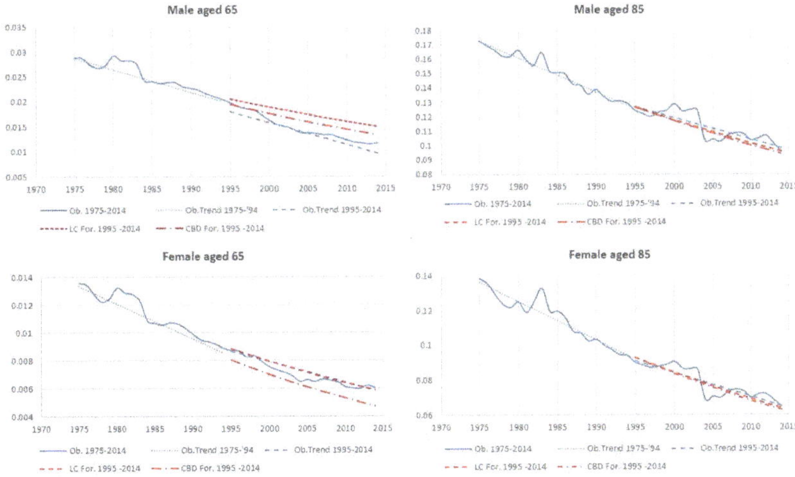

Figure 5. LC and CBD models: comparisons between observed and forecast mortality trends.

As far as men are concerned, the LC model initially overestimates $q^O_{x,t}$ from ages 57 to 80 (approximately), with persistence across years. In particular, the overestimation errors become sharply evident as the projection is extended to the last year of the forecast horizon. Figure 6 multi-dimensionally shows the ratio between projected and the real death probabilities. The described LC performance trend is also graphically reported by the Figure 7, comparing projections at ages 65 and 85 to the observed data. The overestimation starts decreasing from age 80, pointing out that the divergence between $q^O_{x,t}$ and $q^P_{x,t}$ is really close to zero. However, for high ages at the extreme of the interval, LC forecasts systematically underestimate $q^O_{x,t}$.

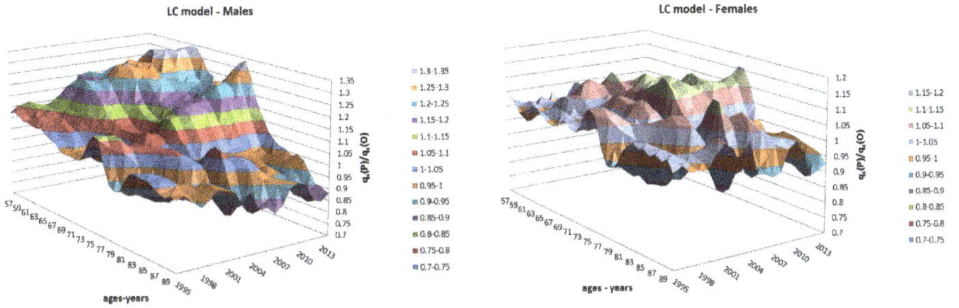

Figure 6. Lee–Carter Fixed Horizon Backtest: $\frac{q^P_{x,t}}{q^O_{x,t}}$ ratio.

As for women, the divergence between $q^O_{x,t}$ and $q^P_{x,t}$ is sharply smaller than for men. This is particularly evident in Figure 6, which shows that the forecast initially underestimates real data converging at the age 65 and then starts overestimating for a wide span of ages. Furthermore, the last part of the age range is again characterized by an underestimation path. However, the overestimation experienced at higher ages is smaller than the one observed in the male case.

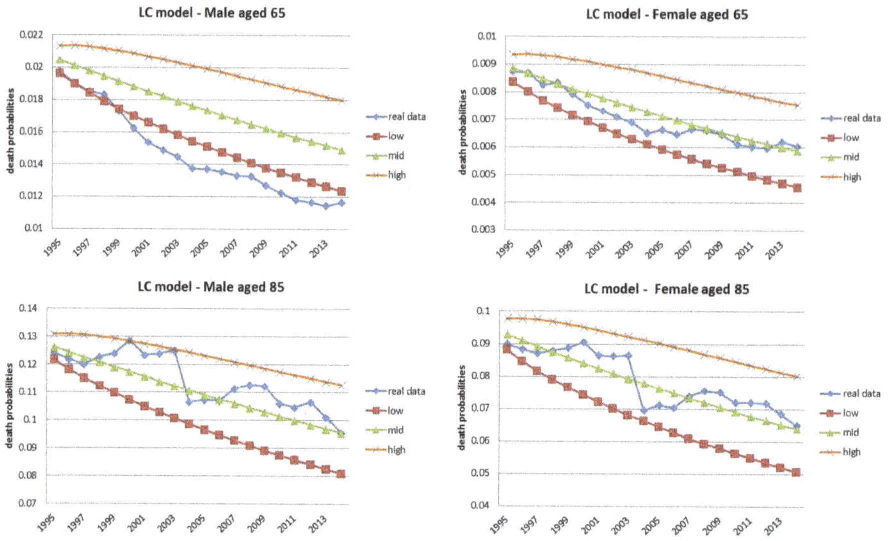

Figure 7. LC Fixed Horizon Backtest forecast: comparison between observed death rates and the corresponding 95% confidence interval of the forecast based on the time series 1975–1994.

The CBD forecast greatly overestimates the male mortality historical evolution, particularly for the central and last years of projection. The error is evident in the full range of ages, although it becomes smaller at the age 80, after which forecasts start underestimating $q^O_{x,t}$ with an increasing magnitude until the last age and the last projection year (i.e., $x = 90$ and $t = 2014$) (Figure 8).

When we look at the female case, the accuracy of the CBD forecast is worse. In this case, in fact, we can notice a wide and systematic underestimation on approximately all of the first half of the age range for almost the totality of the forecast horizon. In particular, the forecast error reduces around the age 68, then it starts overestimating until $x = 85$, after which it underestimates again. However, at $x = 85$, the forecast is relatively accurate, with values of $q^O_{x,t}$ all inside the confidence interval (Figure 9).

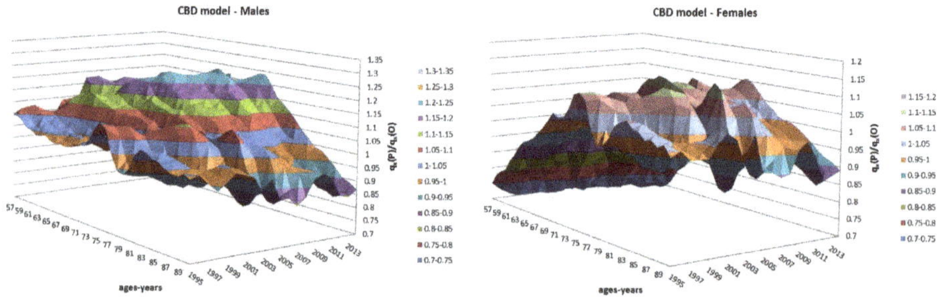

Figure 8. Cairns–Blake–Dowd Fixed Horizon Backtest: $\frac{q^P_{x,t}}{q^O_{x,t}}$ ratio.

In conclusion, both models make similar forecast errors. On the one hand, regarding males, the error is represented by an initial overestimation that smoothly converges to the real data and then starts underestimating, although the divergences experienced with the CBD model are characterized by a smaller variability with respect to the LC model. On the other hand, the female case shows an initial underestimation converging to the real data and then a fluctuation of overestimation and final underestimation. In general, the LC model provides a better fit over a wide range of ages, showing lower variability in both over and underestimation.

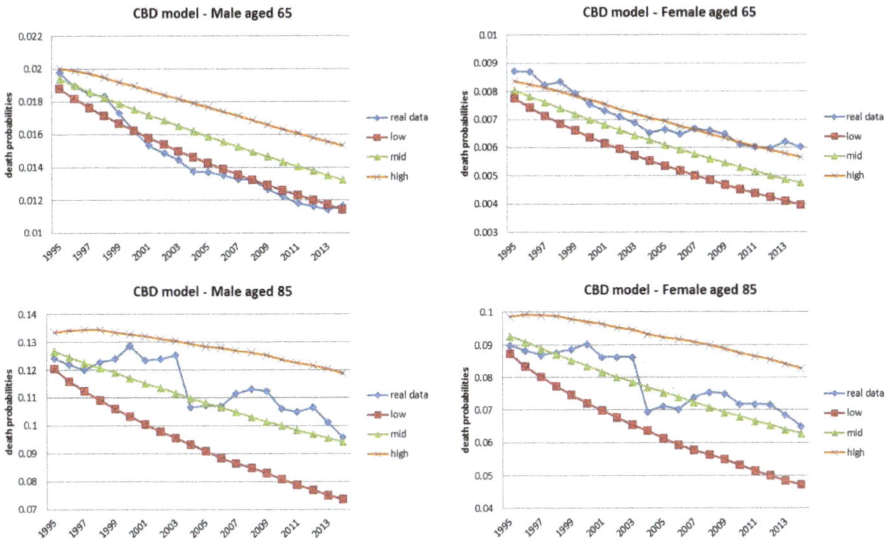

Figure 9. CBD Fixed Horizon Backtest forecast: comparison between observed death rates and the corresponding 95% confidence interval of the forecast based on the time series 1975–1994.

In any case, the choice between the models becomes difficult at particular ages. Figure 10 shows the high and low confidence intervals for both models. Even though LC curves are nested into the CBD lines with greater differences shown in the male case, both models' confidence intervals include the observed data, providing theoretical robustness to the projections.

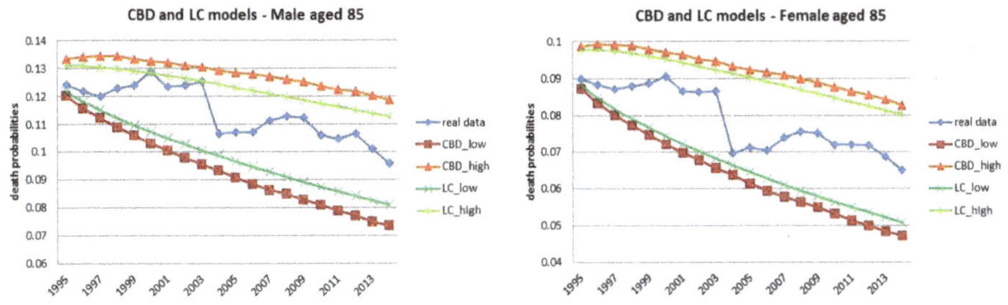

Figure 10. Fixed Horizon Backtest forecast: comparison between CBD and LC confidence intervals at age 85.

Table 4. Root Mean Squared Errors (RMSE) between observed $q^O_{x,t}$ and forecast $q^P_{x,t}$.

Fixed Horizon Backtest				
	CBD model		LC model	
Prediction Years	Male	Female	Male	Female
1995-2014	0.00625	0.00401	0.00596	0.00274
Jumping Fixed-Length Horizon Backtests				
	CBD model		LC model	
Prediction Years	Male	Female	Male	Female
1995–1999	0.00321	0.00201	0.00386	0.00210
2000–2004	0.00470	0.00411	0.00532	0.00369
2005–2009	0.00373	0.00366	0.00455	0.00301
2010–2014	0.00250	0.00229	0.00299	0.00219

4.2. *Jumping Fixed-Length Horizon Backtests*

From the results shown in Table 4, it is clear that the two models best capture the trend of female mortality. More specifically, the accuracy of the prediction about the next five years, using the periods 1975–1994 and 1990–2009 as the database, is far higher than the other two sub-groups of forecast. On the contrary, neither model shows the underestimating and overestimating path of the $q^O_{x,t}$ at various ages, which was peculiar in characterizing the result in the previous backtesting case. Only the results of the CBD model show a similar pattern, although in this case with overestimates and underestimates staggered by age differently from period to period. This point will be discussed in detail hereafter.

The analysed models should be assessed on a long-term prediction, but in this case, it is particularly noticeable how a change in the starting point of the time series makes the models differently incorporate the changes in mortality that occurred in the past 20 years. This is generally accomplished through the parameter estimates, which are also reflected throughout the extrapolation process associated with the model. However, an estimation procedure cannot guarantee a priori a constant performance of the forecast. This is also due to the fact that the dynamic of mortality varies in accordance with a multiplicity of social factors that affect the life of every person. Unfortunately, mathematical models are not always able to capture such factors[11]. "We conclude that the deviations from exponential law at young ages can be explained by heterogeneity, namely by the presence of a subpopulation with a high initial mortality rate presumably due to congenital defects, while those for old ages can be viewed as fluctuations and explained by stochastic effects" (Avraam et al. 2013, p. 1).

Now, we analyse the immediate effects of these estimates, starting with the LC model (1). The parameters α_x and β_x are time-independent age-specific constants, so their estimations will depend on the historical period used as the database and do not need to be predicted. The k_t index captures the time-series common risk factor in that same period, showing the main mortality trend for all ages at time t. Forecasts are produced by extrapolating the time index k_t, and the mortality projections at each age are all linked together by the product[12] $\beta_x k_t$ (1).

In this backtesting framework, the shift forward of the database shows a continuous decline in mortality provided by the estimates of the parameter α_x and k_t. Moreover, the estimations for the parameter β_x referring to the male case show greater values at the beginning of the age range ($57 \le x \le 90$) than at the end. This result describes a greater decrease in mortality for those ages with respect to the others, at which β_x presents smaller estimated values (Figure 11, male).

[11] Even though the LC and CBD models do not take into account social factors in their original formulation, several other studies have considered heterogeneity and vitality factors (Li and Anderson 2009; Li and Anderson 2013).

[12] For this reason, we decided to plot exclusively the β_x dynamics, since they show a more interesting variability with respect to the k_t parameters that, in this case, are barely distant parallel and smooth curves among backtest jumps.

This scenario is in line ex ante with the historical experience. However, the forecast for the period 2000–2004 shows a systematic overestimation of the $q^O_{x,t}$ for both men and women until the age $x = 80$ (Figure 12, LC model). Taking into consideration the female case, the estimates of the parameter β_x are more susceptible to changes in the starting point of the time series. Figure 11 shows this for the female case. Needless to say, the female β_x trend improved the accuracy of the forecast for the periods 1995–1999 and 2010–2014 (Figure 12, LC model).

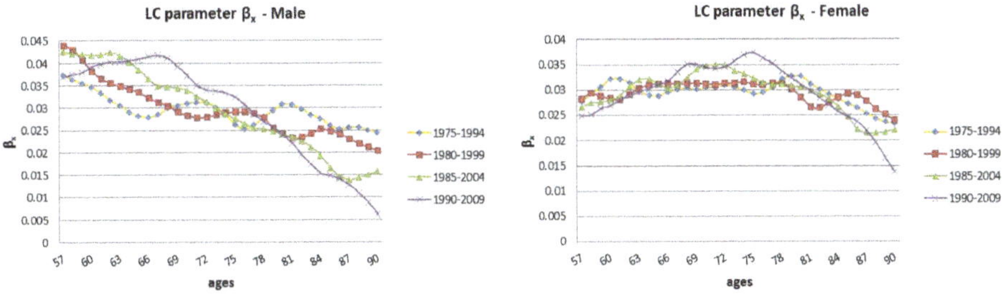

Figure 11. LC Jumping Fixed-Length-Horizon: β_x parameter estimates.

In the case of CBD model (2), the presence of two time-varying parameters $k_t^{(1)}$ and $k_t^{(2)}$ should increase at least a priori the forecasting performance with respect to the LC model. This result is evident for the male forecast in the short-run (Table 4). As mentioned, in the CBD model, the $k_t^{(1)}$ mortality index represents the level of the mortality curve, after the logit transformation. A reduction in $k_t^{(1)}$ entails a parallel downward shift of the logit-transformed mortality curve, which represents an overall mortality improvement. In particular, this is what occurred in practice, with greater effects for the female case that are enhanced by the smooth divergences of $k_t^{(1)}$ trends between sexes. This is clear on the left-hand side of Figure 13 below, in which we also checked for the new-data-invariant property of the model (Chan et al. 2014).

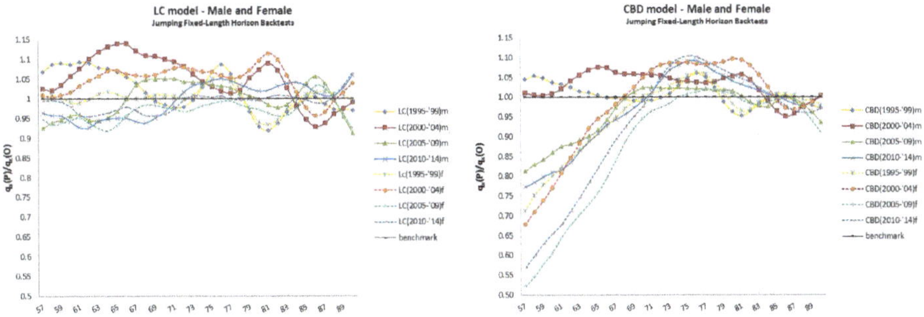

Figure 12. LC and CBD $\frac{q^P_{x,t}}{q^O_{x,t}}$ ratio: comparison between models. Note: the curves represent the average of the $\frac{q^P_{x,t}}{q^O_{x,t}}$ ratio over the five-years forecast horizon.

In this case, the jumps of five years ahead do not seem to affect the $k_t^{(1)}$ trend. This is also evidenced by the substantial continuity of the overall reduction in mortality. This is not the case as far as the the $k_t^{(2)}$ mortality index is concerned. Its path drafts the slope of the logit-transformed mortality curve. An increase in $k_t^{(2)}$ entails an increase in the steepness of the logit-transformed mortality curve, which means that mortality at younger ages i.e., those below the mean age $\bar{x}$ (here $\bar{x} = 73.5$) improves more rapidly than at older ages. This is clear on the right-hand side of Figure 13. Regarding the male case, we find that the speed of increase in $k_t^{(2)}$ is greater for the periods 1985–2004 and 1990–2009 than for the other two. For this reason, the projected $q_{x,t}^P$ shows stronger improvements in mortality for the periods 2005–2009 and 2010–2014 than for the others, particularly for the ages lower than $x = 69$. More in depth, results show an underestimation of the $q_{x,t}^O$ for the ages lower than $x = 69$ and a smooth overestimation path for those higher. Despite the fact that the growth of $k_t^{(2)}$ between 1980 and 1999 is higher than that of 1975–1994 and that the reduction of $k_t^{(1)}$ is greater, we find that $q_{x,t}^P$ sharply overestimates $q_{x,t}^O$ in the period 1995–1999 and particularly in 2000–2004 for the full range of ages.

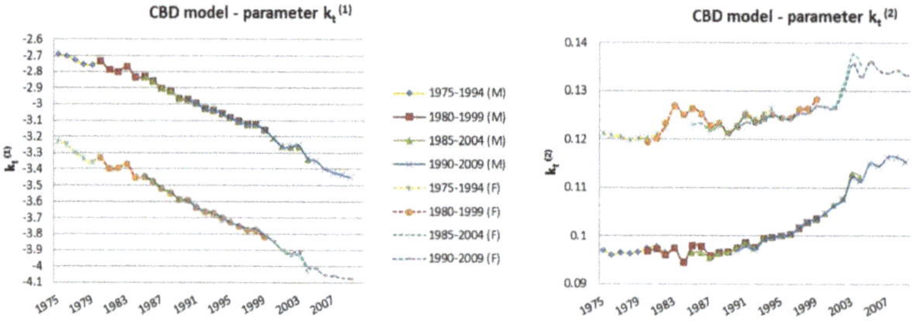

Figure 13. CBD Jumping Fixed-Length-Horizon: parameter estimates.

Regarding women, $k_t^{(2)}$ presents similar records to men, whereas for the period 1990–2009, the growth rate of $k_t^{(1)}$ is slightly attenuated. In contrast with the male scenario, in this case, $q_{x,t}^P$ systematically and significantly underestimates $q_{x,t}^O$ from the age $x = 57$, converging gradually to the observed data as x moves towards $\bar{x}$. Moreover, Figure 14 shows that the underestimations are larger for the projection periods 2005–2009 and 2010–2014. This error path does not influence the forecasts of ages higher than $\bar{x}$ that generally overestimate $q_{x,t}^O$. In particular, for ages higher than $\bar{x}$, forecasts of the periods 1995–1999 and 2010–2014 show better results than those of the other two projection windows (Figure 12, CBD model).

Hence, comparatively, we conclude that a good result for the performance index RMSE (Table 4) can hide some compensation for the forecast error in terms of age and time. Figure 14 graphically shows the described scenario.

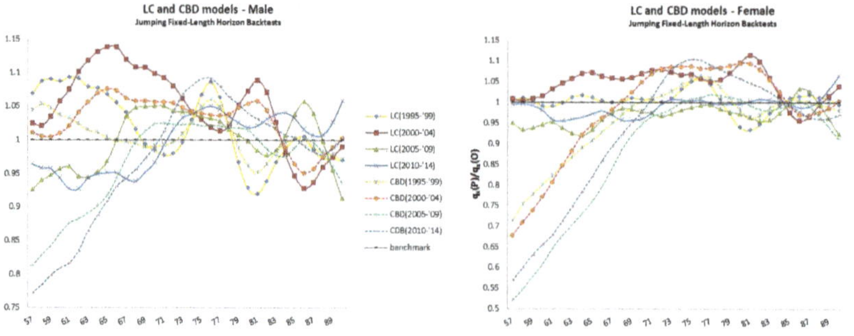

Figure 14. LC and CBD $\frac{q_{x,t}^P}{q_{x,t}^O}$ ratio: comparison between models on the same gender. Note: the curves represent the average of the $\frac{q_{x,t}^P}{q_{x,t}^O}$ ratio over the five-years forecast horizon.

4.3. Rolling Fixed-Length Horizon Backtests

Finally, the analysis concludes with the study of the forecast convergence to the observed $q^O_{x,t}$ in the year[13] 2014. For this reason, we build a framework of 19 groups of estimations and projections, rolling the database (fixed-length of 20 years) sequentially forward from[14] 1975 to 1993. Then, we compare the 2014 forecast obtained in each group with the realized mortality for that year. We observe that the comparison enhances the same critical issues analysed in the previous paragraphs, with particular emphasis on two main aspects.

Firstly, scrolling the database over time year by year gives rise to strong fluctuations in the performance of the prediction measured by the ratio of $q^P_{x,t}$ and $q^O_{x,t}$. These oscillations (Figures 15 and 16) are evident for both sexes in the results of both the LC and the CBD models. Moreover, the trend is interrupted by a deep break in correspondence of the 1985–2004 database. In particular, the previous base (1984–2003) provided a strong overestimation of $q^O_{x,t}$ especially at old ages. The base 1985–2004 data has then reduced the size, while the next one (1986–2005) moved closer to $q^O_{x,t}$.

One the one hand, this result may be related to the cohort effect described at the beginning of paragraph 4, since the cohort effect is proportionally greater on the base of data including years before 1985. On the other hand, they can be partially justified by also recalling that the year 2003 was characterized by a sharp rise in mortality, especially at old ages. Therefore, this historical event may have affected the estimated parameters. However, in the male case, both models systematically underestimate $q^O_{x,t}$ when the age is lower than $x = 73$, and overestimate when it is higher.

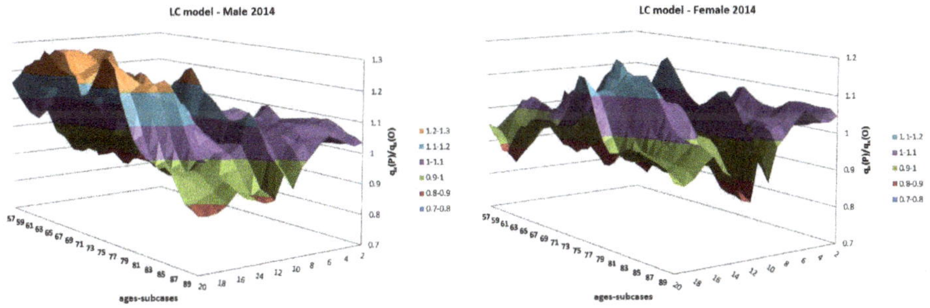

Figure 15. LC Rolling Fixed-Length Horizon Backtests: $\frac{q^P_{x,t}}{q^O_{x,t}}$ ratio 2014.

This result is particularly evident when the "lookback" horizon is 1985–2004, and also for the following cases. In particular, CBD underestimates when the database refers to the period 1981–2000. However, for the period 1985–2004, the divergence becomes greater compared to the LC model (Figures 15 and 16). As is shown, the choice of the database plays a crucial role in forecasting mortality.

Figure 15 shows the ratio between the projected and observed death probabilities for the year 2014. Table 3 shows the projections obtained for that year on each pair of "Lookback" and "Lookforward" horizons.

---

13 The choice for the year 2014 was motivated by the observed regular mortality path. The 2015 mortality trend is expected to be increased, particularly at old ages (Istat 2016).

14 These represent the initial years of the 20-year-long database; i.e., 1975 refers to the estimation period 1975–1994, and so on.

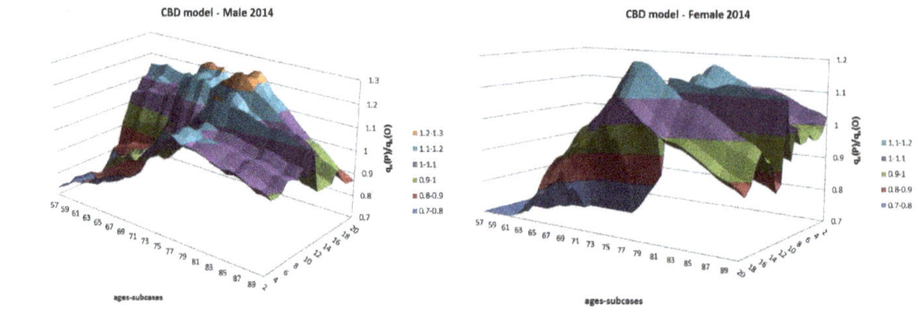

Figure 16. CBD Rolling Fixed-Length Horizon Backtests: $\frac{q^P_{x,t}}{q^O_{x,t}}$ ratio 2014.

In particular, the sub-case index of the graph shows the position of that year on the projection horizon (i.e., 20 means that the year 2014 was the 20th year of the projection, 19 means the 19th, and so on). Since the dataset is rolling over time and decreasing the projection horizon, we decided to show the position of the year 2014 to take into account both the specific sub-case and the related length of the forecast horizon. Figure 16 shows the same for the CBD model with an inverted order of sub-cases for males to better show the shape of each curve.

Secondly, we detected substantial differences between the performances of the two models by analysing female mortality. Figure 16 shows how the CBD model systematically underestimates real mortality until the age of 75 and then starts converging to $q^O_{x,t}$ after that "threshold" age. This result, which was already evident in the previous analysis, is likely linked to the combined effects on the CBD model (2) of the role of the mean age $\bar{x}$ (in our case $\bar{x} = 73.5$) of the age group, for which the forecast is made, and of the observed female mortality pattern. These results are also confirmed from the analysis of the confidence interval referred to the forecast. Figure 17 shows that, in the female case at age 65 ($t = 2014$), $q^O_{x,t}$ is always outside the confidence interval, while at age 85, it is inside with central values almost converged to the real data in each sub-case (Figure 18). In the case of the LC model, the initial underestimation of the $q^O_{x,t}$ is much less pronounced with respect to the previous case. Moreover, the "threshold" age, with respect to which the forecast underestimates and then overestimates $q^O_{x,t}$, increases as the database moves forward (Figure 15).

Figures 17 and 18 show the convergence of the projections to the observed data for the year 2014, at ages 65 and 85. The x-axis shows the position of the year on the forecast horizon as before. Figures 19 and 20 present the same for the Lee–Carter model.

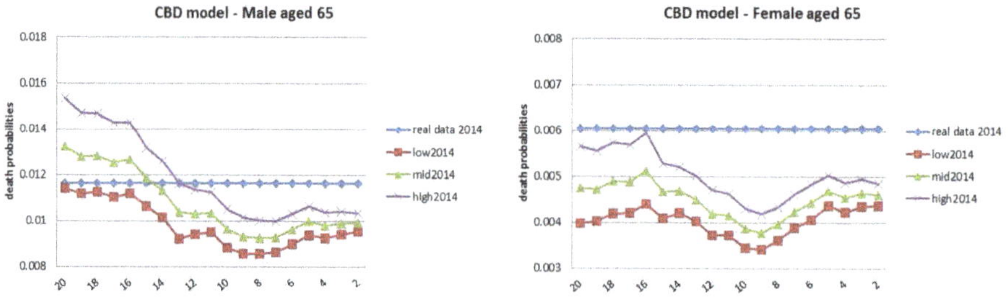

Figure 17. CBD Rolling Fixed-Length Horizon Backtests (age 65): convergence to real data (2014).

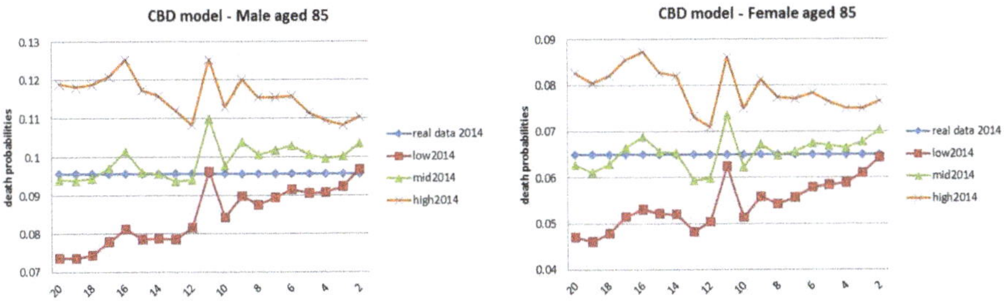

Figure 18. CBD Rolling Fixed-Length Horizon Backtests (age 85): convergence to real data (2014).

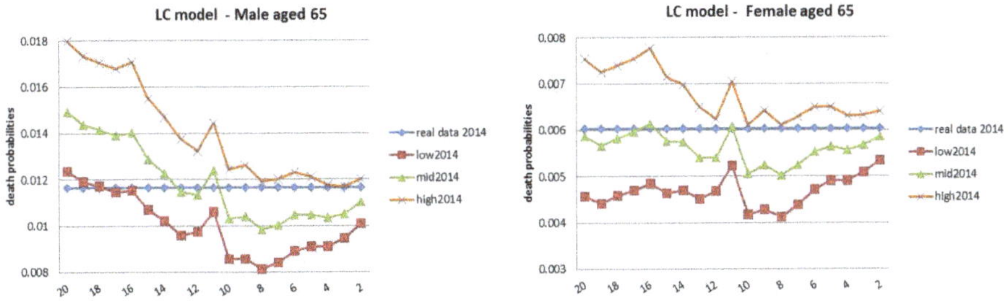

Figure 19. LC Rolling Fixed-Length Horizon Backtests (age 65): convergence to real data (2014).

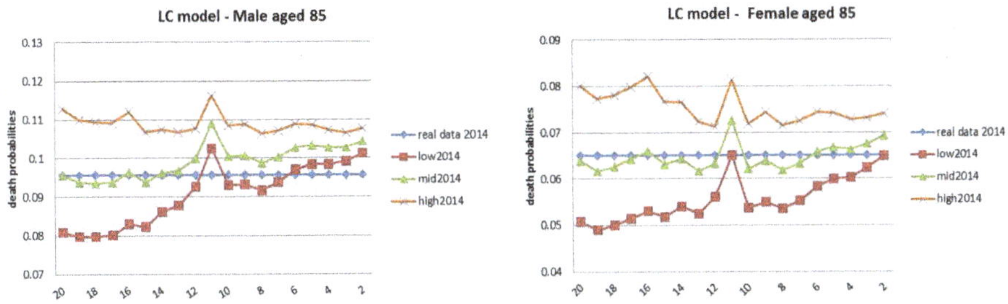

Figure 20. LC Rolling Fixed-Length Horizon Backtests (age 85): convergence to real data (2014).

5. Conclusions

The main aims of this paper are to scrutinize the forecast for both sexes proposed by the original formulation of the models, given the wide use of LC at the national level, and to analyse the long-term forecast with respect to the short term, observing qualitative differences in the estimation of the parameter accordingly to changes in the starting point of the database.

Regarding the former, we find that, basically, neither model was able to capture the shock in terms of improvements on the male mortality trend, with greater biases for ages lower than $x = 75$, which were those more affected by the improvement. In this sense, CBD forecasts for those ages are more biased than LC projections in terms of overestimations. The limited capacity of the models to predict male mortality is evident in all of the three backtesting frameworks. Table 4 numerically summarizes the difference in terms of performances between sexes for the first two backtesting approaches. In addition, the analysis of the forecast for the year 2014 that we provided with the third approach confirms this result. Moreover, women's forecasts are widely more accurate than men's, with small biases observed both in the short and the medium-term. However, in the female case, CBD projections showed particularly deep and systematic underestimations with respect to ages lower than 75.

From the comparison between the short-term and the medium-term forecast, we find that changes in the starting point of the database widely affect the estimation of the LC parameters, particularly for β_x with observable impacts on the projections. The female forecasts are more influenced by those changes in β_x. The CBD model satisfies the "new-data-invariant" property for the estimation of the parameter $k_t^{(1)}$, while $k_t^{(2)}$ presents persistent changes for the same year as the dataset slides forward. This aspect is more evident in males than in females. In particular, the adjustment of the parameter $k_t^{(2)}$ (i.e., $x - \bar{x}$) affects mortality forecasts with weights of the opposite sign at the extremes of the considered age range. The weight is greater the larger the age range. This structural characteristic of the model, albeit simultaneously with $k_t^{(1)}$, results in a systematic underestimation of the $q_{x,t}^{O}$ for ages lower than $\bar{x}$ that gradually decrease as x moves towards $\bar{x}$. Moreover, mortality forecasts around $\bar{x}$ are almost exclusively explained by $k_t^{(1)}$, since $(x - \bar{x})$ is really close to 0 in that case. On the contrary, as x gets closer to the upper limit of the age range, the weight of $(x - \bar{x})$ on mortality forecasts changes with the opposite sign, with resulting overestimation of the $q_{x,t}^{O}$. For these reasons, the risk in terms of application of the models is conspicuous because it could potentially affect both the mortality risk and the longevity risk. Taking into consideration the variability of both the parameters β_x (LC) and $k_t^{(2)}$ (CBD), it is difficult to judge a priori what these two rigidities penalize more in the mortality forecast.

As far as the CBD model is concerned, we find that projections are not reliable for describing mortality at ages before $x = 75$. For this reason, LC projections are preferable for describing Italian mortality in this particular framework of years and ages. However, CBD forecasts showed a more restrained variability of the forecast error at higher ages with respect to LC. This result and the fact that usually the CBD confidence interval at higher ages is wider (i.e., LC is nested in CBD) than LC ones provide a more accurate theoretical robustness to the CBD for ages greater than $x = 75$.

We would like to make clear that we examined the models in their original form, so we cannot rule out the possibility that some extensions of the models might resolve these issues on Italian data (1975–2014). In particular, we expect that the results of both models may be improved with the adoption of the model extensions, including a cohort component, in order to reduce the bias caused by the cohort effect of those born during the First World War. Moreover, the CBD extension, including the quadratic term of the age component, may solve the weighting issue of the model over the considered interval of ages on this data.

In conclusion, the results seem to be relevant for private and public Italian annuity providers that use LC forecasts as demographic bases. From this perspective, the choice between the two models may vary in accordance with the purpose of the use of the model (e.g., the age and the sex of the insured). Even though we limited our analysis to the study of the forecast $q_{x,t}$, we can infer that a backtesting analysis of annuity prices, based on the forecast obtained by the original formulations of the models, would show evidence of a distortion caused by the forecast error on the money's worth of an annuity and on reserves.

Acknowledgments: The authors want to thank the Center for Research on Pensions and Welfare Policies (CeRP) for supporting this study. It is one of the CeRP's contributions to the hackUniTO research project about aging, promoted by the University of Turin.

Author Contributions: The authors contributed equally to this work.

Conflicts of Interest: The authors declare no conflict of interest.

Appendix A. Lee–Carter Estimation and Projection

Appendix A.1. Parameter Estimations

The parameter estimation was computed with respect to the *Ordinary Least Square* (OLS) estimation method in accordance with the original approach suggested by the authors.

The following constraints were used to find a unique solution for the parameters:

$$\sum_{x=x_1}^{x_m} \beta_x = 1 \qquad and \qquad \sum_{t=t_1}^{t_n} k_t = 0. \tag{A1}$$

To obtain the estimation for the variable $\hat{\alpha}_x$, it was necessary to compute the partial derivative of the equation $LS(\alpha,\beta,k) = \sum_x \sum_t (\ln(m_{x,t}) - \alpha_x - \beta_x k_t)^2$, with respect to α_x. Then, as a first order condition, we get:

$$\hat{\alpha}_x = \frac{1}{t_n - t_1 + 1} \sum_t \ln(m_{x,t}), \tag{A2}$$

where the denominator simply represents the number of years considered in the dataset, and $x = x_1, ..., x_m$ is the considered range of ages. As is expressed by the Equation (A2), the estimation for the first parameter α_x was given by the average of the logarithms of the central rate of mortality over time t. Furthermore, the estimations of $\hat{\beta}_x$ and $\hat{k}_t$ for the parameters β_x and k_t were obtained by adopting the Singular Value Decomposition of the matrix A of elements $(\ln m_{x_i,t_j} - \alpha_{x_i})$, with i as age index and j as time index (years considered in the data).

At this point, the estimated parameters were recalibrated so the differences between the actual and the estimated total deaths in each year were zero. This implies that the recalibrated $\hat{k}_t^*$ solves the equation[15]:

$$\sum_x d_{x,t} = \sum_x e^{(\hat{\alpha}_x^* + \hat{\beta}_x^* \hat{k}_t^*)} L_{x,t}. \tag{A3}$$

Finally, the estimated parameters were adjusted to satisfy the constraint at (A1) for the parameter $\hat{k}_t^*$. Then:

$$a_x^* = \hat{\alpha}_x + \hat{\beta}_x \bar{k}, \tag{A4}$$

$$\beta_x^* = \hat{\beta}_x \left(\sum_{j=1}^{x_m - x_1 + 1} \hat{\beta}_{1j} \right), \tag{A5}$$

$$k_t^* = (\hat{k}_t^* - \bar{k}) \left(\sum_{j=1}^{x_m - x_1 + 1} \hat{\beta}_{1j} \right), \tag{A6}$$

where $\bar{k} = \frac{1}{t_n - t_1 + 1} \sum_{t=1}^{t_n} \hat{k}_t^*$ is the arithmetic average of $\hat{k}_t^*$ with respect to time t, and $\left(\sum_{j=1}^{x_m - x_1 + 1} \hat{\beta}_{1j} \right)$ is simply the sum of all the estimated $\hat{\beta}$, which sum to 1. The fitted model is then used to estimate the median and the 95% prediction interval.

---

15 Equation (A3) has no explicit solution, so it has to be solved numerically.

Appendix A.2. Parameter Projection

We projected the estimated[16] parameters k_t^* of the Lee–Carter model using a *Random Walk with Drift* equation:

$$k_t = k_{t-1} + d + \eta_t \qquad with \qquad \eta_{x,t} \sim \mathcal{N}(0,1) \;\; and \;\; E(\eta_s, \eta_t) = 0, \tag{A7}$$

where the drift d is estimated by the formula:

$$\hat{d} = \frac{(k_2^* - k_1^*) + (k_3^* - k_2^*) + ... + (k_T^* - k_{T-1}^*)}{t_n - t_1} = \frac{(k_T^* - k_1^*)}{t_n - t_1},$$

with k_T^* and k_1^*, respectively, given by the first and the last elements of the vector $k_t^* = [k_1^*, ..., k_T^*]$. The drift is simply the arithmetic mean of the differenced series of estimated parameters.

After having solved Equation (A7) of the RWD model, we describe the projection of the parameter k_t at time $T + \Delta t$ as follows:

$$\hat{k}_{T+\Delta t} = k_T^* + (\Delta t)\hat{d} + \sqrt{\Delta t}\eta_t.$$

At this point, it was possible to get the equation for the projection of the central rates of mortality as follows:

$$\hat{m}_{x,T+\Delta t} = e^{a_x^* + b_x^* \hat{k}_{T+\Delta t}}.$$

Finally, we transformed the central mortality rates into probabilities by adopting the Reed and Merrell (1939) method. The relation is expressed by the equation:

$$_n q_{x,t} = 1 - e^{-n(m_{x,t}) - n^3 0.008 (m_{x,t})^2}.$$

Appendix B. Cairns–Blake–Dowd Estimation and Projection

According to the original formulation of the model proposed by Cairns et al. (2006), Equation (2) is the result of the logit transformation of the following model equation:

$$q_{x,t} = \frac{e^{k_t^{(1)} + k_t^{(2)}(x - \bar{x})}}{1 + e^{k_t^{(1)} + k_t^{(2)}(x - \bar{x})}}. \tag{A8}$$

Fitted values for the stochastic processes $k_t^{(1)}$ and $k_t^{(2)}$ were obtained using least squares applied to the Equation (A8). The fitted model is then used to estimate the median and the 95% prediction interval.

The parameters vector $\vec{k}_t = \left[k_t^{(1)}, k_t^{(2)}\right]'$ has been projected by considering the following equation of a two-dimensional random walk with drift:

$$\vec{k}_{t+1} = \vec{k}_t + \mu + CN(t+1), \tag{A9}$$

where

- μ is a constant 2×1 vector of drifts, computed as the arithmetic mean of the differenced series of estimated parameters;
- C is a constant 2×2 upper triangular matrix, derived by the unique Cholesky decomposition of the variance–covariance matrix $V = CC'$ of the parameters vector $\vec{k}_{t+1}$; and
- $N(t+1)$ is a two-dimensional standard normal random variable.

---

16 We used MATLAB (R2010b, The MathWorks, Inc., Natick, Massachusetts 01760 USA) for estimation and forecast.

The adopted forecast method treats the estimated parameters as if they were the true parameter values (parameters certainty). In particular, the presented projections were computed[17] considering parameter certainty based on 5000 simulation trials.

References

ANIA. 2014. *Le Basi Demografiche Per Rendite Vitalizie a 1900–2020 e a62*. Technical report. Roma: Associazione Nazionale fra le Imprese Assicuratrici (ANIA).

Avraam, Demetris, Joao Pedro de Magalhaes, and Bakhtier Vasiev. 2013. A mathematical model of mortality dynamics across the lifespan combining heterogeneity and stochastic effects. *Experimental Gerontology* 48: 801–11.

Booth, Heather, Rob Hyndman, Leonie Tickle, and Piet De Jong. 2006. Lee-carter mortality forecasting: A multi-country comparison of variants and extensions. *Demographic Research* 15: 289–310.

Cairns, Andrew J. G., David Blake, and Kevin Dowd. 2006. A two-factor model for stochastic mortality with parameter uncertainty: Theory and calibration. *Journal of Risk and Insurance* 73: 687–718.

Cairns, Andrew J. G., David Blake, Kevin Dowd, Guy D. Coughlan, David Epstein, Alen Ong, and Igor Balevich. 2009. A quantitative comparison of stochastic mortality models using data from england and wales and the united states. *North American Actuarial Journal* 13: 1–35.

Chan, Wai-Sum, Johnny Siu-Hang Li, and Jackie Li. 2014. The cbd mortality indexes: Modeling and applications. *North American Actuarial Journal* 18: 38–58.

Dowd, Kevin, Andrew J. G. Cairns, David Blake, Guy D Coughlan, David Epstein, and Marwa Khalaf-Allah. 2010a. Backtesting stochastic mortality models: An ex post evaluation of multiperiod-ahead density forecasts. *North American Actuarial Journal* 14: 281–98.

Draper, Norman R., and Harry Smith. 2014. *Applied Regression Analysis*. New York: John Wiley & Sons.

Istat. 2001. *Tavole di mortalità della popolazione italiana per provincia e regione di residenza. anno 1998.* Roma: Servizio Popolazione Istruzione e Cultura.

Istat. 2008. *Previsioni demografiche*. 1 gennaio 2007-1 gennaio 2051. Nota informativa, Popolazione. Technical report. Roma: Istat.

Istat. 2016. *Indicatori Demografici: Stime Per L'anno 2015*. Technical report. Roma: Istat.

Keyfitz, Nathan, and Hal Caswell. 2005. *Applied Mathematical Demography*. New York: Springer, vol. 47.

Kullback, Solomon, and Richard A. Leibler. 1951. On information and sufficiency. *The Annals of Mathematical Statistics* 22: 79–86.

Lee, Ronald. 2000. The lee-carter method for forecasting mortality, with various extensions and applications. *North American Actuarial Journal* 4: 80–91.

Lee, Ronald, and Timothy Miller. 2001. Evaluating the performance of the lee-carter method for forecasting mortality. *Demography* 38: 537–49.

Lee, Ronald D., and Lawrence R Carter. 1992. Modeling and forecasting US mortality. *Journal of the American Statistical Association* 87: 659–71.

Li, Jackie. 2010. Projections of new zealand mortality using the lee-carter model and its augmented common factor extension. *New Zealand Population Review* 36: 27–53.

Li, Nan, and Ronald Lee. 2005. Coherent mortality forecasts for a group of populations: An extension of the lee-carter method. *Demography* 42: 575–94.

Li, Ting, and James Anderson. 2013. Shaping human mortality patterns through intrinsic and extrinsic vitality processes. *Demographic Research* 28: 341–72.

Li, Ting, and James J Anderson. 2009. The vitality model: A way to understand population survival and demographic heterogeneity. *Theoretical Population Biology* 76: 118–31.

Loisel, Stéphane, and Daniel Serant. 2007. In the core of longevity risk: Hidden dependence in stochastic mortality models and cut-offs in prices of longevity swaps. *Cahier de Recherche de l'ISFA WP2044*. Working Paper. Available online: http://isfaserveur.univ-lyon1.fr/ stephane.loisel/Loisel-Serant-ISFA-WP2044.pdf

[17] We used MATLAB for estimation and forecast.

Maccheroni, Carlo. 2014. Diverging tendencies by age in sex differentials in mortality in italy. *South East Journal of Political Science (SEEJPS)* 2: 42–58.

Maccheroni, Carlo. 2016. *The Actuarial Aging of Italian Veterans of World War I Born 1889-1906 and a Comparison to the Cohorts Born During the Years Immediately Following*. Technical report. Torino: Department of Economics and Statistics (WP36), University of Torino.

Mavros, George, Andrew J.G. Cairns, Torsten Kleinow, and George Streftaris. 2014. *A Parsimonious Approach to Stochastic Mortality Modelling with Dependent Residuals.* Technical report. Edinburgh: Citeseer.

Pitacco, Ermanno, Michel Denuit, Steven Haberman, and Annamaria Olivieri. 2009. *Modelling Longevity Dynamics for Pensions and Annuity Business.* London: Oxford University Press.

Reed, Lowell Jacob, and Margaret Merrell. 1939. A short method for constructing an abridged life table. *American Journal of Epidemiology* 30: 33–62.

Thatcher, A. Roger, Väinö Kannisto, and James W. Vaupel. 1998. The force of mortality at ages 80 to 120. *Odense Monographs on Population Aging* 5: 104-20.

Vaupel, James W. 2010. Biodemography of human ageing. *Nature* 464: 536–42.

Whitehouse, Edward. 2007. Life-expectancy risk and pensions: Who bears the burden? OECD Social, Employment, and Migration Working Papers.(60): 46 pp. Working Paper. Retrieved from: http://www.oecd.org/social/soc/39469901.pdf

risks MDPI

Article

Minimum Protection in DC Funding Pension Plans and Margrabe Options

Pierre Devolder * and Sébastien de Valeriola *

Institute of Statistic, Biostatistic and Actuarial Science (ISBA), Université catholique de Louvain (UCL), Voie du Roman Pays, 20, 1348 Louvain-la-Neuve, Belgium
* Correspondence: pierre.devolder@uclouvain.be (P.D.); sebastien.devaleriola@uclouvain.be (S.d.V.)

Academic Editor: Luca Regis
Received: 14 November 2016; Accepted: 10 January 2017; Published: 18 January 2017

Abstract: The regulation on the Belgian occupational pension schemes has been recently changed. The new law allows for employers to choose between two different types of guarantees to offer to their affiliates. In this paper, we address the question arising naturally: which of the two guarantees is the best one? In order to answer that question, we set up a stochastic model and use financial pricing tools to compare the methods. More specifically, we link the pension liabilities to a portfolio of financial assets and compute the price of exchange options through the Margrabe formula.

Keywords: pensions; Defined Contributions; guaranteed rate; option theory; Margrabe formula

1. Introduction

In most European countries, the sustainability of the pension system has become a major concern. The past few decades have therefore seen an evolution of the pension plan designs (as remarked e.g., by the European Commission, [1]). On one hand, more and more plans are financed through funding by pension funds or group/life insurance contracts (as opposed to plans financed through pay-as-you-go mechanisms). On the other hand, Defined Contribution (DC) schemes have tended to overtake Defined Benefit (DB) schemes. This new pension plan model (funding and DC) addresses—at least partially—the sustainability problem. However, it generates another issue, which is related to the adequacy of the benefits: in such a plan, the affiliates bear all of the financial risk.

To protect the affiliates and make these plans politically acceptable, many European countries have enacted legislations. Among various types of guarantees (presented e.g., in [2]), some of them impose on pension sponsors ensuring a minimum financial performance on plan contributions. The Swiss system is one of them, and an early and interesting example. Dating back to 1985, it imposes a minimal guaranteed rate that can be revised every other year by the Federal Council, which takes into account financial markets to do so. Accordingly, the rate was progressively lowered from 4% (its value between 1985 and 2002) to its current level of 1.25%.

In 2003, Belgian authorities implemented the *Law on Complementary Pension* (LCP), obliging sponsors to guarantee a minimum rate of 3.25% on the employer's contributions and of 3.75% on employees' contributions. Since then, these values have proven to be unsustainable in the context of a decreasing interest rates market.

A reform act [1] has therefore been passed by the government (applicable since the beginning of 2016), that transforms the fixed minimum guaranteed rate into a variable rate, linked to the yield rate

[1] "Loi du 18 décembre 2015 visant à garantir la pérennité et le caractère social des pensions complémentaires et visant à renforcer le caractère complémentaire par rapport aux pensions de retraite", published in the *Moniteur Belge* on 24 December 2015.

of the 10 year Belgian governmental bond. As it is fluctuating, one needs to indicate how the guarantee is applied to the previously paid contributions. Two different computation approaches are described in the new legal text, designated as the *horizontal* and *vertical* methods. In the case of newly created plans, sponsors are allowed to choose between them. On the contrary, in the case of already existing plans, the method that has to be used depends on the funding vehicle of the plan.

The existence of two computation methods raises the natural question of their comparison. In this paper, we address it by setting a stochastic framework for the interest rates and considering the evolution of the pension liability over the years. In order to compare the amounts obtained from one initial contribution using the horizontal and vertical methods, we embrace two distinct approaches. On one hand, we simply compute the expectations of the corresponding stochastic processes and determine which method leads to the best results. This approach can be associated with the affiliates' point of view, as it estimates how much the affiliates will earn from the initial contribution.

On the other hand, we take the pension sponsor's point of view and compute the price of both pension guarantees. The topic of pension guarantee pricing has been much studied in the literature (starting with the seminal papers of Pennacchi and Fischer [3,4] and going on after that with [5,6], among many others). More specifically, we follow an Asset and Liability Management-driven methodology (as done for example in [7–9]): we suppose that the sponsor has an asset investment portfolio in front of its pension liabilities, and we try to determine which method is preferable for him, taking into account its investment preferences. In order to do so, we consider options allowing for exchanging the asset portfolio for the horizontal (respectively vertical) liability and compute their prices: the best method is the one associated to the cheapest option. This methodology has already been used, for example in [10]. The pricing of these exchange options is achieved using the *Margrabe formula* (see [11]). More precisely, we use a generalization of this formula to a stochastic interest rates framework obtained (in the general case, where assets and rates are not independent) by Bernard and Cui [12] (see also [13]).

The paper is organized as follows: in Section 2, we present the details of the reform act, such as the definition of the guaranteed rate, and describe the horizontal and vertical computation methods. Then, we set up a stochastic framework and perform the first comparison of the two methods in Section 3. Section 4 is devoted to our second comparison approach, using option prices and the Margrabe formula. Finally, we comment on the results and conclude in Section 5.

2. Detailed Design of the Reform Act

The new LCP links the guaranteed rate to a 24-month moving average of the 10-year OLO (i.e., Belgian governmental bond) yield rate . A cap and a floor is applied to this average, and the result is multiplied by a constant:

$$r_{\text{guaranteed}}(t_0) = \max\left(1.75\%; \min\left(\pi \frac{1}{24} \sum_{t=0\text{ months}}^{23\text{ months}} r_{\text{OLO 10}}(t_0 - t); 3.75\%\right)\right).$$

The value of π is defined as 65%, but the law states that, under some circumstances (which are linked to the evolution of the maximum rate of long-term insurance contracts), the National Bank of Belgium can decide to raise this percentage to 75% in 2018 and to 85% in 2020. Figure 1 shows the evolution of these rates between January 1991 and September 2015.

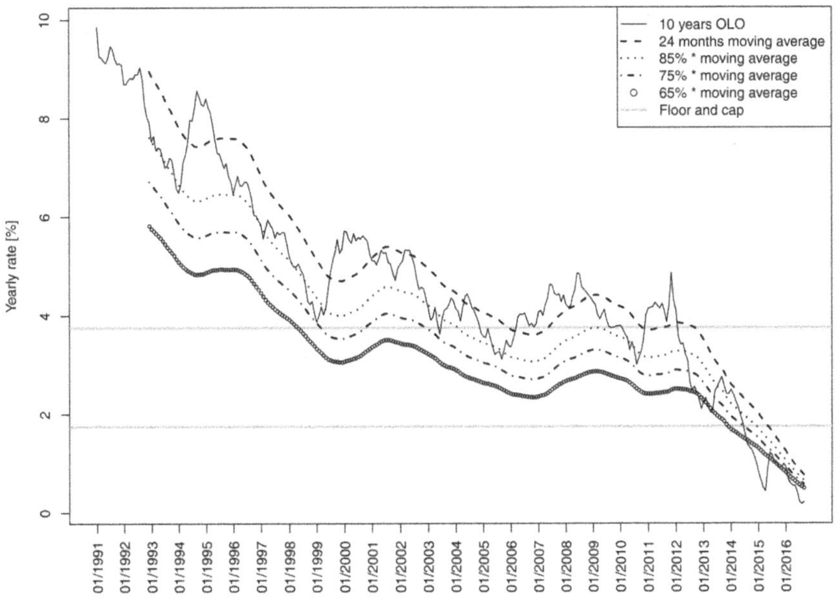

Figure 1. Different rates appearing in the definition of the reference rate.

Let us now present the two computation methods, which are summarized in Figure 2. The *vertical method* is used when the vehicle of an existing pension scheme is a pension fund (or a pure unit linked product sold by an insurance company), or when the sponsor of a new pension scheme (i.e., created before 1 January 2015) chooses so. In this case, the guaranteed rate of year t is applied to the whole amount of cotisations already paid by the affiliated up to year t. The *vertical liability* is then similar to the one produced by a savings product where the contributions are deposited, whose interest rate is the guaranteed rate, susceptible to be different from year to year.

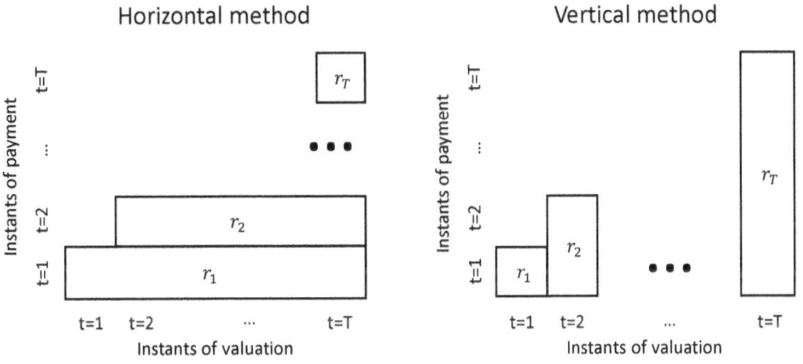

Figure 2. The two different methods of guaranteed rate application.

The *horizontal method* is used when the financing vehicle is a life insurance contract with interest rate guarantee or when the sponsor of a new pension scheme chooses so. Remark that, in this case, the guarantee level offered by the insurer can be different from the guarantee level that the sponsor must legally ensure to its affiliates. The guaranteed rate of year t is then applied to the new cotisations paid in year t, the cotisations already paid in years $t-1$ being accounted for with the guaranteed rate of year $t-1$, etc. The resulting *horizontal liability* is similar to the one produced by a standard life insurance product.

Let us first consider a very simple example to illustrate the two methods: assume that an affiliate successively pays two contributions of 1 Euro in 2016 and 2017, and retires in 2018. In Table 1, we consider two scenarios for the evolution of the guaranteed interest rate.

Table 1. Simple example illustrating how the horizontal and vertical methods are applied to the plan contributions.

	Scenario 1	Scenario 2
2016 guaranteed rate	2.5%	2.5%
2017 guaranteed rate	3.5%	2%
2018 liability (horizontal)	$1.025^2 + 1.035 = 2.086$	$1.025^2 + 1.02 = 2.071$
2018 liability (vertical)	$1.025 \cdot 1.035 + 1.035 = 2.096$	$1.025 \cdot 1.02 + 1.02 = 2.066$
Highest liability	vertical	horizontal

Although very simple, this small toy example provides some intuition about the relation between the two computation methods and the market evolution. If the interest rates are increasing, the vertical method leads to a larger amount. If, on the contrary, the interest rates are decreasing, the horizontal liability is larger.

3. Direct Comparison

In this section, we set up a stochastic framework for the interest rates and use it to compare the level of the two guarantees in absolute terms.

3.1. Interest Rate Framework

We assume that the short rate r_t is modelled with a Vasicek one-factor model, i.e., that in the risk-neutral world

$$\mathrm{d}r_t = k(\theta - r_t)\mathrm{d}t + \sigma \mathrm{d}W_t^r, \tag{1}$$

where $k > 0$, $\sigma > 0$ and θ are real constants and W^r is a standard Brownian motion. It is well-known (see e.g., [14]) that the solution of this stochastic differential equation is

$$r_t = r_0 e^{-kt} + \theta(1 - e^{-kt}) + \sigma \int_0^t e^{-k(t-s)} \mathrm{d}W_s^r, \tag{2}$$

and that the K-years zero-coupon bond yield is given by

$$r_t^K = \frac{C(K) + D(K) r_t}{K} = A(K) + B(K) r_t, \tag{3}$$

where

$$\begin{aligned} A(K) &= \frac{C(K)}{K}, \\ B(K) &= \frac{D(K)}{K}, \\ C(K) &= \left(\frac{\sigma^2}{2k^2} - \theta\right)(D(K) - K) + \frac{\sigma^2}{4k} D^2(K), \\ D(K) &= \frac{1}{k}\left(1 - e^{-kK}\right). \end{aligned} \tag{4}$$

Note that, in the following, we will drop the K dependence and write $A = A(K)$ and $B = B(K)$ when the context is clear.

For simplicity reasons, and in order to obtain closed formula, we now make four assumptions. First, we replace the coupon-bearing reference bond instrument by a standard zero-coupon bond, i.e., we assume that the OLO bonds do not bear coupons. Second, we define the reference rate R as a three-year moving average of the market rate, instead of a 24-month moving average. This assumption strongly simplifies the notations but does not make the mathematical development easier. It also limits the smoothing effect of the moving average, but we think that it does not affect the hierarchy between the two methods. Third, we neglect the cap and floor applied to the market rate. It then follows from previous expressions that

$$R_t = \pi \frac{r_{t-2}^{10} + r_{t-1}^{10} + r_t^{10}}{3}.$$

Finally, we consider that the parameter π is constant, i.e., that the National Bank does not modify it during the considered period of time.

Note that we assume that the quantities r_{-2}, r_{-1} and r_0 are known at $t = 0$.

We consider a unique unitary payment made at time $t = 0$ and look at the capital generated by this payment after T years (with $T \geq 4$).

3.2. *Expression of the Liability*

When the horizontal method is used, the expression of the liability is very simple:

$$L_T^h = e^{R_0 T} = \exp\left(\pi A(10)T + \frac{B(10)\pi T}{3}(r_{-2} + r_{-1} + r_0)\right),$$

which is a deterministic quantity.

When, on the contrary, the vertical method is preferred, the liability is given by

$$L_T^v = \prod_{t=0}^{T-1} e^{R_t} = \exp\left(\sum_{t=0}^{T-1} R_t\right). \tag{5}$$

The following proposition gives the distribution of this liability.

Proposition 1. *Under the assumptions stated above, the vertical liability at time T is given by*

$$L_T^v = \exp\left\{\pi AT + \pi B\left(\frac{1}{3}r_{-2} + \frac{2}{3}r_{-1} + (1+\Lambda(1))r_0 + \theta(T-2-\Lambda(1))\right)\right.$$
$$\left. + \pi B\sigma \sum_{t=1}^{T-1} \Lambda(t) \int_{t-1}^{t} e^{ks} dW_s^r \right\}, \tag{6}$$

where

$$A = A(10) \text{ and } B = B(10),$$

$$\lambda(t) = \begin{cases} 1 & \text{if } t = 1,2,\ldots,T-3 \\ \frac{2}{3} & \text{if } t = T-2 \\ \frac{1}{3} & \text{if } t = T-1 \end{cases}, \tag{7}$$

$$\Lambda(t) = \sum_{u=t}^{T-1} \lambda(u) e^{-ku}. \tag{8}$$

In particular, $L_T^v \sim \mathcal{LN}\left(m_v(T), s_v^2(T)\right)$ *with*

$$m_v(T) = \pi A T + \pi B\left(\frac{1}{3}r_{-2} + \frac{2}{3}r_{-1} + (1+\Lambda(1))r_0 + \theta(T-2-\Lambda(1))\right),$$

$$s_v^2(T) = \frac{\pi^2 B^2 \sigma^2 (1-e^{-2k})}{2k} \sum_{t=1}^{T-1} \Lambda^2(t) e^{2kt}.$$

The proof of this result is given in the Appendix A.

3.3. Comparison of the Expectations

Intuition, guided by the example given in Table 1, suggests that the hierarchy between the two methods depends on the evolution of the markets: if they are increasing (resp. decreasing), the vertical (resp. horizontal) method produces a larger amount. An analysis of the results obtained in the less trivial stochastic framework presented in the preceding section shows that they go in that direction.

Table 2 gives the parameters that were used in the computations. Remark that the Vasicek parameters (namely, k, σ and r_0) have been calibrated using historical OLO yield curves from 1991 to 2015.

Table 2. Parameters used in the computations of the direct comparison.

k	σ	r_0	r_{-1}	r_{-2}
0.15	0.41%	1.34%	1.34%	1.34%

In Figure 3, we show the values of the four expectations:

$$\mathbb{E}\left[\log(L_T^h)\right] = m_h(T) \quad ; \quad \mathbb{E}\left[L_T^h\right] = \exp\left(m_h(T) + \frac{s_h^2(T)}{2}\right) = \exp\left(m_h(T)\right),$$

$$\mathbb{E}\left[\log(L_T^v)\right] = m_v(T) \quad ; \quad \mathbb{E}\left[L_T^v\right] = \exp\left(m_v(T) + \frac{s_v^2(T)}{2}\right),$$

when the parameter θ varies (the values of the other parameters are given in the appendix). We observe in the upper plot that, in accordance with the intuition, r_0 acts as a *turning point*:

$$\begin{cases} m_h(T) > m_v(T) & \text{if } \theta < r_0, \\ m_h(T) = m_v(T) & \text{if } \theta = r_0, \\ m_h(T) < m_v(T) & \text{if } \theta > r_0. \end{cases}$$

However, as is shown in the lower plot, another conclusion can be made for the expectations of the liabilities themselves, though the difference is not huge. There exists indeed another turning point, which is related but not equal to r_0. The reason for this phenomenon is the difference of volatility between the two liabilities ($0 = s_h(T) < s_v(T)$).

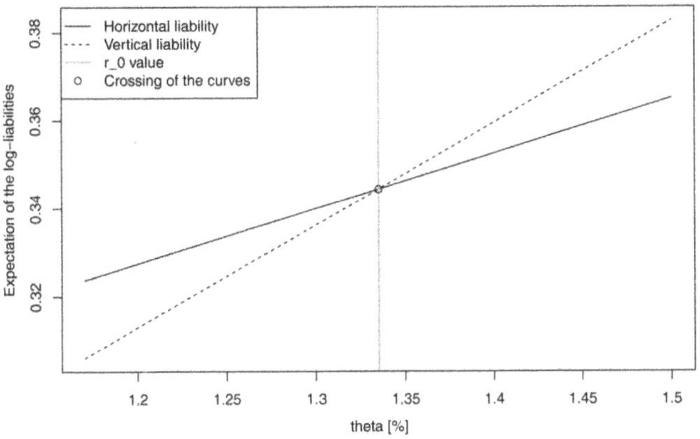

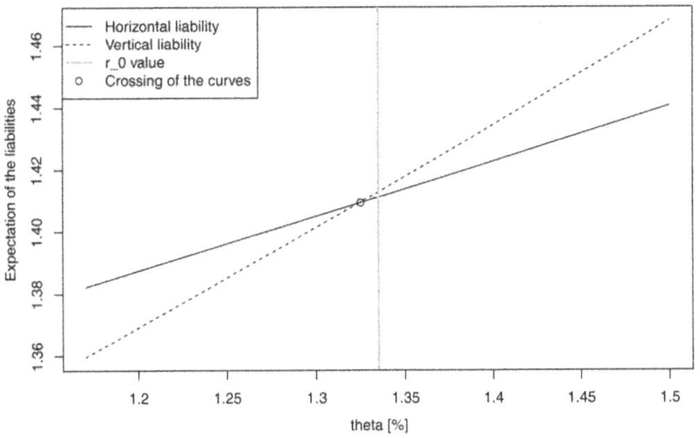

Figure 3. Comparison of the expectations of the log-liability (upper graph) and of the liability (lower graph) obtained using the horizontal and the vertical methods.

4. ALM-Based Comparison

In this section, we compare the horizontal and vertical liabilities using an Asset and Liability Management approach. For this purpose, we assume that the organization offering the pension scheme to the affiliated invests the paid contributions in an investment portfolio. In order to compare the two methods, we compute the prices of two options giving the right to exchange the asset portfolio for the horizontal (resp. vertical) liability.

This is done using the well-known Margrabe formula (see [11]), which has been extended to a stochastic interest rates environment by [12]:

Proposition 2. *Let U and V be two non-dividend paying assets whose distributions are log-normal. If the short rate is a Brownian diffusion, the price of the European option whose pay-off at time T has the form* $(U_T - V_T)_+$ *is given by*

$$M = U_0 \Phi\left(\frac{\log \frac{U_0}{V_0} + \frac{1}{2}\nu^2(T)}{\nu(T)}\right) - V_0 \Phi\left(\frac{\log \frac{U_0}{V_0} - \frac{1}{2}\nu^2(T)}{\nu(T)}\right), \tag{9}$$

with

$$\nu(T) = \sqrt{\sigma_U^2(T) + \sigma_V^2(T) - 2c_{U,V}(T)},$$

where Φ *is the cumulative distribution function of the standard normal,* $\sigma_U(T)$ *and* $\sigma_V(T)$ *are the standard deviations of* $\log(U_T)$ *and* $\log(V_T)$*, respectively, and* $c_{U,V}(T)$ *is the covariance between* $\log(U_T)$ *and* $\log(V_T)$.

Note that, in the case of the horizontal liability (which is constant), the exchange option is identical to a standard put option. If the asset is log-normally distributed, the Margrabe formula thus reduces to the standard Black and Scholes formula (with stochastic interest rates).

4.1. Assets

We consider that the pension organizer has three investment opportunities: a bank deposit account, a rolling bond with fixed maturity and a stock. We first need to define the portfolio's dynamics under the risk-neutral measure. The dynamics of the cash C is straightforwardly obtained from the short rate:

$$\mathrm{d}C_t = C_t r_t \mathrm{d}t.$$

The price of the rolling bond P with maturity K is related to the forward rate given in Equations (3) and (4):

$$P_t = \exp\left(-C(K) - D(K)r_t\right),$$

so that, using the Itô formula, we easily obtain its dynamics:

$$\mathrm{d}P_t = P_t\left(r_t \mathrm{d}t - \sigma D \mathrm{d}W_t^r\right).$$

Finally, we assume that the stock S follows a geometric Brownian motion:

$$\mathrm{d}S_t = S_t\left(r_t\,\mathrm{d}t + \eta\rho\,\mathrm{d}W_t^r + \eta\sqrt{1-\rho^2}\,\mathrm{d}W_t^S\right),$$

where $\eta > 0$ and $\rho \in [-1,1]$ are real parameters and W^S is a standard Brownian motion that is independent from W^r.

We assume that the proportion of each asset in the portfolio A is kept constant over time, being $x \in [0,1]$ for stock, $y \in [0,1]$ for bond and $(1-x-y) \in [0,1]$ for cash. Obtaining an expression for the portfolio value is easy. First, we write its value as

$$A_t = N_t^C C_t + N_t^P P_t + N_t^S S_t,$$

where N^C, N^P and N^S are, respectively, the number of cash, rolling bond and stock units held at time t in the portfolio. Considering a self-financing portfolio, we obtain that

$$\mathrm{d}A_t = N_t^C \mathrm{d}C_t + N_t^P \mathrm{d}P_t + N_t^S \mathrm{d}S_t,$$

or, equivalently, that

$$\begin{aligned} N_t^C &= (1-x-y)\frac{A_t}{C_t}, \\ N_t^P &= y\frac{A_t}{P_t}, \\ N_t^S &= x\frac{A_t}{S_t}. \end{aligned}$$

The dynamics of A are therefore given by

$$\frac{\mathrm{d}A_t}{A_t} = r_t \mathrm{d}t + x\eta\sqrt{1-\rho^2}\mathrm{d}W_t^S + (x\eta\rho - y\sigma D)\mathrm{d}W_t^r.$$

The solution of the preceding equation can be easily obtained using the Itô formula:

$$
\begin{aligned}
A_T &= A_0 \exp\left(\int_0^T r_s \mathrm{d}s - \frac{1}{2}(x^2\eta^2 + y^2\sigma^2 D^2 - 2\rho x y \eta \sigma D)T \right. \\
&\qquad \left. + x\eta\sqrt{1-\rho^2}W_T^S + (x\eta\rho - y\sigma D)W_T^r \right) \\
&= A_0 \exp\left(\theta T + \frac{r_0 - \theta}{k}(1 - e^{-kT}) - \frac{1}{2}(x^2\eta^2 + y^2\sigma^2 D^2 - 2\rho x y \eta \sigma D)T \right. \\
&\qquad \left. + \int_0^T \left(\gamma - \frac{\sigma}{k}e^{-k(T-s)}\right) \mathrm{d}W_s^r + x\eta\sqrt{1-\rho^2}W_T^S \right),
\end{aligned}
$$

where

$$
\gamma = \frac{\sigma}{k} + x\eta\rho - y\sigma D
$$

so that $A_T \sim \mathcal{LN}\left(m_a(T), s_a^2(T)\right)$ with

$$
\begin{aligned}
s_a^2(T) &= \int_0^T \left(\gamma - \frac{\sigma}{k}e^{-k(T-s)}\right)^2 \mathrm{d}s + x^2\eta^2(1-\rho^2)T \\
&= \frac{\sigma^2}{2k^3}(1 - e^{-2kT}) - 2\frac{\sigma\gamma}{k^2}(1 - e^{-kT}) + \left(\gamma^2 + x^2\eta^2(1-\rho^2)\right)T.
\end{aligned}
$$

Remark that the asset allocation we consider here is constant over time. This is consistent with the investment habits of many Belgian pension funds and insurance companies. Some other pension funds around the world implement different strategies, e.g., following the affiliates' risk preferences, and decreasing the volatility of the asset portfolios as the affiliates grow old. Generalizing the results, we obtain in the following sections that such a situation is not conceptually difficult, as we only have to replace the constants x and y by deterministic functions $x(t)$ and $y(t)$ in A's dynamics. In particular, the asset random variable remains log-normally distributed.

4.2. Liabilities

As we have previously seen, the variables A_T and L_T^v are log-normally distributed under our asset and interest rate assumptions, and L_T^h is constant. However, as L^v and L^h are not tradable assets, we have to define their fair values in order to apply the Margrabe formula (9):

$$
U_t^h = \mathbb{E}_Q\left[\exp\left(-\int_t^T r_s \mathrm{d}s\right) L_T^h \,\middle|\, \mathcal{F}_t\right] \quad \text{and} \quad U_t^v = \mathbb{E}_Q\left[\exp\left(-\int_t^T r_s \mathrm{d}s\right) L_T^v \,\middle|\, \mathcal{F}_t\right].
$$

The processes U^h and U^v will successively play the role of U in Proposition 2, while the asset portfolio A will play the role of V. The payoffs of the considered options become then, respectively, $(U_T^h - A_T)^+$ and $(U_T^v - A_T)^+$. To apply Proposition 2 and compute their prices, we only have to compute three supplementary quantities: the initial fair values U_0^h and U_0^v and the covariance between the (logarithms of) A_T and L_T^v.

To obtain U_0^v, we first integrate Equation (2) to obtain

$$
\int_0^T r_s \mathrm{d}s = \theta T + \frac{r_0 - \theta}{k}(1 - e^{-kT}) + \frac{\sigma}{k}\int_0^T \left(1 - e^{-k(T-s)}\right) \mathrm{d}W_s^r.
$$

Putting this expression together with Formula (6) leads to

$$
\begin{aligned}
\tilde{L}_T^v &= \exp\left(-\int_0^T r_s \mathrm{d}s\right) L_T^v \\
&= \exp\Bigg\{\pi AT + \pi B\left(\frac{1}{3}r_{-2} + \frac{2}{3}r_{-1} + (1+\Lambda(1))r_0 + \theta(T-2-\Lambda(1))\right) \\
&\quad - \theta T - \frac{r_0-\theta}{k}(1-e^{-kT}) \\
&\quad + \sum_{t=1}^{T-1}\int_{t-1}^{t}\left(\pi B\sigma\Lambda(t)e^{ks} - \frac{\sigma}{k}(1-e^{-k(T-s)})\right)\mathrm{d}W_s^r \\
&\quad - \frac{\sigma}{k}\int_{T-1}^{T}\left(1-e^{-k(T-s)}\right)\mathrm{d}W_s^r\Bigg\},
\end{aligned}
$$

so that the discounted vertical liability $\tilde{L}_T^v \sim \mathcal{LN}\left(\tilde{m}_v(T), \tilde{s}_v^2(T)\right)$ with

$$
\begin{aligned}
\tilde{m}_v(T) &= \pi AT + \pi B\left(\frac{1}{3}r_{-2} + \frac{2}{3}r_{-1} + (1+\Lambda(1))r_0 + \theta(T-2-\Lambda(1))\right) - \theta T - \frac{r_0-\theta}{k}(1-e^{-kT}), \\
\tilde{s}_v^2(T) &= \frac{\sigma^2}{k^2}T + \sum_{t=1}^{T-1}\Bigg\{\frac{(\pi B\sigma\Lambda(t) + \frac{\sigma}{k}e^{-kT})^2}{2k}e^{2kt}\left(1-e^{-2k}\right) \\
&\quad - \frac{2\sigma(\pi B\sigma\Lambda(t) + \frac{\sigma}{k}e^{-kT})}{k^2}e^{kt}\left(1-e^{-k}\right)\Bigg\} + \frac{\sigma^2}{k^3}\left(-\frac{3}{2} + 2e^{-k} - \frac{1}{2}e^{-2k}\right).
\end{aligned}
$$

Now, U_0^v is straightforwardly obtained, as it is the expectation of a log-normally distributed random variable

$$
U_0^v = \mathbb{E}\left[\mathcal{LN}\left(\tilde{m}_v(T), \tilde{s}_v^2(T)\right)\right] = \exp\left(\tilde{m}_v(T) + \frac{\tilde{s}_v^2(T)}{2}\right).
$$

In addition, the initial value of the horizontal liability is easy to obtain, as

$$
\begin{aligned}
U_0^h &= \mathbb{E}_Q\left[\exp\left(-\int_0^T r_s \mathrm{d}s\right) L_T^h\right] = L_T^h \mathbb{E}_Q\left[\exp\left(-\int_0^T r_s \mathrm{d}s\right)\right] \\
&= L_T^h P(0,T) = L_T^h \exp\left(-C(T) - D(T)r_0\right).
\end{aligned}
$$

Finally, we compute, using Proposition 1,

$$
\begin{aligned}
c_{v,a}(T) &= \mathrm{cov}\left[\log(A_T), \log(L_T^v)\right] \\
&= \mathbb{E}\Bigg[\left(\int_0^T\left(\gamma - \frac{\sigma}{k}e^{-k(T-s)}\right)\mathrm{d}W_s^r + x\eta\sqrt{1-\rho^2}W_T^S\right) \\
&\qquad \cdot\left(\pi B\sigma\sum_{t=1}^{T-1}\Lambda(t)\int_{t-1}^{t}e^{ks}\mathrm{d}W_s^r\right)\Bigg] \\
&= \pi B\sigma\sum_{t=1}^{T-1}\Lambda(t)\int_{t-1}^{t}\left(\gamma - \frac{\sigma}{k}e^{-k(T-s)}\right)e^{ks}\mathrm{d}s \\
&= \pi B\sigma\sum_{t=1}^{T-1}\Lambda(t)\left(\frac{\gamma}{k}(e^{kt} - e^{k(t-1)}) - \frac{\sigma}{2k^2}e^{-kT}(e^{2kt} - e^{2k(t-1)})\right).
\end{aligned}
$$

4.3. Comparison of Margrabe Option Prices

We are now able to compare the two liabilities using the ALM methodology explained supra. On one hand, the price of the option giving the right at time T to exchange the asset portfolio for the vertical liability is equal to

$$p_0^v = \exp\left(\tilde{m}_v(T) + \frac{1}{2}\tilde{s}_v^2(T)\right)\Phi\left(\frac{\tilde{m}_v(T) + \frac{1}{2}\tilde{s}_v^2(T) + \frac{1}{2}\left(s_v^2(T) + s_a^2(T) - 2c_{v,a}(T)\right)}{\sqrt{s_v^2(T) + s_a^2(T) - 2c_{v,a}(T)}}\right) - \Phi\left(\frac{\tilde{m}_v(T) + \frac{1}{2}\tilde{s}_v^2(T) - \frac{1}{2}\left(s_v^2(T) + s_a^2(T) - 2c_{v,a}(T)\right)}{\sqrt{s_v^2(T) + s_a^2(T) - 2c_{v,a}(T)}}\right).$$

On the other hand, the price of the option giving the right at time T to exchange the asset portfolio for the horizontal liability, which reduces to a standard put option on the asset portfolio with the strike being equal to the final value of the horizontal liability, is equal to

$$p_0^h = -\Phi\left(\frac{\log\left(L_T^h P(0,T)\right) - \frac{1}{2}s_a^2(T)}{s_a(T)}\right) + L_T^h P(0,T)\Phi\left(\frac{\log\left(L_T^h P(0,T)\right) + \frac{1}{2}s_a^2(T)}{s_a(T)}\right).$$

We can now compute these option prices for a set of various investment portfolios, using the parameters of Tables 2 and 3. Table 4 gathers the results of the comparison. Among the example portfolios that we have considered, the "Typical insurer portfolio" is meant to mimic the investment habits of Belgian insurers. The prices of the two options are given in this case in Table 5.

Table 3. Supplementary parameters used in the computations of the ALM comparison.

θ	K	η	μ
1.34%	10	25%	5%

Table 4. Results of the ALM comparison for some example portfolios. The cheapest liability is the horizontal one when H is displayed, and the vertical one when V is displayed.

Description	**Composition**			**Cheapest Liability**				
	x	y	z	$\rho = -1$	$\rho = -0.5$	$\rho = 0$	$\rho = 0.5$	$\rho = 1$
Only stocks	100%	0%	0%	H	H	V	V	V
Only bonds	0%	100%	0%	H	H	H	H	H
Only cash	0%	0%	100%	V	V	V	V	V
Stocks and bonds	50%	50%	0%	H	H	V	V	V
Stocks and cash	50%	0%	50%	H	H	V	V	V
Bonds and cash	0%	50%	50%	V	V	V	V	V
Equal repartition	33%	33%	33%	H	H	V	V	V
Typical insurer portfolio	10%	80%	10%	H	H	V	V	V

Table 5. Prices of the options giving the right to exchange the "Typical insurer" asset portfolio (as defined in Table 4) for the horizontal (resp. vertical) liability.

	$\rho = -1$	$\rho = -0.5$	$\rho = 0$	$\rho = 0.5$	$\rho = 1$
p_0^h	0.0044	0.0077	0.0112	0.0148	0.0183
p_0^v	0.0108	0.0099	0.0090	0.0082	0.0073
$p_0^h - p_0^v$	−0.0065	−0.0023	0.0022	0.0066	0.0111

Let us first consider portfolios without any stock. In the case of the "only bonds" one, the horizontal liability is cheaper. This result is not really surprising, as this method looks like the way bonds produce money. On the contrary, in the case of the "only cash" portfolio, the vertical option price is smaller. Again, this conclusion is not unexpected because this method is similar to a savings product.

When stocks are included in the portfolio, the hierarchy between the methods depends on the correlation between stocks and rates. If $\rho > 0$, the stock and the cash are similar in some sense. The vertical method is thus the cheapest one, as in the case of portfolios without stock. If, on the contrary, $\rho < 0$, the asset portfolio is very different from cash, and the horizontal method is preferred.

The funding vehicle of the pension plan in question is therefore an important feature to consider when comparing the two computation methods. The nature of this institution has indeed a strong influence on its investment habits: insurers tend to invest a lot in bonds, while pension funds often prefer stocks.

5. Conclusions

The two comparison methodologies give different points of view of the two computation methods. The first one confirms what was trivially suggested by the intuition: the horizontal liability is larger than the vertical liability in the case of a decreasing rates market, and vice versa. The second methodology yields more interesting conclusions, as it connects the hierarchy between the two methods to the investment profile of the institution granting the guarantee. We have seen that two methods represent two different philosophies: the horizontal one is closer to the insurers' asset management habits, while the vertical one is closer to pension funds' investment preferences. For this reason, the reform act will possibly have consequences regarding the investment strategies of the Belgian pensions plans' funding vehicles.

We have chosen to consider a valuation framework in order to be consistent with the IAS philosophy, and thus with the funding vehicles' interests. It should, however, be noted that other methodologies would make sense. For example, it is possible to compute, instead of exchange option prices, risk measures (such as VaR or TVaR) applied to the gap between the asset portfolio value and the liability value.

Political circumstances have led Belgian authorities to let the choice for new pensions schemes, but, as the results generated by the two methods are different, a whole set of legal questions arise (out of scope here). Among them, we can mention discrimination problems (possible arbitrage by the sponsor, see e.g., [15–17]).

Our work leaves some questions open for further research, mainly in two directions. On one hand, we could consider the exact definition of the guaranteed rate, i.e., take into account the cap and the floor as defined in the legal text. In order to compute options prices similar to the ones that we have obtained with closed formulas, it would then be necessary to use numerical methods. On the other hand, we could consider more complex models for the interest rate and the stock price, including a more complete dependence structure between the two risk factors.

Acknowledgments: We would like to thank the anonymous referees for their useful remarks. This work has been done in the context of the *Chaire d'excellence sur les pensions* of the Université catholique de Louvain.

Author Contributions: Both authors have contributed equally to this paper.

Conflicts of Interest: The authors declare no conflict of interest.

Appendix A. Proof of Proposition 1

Proof. First, we rewrite the sum of R's consecutive values:

$$\begin{aligned}
\frac{1}{\pi}\sum_{t=0}^{T-1} R_t &= \sum_{t=0}^{T-1} \frac{r_{t-2}^{10} + r_{t-1}^{10} + r_t^{10}}{3} \\
&= \sum_{t=0}^{T-1} \frac{A + Br_{t-2} + A + Br_{t-1} + A + Br_t}{3} \\
&= AT + B\left(\frac{1}{3}r_{-2} + \frac{2}{3}r_{-1} + r_0 + \sum_{t=1}^{T-3} r_t + \frac{2}{3}r_{T-2} + \frac{1}{3}r_{T-1}\right) \\
&= \alpha + B\sum_{t=1}^{T-1} \lambda(t) r_t,
\end{aligned}$$

where we denoted the sum of the deterministic terms by α and introduced the notation $\lambda(t)$ defined in Formula (7). Using the expression for r_t given by Equation (2),

$$\begin{aligned}
\frac{1}{\pi}\sum_{t=0}^{T-1} R_t &= \alpha + B(r_0 - \theta)\sum_{t=1}^{T-1}\lambda(t)e^{-kt} + B\theta\sum_{t=1}^{T-1}\lambda(t) + B\sigma\sum_{t=1}^{T-1}\lambda(t)e^{-kt}\int_0^t e^{ks}\mathrm{d}W_s^r \\
&= \alpha + B(r_0 - \theta)\Lambda(1) + B\theta(T-2) + B\sigma\sum_{t=1}^{T-1}\Lambda(t)\int_{t-1}^t e^{ks}\mathrm{d}W_s^r,
\end{aligned}$$

where we have used the notation $\Lambda(t)$ defined in Formula (8), as

$$\begin{aligned}
&\sum_{t=1}^{T-1}\lambda(t)e^{-kt}\int_0^t \# \\
&= \lambda(1)e^{-k}\int_0^1 \# + \lambda(2)e^{-k2}\int_0^2 \# + \cdots + \lambda(T-1)e^{-k(T-1)}\int_0^{T-1} \# \\
&= \left(\lambda(1)e^{-k} + \lambda(2)e^{-k2} + \cdots + \lambda(T-1)e^{-k(T-1)}\right)\int_0^1 \# \\
&\quad + \left(\lambda(2)e^{-k2} + \cdots + \lambda(T-1)e^{-k(T-1)}\right)\int_1^2 \# \\
&\qquad + \ldots \\
&\qquad\qquad + \lambda(T-1)e^{-k(T-1)}\int_{T-2}^{T-1} \#,
\end{aligned}$$

where # denotes any integrand. These notations seem cumbersome, but allow handling the sum of independent stochastic integrals, which is much easier for the following computations than dependent stochastic integrals.

The $m_v(T)$ parameter is straightforwardly obtained from the expression obtained for the sum of R's values. For the volatility, we compute

$$\begin{aligned}
s_v^2(T) &= \mathbb{E}\left[\left(\pi B\sigma\sum_{t=1}^{T-1}\Lambda(t)\int_{t-1}^t e^{ks}\mathrm{d}W_s^r\right)^2\right] \\
&= \pi^2B^2\sigma^2\sum_{t=1}^{T-1}\Lambda^2(t)\int_{t-1}^t e^{2ks}\mathrm{d}s \\
&= \frac{\pi^2B^2\sigma^2}{2k}\sum_{t=1}^{T-1}\Lambda^2(t)\left(e^{2kt} - e^{2k(t-1)}\right),
\end{aligned}$$

which completes the proof of Proposition 1. □

References

1. European Commission. *An Agenda for Adequate, Safe and Sustainable Pensions*; White Paper COM(2012)55; European Commission: Brussels, Belgium; Luxembourg, 2012; Volume 55.
2. Antolín, P.; Payet, S.; Whitehouse, E.; Yermo, J. *The Role of Guarantees in Defined Contribution Pensions*; OECD Working Papers on Finance, Insurance and Private Pensions; OECD Publishing: Paris, France, 2011; Volume 11.
3. Pennacchi, G. The Value of Guarantees on Pension Fund Returns. *J. Risk Insur.* **1999**, *66*, 219–237.
4. Fischer, K. Pricing Pension Fund Guarantees: A Discrete Martingale Approach. *Can. J. Adm. Sci.* **1999**, *16*, 256–266.
5. Lachance, M.E.; Mitchell, O.; Smetters, K. Guaranteeing Defined Contribution Pensions: The Option to Buy Back a Defined Benefit Promise. *J. Risk Insur.* **2003**, *70*, 1–16.
6. Yang, S.; Yueh, M.L.; Tang, C.H. Valuation of the interest rate guarantee embedded in defined contribution pension plans. *Insur.: Math. Econ.* **2008**, *42*, 920–934.
7. Deelstra, G.; Grasselli, M.; Koehl, P. Optimal investment strategies in the presence of a minimum guarantee. *Insur.: Math. Econ.* **2003**, *33*, 189–207.
8. Consiglio, A.; Saunders, D.; Zenios, S. Asset and liability management for insurance products with minimum guarantees: The UK case. *J. Bank. Financ.* **2006**, *30*, 645–667.
9. Consiglio, A.; Cocco, F.; Zenios, S. Asset and liability modelling for participating policies with guarantees. *Eur. J. Oper. Res.* **2008**, *186*, 380–404.
10. Consiglio, A.; Tumminello, M.; Zenios, S. Designing and pricing guarantee options in defined contribution pension plans. *Insur.: Math. Econ.* **2015**, *65*, 267–279.
11. Margrabe, W. The Value of an Option to Exchange One Asset for Another. *J. Financ.* **1978**, *33*, 177–186.
12. Bernard, C.; Cui, Z. A Note on Exchange Options under Stochastic Interest Rates. Available online: https://ssrn.com/abstract=1626020 (accessed on 16 June 2010).
13. Huerlimann, W. Option pricing in the multidimensional Black-Scholes market with Vasicek interest rates. *Math. Financ. Lett.* **2013**, *2*, 1–18.
14. Brigo, D.; Mercurio, F. *Interest Rate Models—Theory and Practice. With Smile, Inflation and Credit*; Springer: Berlin, Germany, 2006.
15. Flohimont, V. *Gelijkheid in de Pensioenregelingen voor Ambtenaren, Werknemers en Zelfstandigen*; Die Keure: Bruges, Belgium, 2012.
16. Flohimont, V. Comparaison et comparabilité dans la jurisprudence de la Cour constitutionnelle: Rigueur ou jeu de hasard? *Revue belge de droit constitutionnel* **2008**, *3*, 217–235.
17. Ellis, E.; Watson, P. The principle of equality as applied to pensions. In *EU Anti-Discrimination Law*; Oxford University Press: Oxford, UK, 2012; pp. 195–208.

risks

MDPI

Article

A Discussion of a Risk-Sharing Pension Plan

Catherine Donnelly

Department of Actuarial Mathematics and Statistics, and the Maxwell Institute for Mathematical Sciences, Heriot-Watt University, Edinburgh EH14 4AS, UK; c.donnelly@hw.ac.uk; Tel.: +44-131-451-3251

Academic Editor: Luca Regis
Received: 2 October 2016; Accepted: 27 January 2017; Published: 14 February 2017

Abstract: I show that risk-sharing pension plans can reduce some of the shortcomings of defined benefit and defined contributions plans. The risk-sharing pension plan presented aims to improve the stability of benefits paid to generations of members, while allowing them to enjoy the expected advantages of a risky investment strategy. The plan does this by adjusting the investment strategy and benefits in response to a changing funding level, motivated by the with-profits contract proposed by Goecke (2013). He suggests a mean-reverting log reserve (or funding) ratio, where mean reversion occurs through adjustments to the investment strategy and declared bonuses. To measure the robustness of the plan to human factors, I introduce a measurement of disappointment, where disappointment is high when there are many consecutive years over which benefit payments are declining. Another measure introduced is devastation, where devastation occurs when benefit payments are zero. The motivation is that members of a pension plan who are easily disappointed or likely to get no benefit, are more likely to exit the plan. I find that the risk-sharing plan offers more disappointment than a defined contribution plan, but it eliminates the devastation possible in a plan that tries to accumulate contributions at a steadily increasing rate. The proposed risk-sharing plan can give a narrower range of benefits than in a defined contribution plan. Thus it can offer a stable benefit to members without the risk of running out of money.

Keywords: defined contribution; defined benefit; risk-sharing; pension

1. Introduction

Risk-sharing pension plans offer a middle ground between the extremes of defined benefit (DB) and defined contribution (DC) pension plans. They don't promise a certain level of pension at retirement like DB plans, but neither do they promise something that they may not deliver. They don't give members control over their own investment strategy like DC plans, but neither do they require members to be financial experts. Instead, they try to pay a stable pension to the members. They try to give members an idea of what their pension may be in retirement, but an aim or target amount rather than a guarantee. And they try to actively maintain the sustainability of the plan to adverse investment returns, by adjusting one or more of the investment strategy, benefits and contributions to be paid.

I discuss a model risk-sharing pension plan that adjusts only the investment strategy and retirement benefits. It is closer to a DC plan than a DB plan. In the risk-sharing plan, the retirement benefits are the accumulated value of the contributions. The plan reduces retirement benefit volatility to the plan members, paying a more stable benefit to its members than under a DC plan. It does not require additional contributions to make good a funding deficit. Instead, the benefits paid and investment strategy adjust so that the funding level is self-correcting. Adjusting the investment strategy means adjusting the level of investment risk taken by the plan. Moreover, the structure of the plan is highly flexible. By changing the parameters of the plan, the amount of benefit volatility experienced by different generations of members can be adjusted.

Although DB plans are currently in decline, they have some very appealing features for their members. A retirement "defined benefit" income or lump sum is promised to the plan members without regard to the achieved investment return. This is very attractive to the membership since they are insulated from the ups and downs of investment returns. However, the adverse consequence is that a DB plan can require large cash injections from its sponsoring employer. If the sponsor does not make the cash injections, then the plan may have to wind up and secure whatever fraction of the promised benefits it can for its members. In recent years, poor equity returns and low interest rates have resulted in many DB plans being underfunded [1]. As a result, many employers are closing down their DB plans and replacing them by DC plans [2].

In contrast, DC plans are in the ascendancy in countries such as the UK and USA. They have some very appealing features for the employer who sets them up on behalf of their employees. DC plans require no unexpected contributions to make good a funding deficit. This means that the employer has no uncertainty about their contribution rate to a DC plan, unlike in a DB plan. Typically, members and the employer pay in contributions which are invested in the financial market. The accumulated value of their contributions, which varies directly with the investment return achieved, is the value of the benefit paid to a member at their retirement date. There are no guarantees as to the amount of the retirement benefit, unless a financial guarantee is purchased. Thus members are exposed to the full volatility of their investment choices. If returns are much lower than expected, members may question the value of saving for retirement and not save enough for their retirement. Moreover, in DC plans the member must choose the investment strategy, although many people are financially illiterate [3] and do not consult a financial advisor ([Figure 325], [4]).

They are other types of pension plans, such as collective DC (CDC) plans. They are a type of risk-sharing plan, which can adjust the benefits paid to members in response to achieved investment returns. If annuities are paid as a benefit from a CDC plan, then the benefits can also be adjusted in response to mortality experience. The Dutch hybrid pension plans [5] can be considered as the latter type of CDC plan.

Plans with inter-generational risk-sharing, such as CDC plans and other risk-sharing plans, have been shown to be welfare-improving, compared to the individually optimal lifecycle strategy [6,7]. This is when measuring welfare using an expected utility-of-consumption framework, and maximizing utility across all generations. Inter-generational risk-sharing plans have higher and smoother consumption patterns, averaged across generations, than in a pure DC plan. More generally, risk-sharing in pension plans is discussed in Pugh and Yermo [8] and Blommestein et al. [9], both in terms of types of risk and who bears each risk. For example, in both DB and cash-balance plans the sponsoring employers bear the investment risk, whereas the members bear this risk in DC plans and in the plan analyzed here. Another example are conditional indexation plans: they share investment risk between the sponsor and the members, and the members' basic benefit is guaranteed by the sponsor but benefit increases are not.

Closely related to the idea of risk-sharing plans are participating policies, which are contracts issued by insurance companies. Participating policies typically increase contributions annually at the risk-free rate, and thus provide a minimum guarantee of the benefit paid at retirement. Briys and De Varenne [10] study a model participating policy, focusing on the maturity value of the policy. Other studies including the minimum guarantee are Barbarin and Devolder [11], Graf et al. [12], Grosen and Jørgensen [13], Hieber et al. [14]. Guillén et al. [15] analyze a policy that was launched by a Danish insurance company. The policy smooths investment returns over the contract duration, but does not guarantee a minimum investment return. In these new contracts, there is no direct or indirect inter-generational investment risk-sharing. Baumann and Müller [16] propose a pension plan in which benefits are increased by the risk-free rate plus or minus a proportion of the funding level above or below a desired funding level. They find the static investment strategy that maximizes the discounted expected utility of employees averaged over all generations. They find that their proposed plan increases the risk tolerance and the expected utility of the retirement benefits. Analyses of different surplus appropriation schemes in participating policies are provided by Bohnert and Gatzert [17] and Zemp [18].

The risk-sharing pension plan that I study changes explicitly both the accumulation of contributions and the investment strategy in response to changes in a notional funding level. Thus it is not like a Dutch-style plan, nor a typically considered CDC plan in the literature, in which there is no explicit adjustment to the investment strategy. It is an adaptation of the scheme proposed by Goecke [19], which he proposed in the context of a with-profits contract. Unlike many with-profit contracts, there are no investment guarantees in Goecke's scheme, and hence there is no need for an insurance company to financially underwrite the proposed contract. Thus Goecke's scheme could be considered as a type of CDC plan, since the policyholders collectively bear all of the risk. However, Goecke [19] considers only a single generation of members, all of whom enter the contract at the same time with the same amount of money, and obtain the terminal value of the contract at the same time. In this paper, I analyze how the plan performs over time when there are regular withdrawals from its assets, which is not generally a consideration for with-profits contracts and was thus, unsurprisingly, not considered in Goecke [19].

The risk-sharing plan promises to increase the accumulated value of contributions each year in line with the expected return on assets, adjusted for the plan being over- or under-funded relative to a target funding level. Although the plan uses a notional funding level in its operation, benefits are not guaranteed. While the increase in the accumulation of contributions varies each year, the idea is that the annual variation in the accumulation increase is kept small. The notional funding level is simply a mechanism to determine the investment strategy and accumulation on the contributions at a selected time. The target funding level is fixed and its value helps to determine the spread of investment returns across generations.

The plan invests its money in line with a long-term strategic investment strategy, which would be chosen by the trustees or plan managers. However, if the plan is over-funded, then the investment risk of its strategy is increased (and correspondingly its expected investment return is increased). The opposite happens if the plan is under-funded: the investment risk is decreased. The two adjustments, to the accumulated contributions and the investment strategy, act to encourage the funding level back towards the target funding level.

I examine the robustness of the proposed risk-sharing pension plan from the viewpoint of individual members. I believe this is more appropriate for private pension plans than a social-planning viewpoint. Plans can fail because of what happens to one generation, regardless if they are expected to be a success averaged across all generations.

I focus on the actual retirement benefit payments made to members, as this is the ultimate purpose of the plan, rather than, for example, maximizing the expected utility derived from the payments. To do this, I examine the stability of the retirement benefit payments between generations of members and look at their distribution. Furthermore, in risk-sharing plans, it is inevitable that benefits have to be cut for some generations. However, the benefit cuts should not be too large between generations. A plan structure which means there is a high chance of members getting nothing is unlikely to succeed long-term in the marketplace. Similarly if the benefits decline year-on-year. For this reason, I calculate the probability of the plan's assets being exhausted before all benefits have been paid, which I call devastation, and the probabilities of benefits declining year-on-year between generations, which I call disappointment.

I investigate (i) how changing the parameterization of the risk-sharing plan changes the range of benefits across generations; (ii) the retirement benefit stability across generations of members; (iii) disappointment, namely the frequency of runs of declining accumulation of contributions; and (iv) devastation, namely the chance of the plan exhausting its assets before all members have received their benefit.

I find that a suitably parameterized risk-sharing plan can offer a stable retirement benefit across generations. With a suitable choice of plan-specific parameters, it has a zero chance of running out of money before all members have retired, for the chosen financial market model. The downside is that members must expect that retirement benefits may decrease; there is no guaranteed minimum retirement benefit. While this is also seen in the DC plan, and many people are in DC plans, the risk-sharing plan members may compare themselves with other plan members and feel that they should get more each year.

2. Risk-Sharing Plan

The risk-sharing plan has the aim of paying a reasonable retirement benefit to its members, while maintaining the financial security of the non-retired members. Financial security is measured through the funding level of the plan, namely the ratio of the plan's assets to its liabilities. The most attractive aspect is that each plan can be adjusted to the needs of the beneficiaries and sponsors, if any.

A target funding level is fixed and the plan's managers seek to bring the funding level back to the chosen target, by adjusting the accumulated value of the members' contributions and the investment strategy. The motivation is to maintain a cushion of assets as financial security for the non-retired plan members. This is done through applying the scheme of Goecke [19], and adapting it for use as an inter-generational pension plan.

Rather than pension plans that pay benefits, Goecke [19] studies with-profit contracts and introduces a mechanism for the smoothing of capital market returns in them. This involves changing the bonus declaration and the investment strategy in response to changes in the reserve ratio. A highly attractive property is that the log reserve ratio is mean-reverting to a fixed target log reserve ratio. As Goecke [19] studies with-profits contracts, which are held to the same maturity date, there is naturally no consideration of payments out. However, this must be allowed for in the risk-sharing plan as a pension plan is constantly paying out benefits to its retired members. Furthermore, I do not allow short-selling of any asset, which is a realistic assumption for a pension plan since the plan manager must act as a "prudent investor" [20].

2.1. *Investment Strategy*

Assume that time is measured in years. In the financial market, the plan can invest in a risky stock and a risk-free bond. The annual effective return over the time period $[n-1, n)$ on the risky stock is represented by the random variable $R_n > -1$, for $n = 1, 2, \ldots$. For the risk-free bond, its annual effective return over the time period $[n-1, n)$ is the constant $r > -1$. The plan's investment strategy at time n is represented by the proportion π_n of assets invested in the risky stock, for each $n = 0, 1, 2, \ldots$. The proportion is determined through several elements.

One of the elements is a long-term strategic investment of s^{LT} in the risky stock. This can be decided by reference to the risk attitude of a typical member or, more realistically, the risk attitude of the trustees of the plan, a small group of people who run the plan in the interests of the members. An approach to deciding an investment strategy for a long-term investor like a pension fund is given in de Jong [21].

Another element of the strategy is positive or negative at time n, according to the funding level F_n of the plan. The funding level is defined as the value of assets divided by the value of the liabilities, and it is formally defined in Section 2.3. If the plan is over-funded relative to a fixed target funding level $\overline{F} \geq 1$, then it invests more in the risky stock. The idea is that the plan can risk losing money by following a more risky investment strategy. The reverse is true when the plan is under-funded.

I impose the realistic investment constraints that the plan cannot short-sell the stock and neither can it invest more than 100% of its asset value in the stock. Taking these constraints into account, the total proportion of assets which are invested in the risky stock at time n, for investment over the period $[n, n+1)$ is

$$\pi_n := \max\Big\{0, \min\Big\{1, s^{\mathrm{LT}} + a\big(F_n - \overline{F}\big)\Big\}\Big\},$$

in which $a \geq 0$ is a constant called the *investment risk adjustment* that is chosen when the plan is set up, and F_n is the plan's notional funding level at time n. I state in Section 2.3 how the funding level is calculated. The higher the value of the constant a, the more sensitive is the strategy to over- and under-funding and hence the more volatile is the proportion invested in the risky stock.

2.2. Accumulation of Contributions

The members' contributions are increased each year using a rate calculated via a pre-specified formula. Once each member's retirement benefit, i.e., the accumulated value of their contributions, is paid to them as a lump sum on their retirement date, there is no more plan liability to that member.

The annual accumulation factor (AAF) granted on each member's contributions at time n (i.e., for accumulation from time $n-1$ to time n) is

$$1 + r + \pi_{n-1}(\mathbb{E}(R_n) - r) + \beta(F_{n-} - \overline{F}), \tag{1}$$

for $n = 1, 2, \ldots$. The funding level F_{n-} is the funding level just prior to any payment made at time n and it is defined in Section 2.3. The *AAF adjustment* $\beta \geq 0$ is chosen when the plan is set-up. There are two components to the AAF. The first is a stable return, $r + \pi_{n-1}(\mathbb{E}(R_n) - r)$, equal to the *expected* return on the assets for the current investment strategy.

The second component is a return, $\beta(F_{n-} - \overline{F})$, that is positive or negative according to the funding level of the plan relative to the target. The AAF is higher when the plan is over-funded relative to the target funding level, i.e., when $F_{n-} > \overline{F}$, as the plan can afford to grant higher accumulation factors. The higher value of the accumulated contributions acts to decrease the funding level when the plan is over-funded. The reverse happens when the plan is under-funded. The AAF adjustment β decrees the extent to which the AAF responds to situations of over- and under-funding; the higher the value of β, the greater the sensitivity. Notice that if $\beta = 0$ then the AAF is not affected by deviations in the notional funding level from the target.

Here the funding level just prior to any payment out that is made at time n is used to calculate the AAF. If the funding level at time n was used then the AAF would have to be solved for implicitly, which makes the accumulation calculation more opaque to the members.

Let $B_n^{(k)}$ denote the value of the accumulated contributions of generation k at time n, for $n = 1, \ldots, k$. It is calculated from the previous year's accumulated value, $B_{n-1}^{(k)}$, and any new contributions as

$$B_n^{(k)} = B_{n-1}^{(k)}(1 + r + \pi_{n-1}(\mathbb{E}(R_n) - r) + \beta(F_{n-} - \overline{F})) + C_n^{(k)},$$

in which $C_n^{(k)} \geq 0$ represents the new contribution made at time $n = 1, \ldots, k-1$ by generation $k = 2, \ldots N$. As generation 1 retires at time 1, the only contribution that generation 1 makes is $B_0^{(1)}$ at time 0.

The retirement benefit depends directly on the investment strategy of the risk-sharing plan. This is not quite the same as in a DC plan, in which the contributions are increased at the rate of investment return on the assets. For example, a DC plan has its contributions increasing at the annual rate $r + \pi_{n-1}(R_n - r)$, i.e., with the actual return on the DC plan's assets rather than with the expected return, as in the risk-sharing plans considered here.

2.3. Funding Level

The funding level of the risk-sharing plan is encouraged to move towards the target funding level. The AAF changes in response to deviations in the funding level, in order to bring the funding level back to the target value. Simultaneously, the investment strategy adjusts its investment risk-taking, lowering it if the plan is under-funded and otherwise raising it.

The funding level of the risk-sharing plan at time n is

$$F_n := \frac{A_n}{L_n},$$

where A_n is the value of the assets at time n. The value L_n at time n, is a notional liability, since the plan does not guarantee to pay any benefit. The plan simply accumulates contributions. However, I regard the accumulated contributions as a notional deferred benefit. The notional liability is calculated assuming that the accumulated contributions at time n are increased at every subsequent year by the current expected return on the long-term investment strategy and discounted by the same expected return. In valuing the notional liabilities like this, the idea is that the retirement benefit is intended, but not guaranteed, to be the accumulated contributions that would be obtained from following the strategic long-term investment strategy and receiving the expected return on that strategy. Thus for N starting generations in the plan, of whom generations $n+1,\ldots,N$ will retire after time n,

$$L_n = \sum_{k=n+1}^{N} \left(B_n^{(k)} + C_n^{(k)}\right),$$

i.e., it is a notional liability to pay the current value of accumulated contributions to each currently non-retired generation, including their new contributions. The notional liability at time $n-$ includes the generation who are about to retire at time n, but accumulates their contributions at the expected, long-term strategic return over $[n-1, n)$ rather than the actual return, i.e.,

$$L_{n-} := \left(1 + r + s^{\mathrm{LT}}(\mathbb{E}(R_n) - r)\right) \sum_{k=n}^{N} B_{n-1}^{(k)}.$$

Accumulating the previous's years contributions using the expected return on the long-term strategy is for two reasons: (i) to reflect the investment aim of the plan to invest in line with the long-term strategy; and (ii) to avoid the implicit equation involving L_{n-} (through F_{n-}) that would arise if we used the AAF shown in (**1**).

3. Illustrations

3.1. Model Parameterization

For simplicity, I assume that the risky stock's annual effective random returns $R_1, R_2, \ldots$ are independent, lognormally distributed random variables each with location parameter μ and scale parameter $\sigma > 0$. The continuously-compounded annual risk-free rate is denoted by the constant r. To parameterize the model, I used long-term returns. However, the risk-free bond return is "normalized" to 0% p.a. The reason for the normalization is to make it clear when members get a higher benefit from investing in the plan rather than investing all their money in the risk-free bond. The choice of the risk-free rate of 0% per annum means that, for example, a member who obtains a retirement benefit higher in value than their total contributions has done better than investing their contributions entirely in the risk-free asset. This corresponds to an average AAF which is greater than one.

The annual return on the S&P500 index over the years 1956–1999 is about 12% with an annual volatility of about 15%, based on the values in (Table 2.1, Hardy [22]). Over the same time period, annual 10-year US Treasury bond returns were around 7%[1]. This gives the S&P500 annual return to be about 5% above the 10-year US Treasury bond return.

[1] Based on the average annual 10-year US Treasury bond returns obtained from https://fred.stlouisfed.org/series/IRLTLT01USA156N over the years 1956–1999.

To broadly mimic these historical long-term returns, set the financial market parameters to

$$r = 0, \mu = 0.0375, \sigma = 0.15.$$

Then the mean annual return of the risky asset is $e^{\mu+0.5\sigma^2} - 1 \approx 0.05$ and its annual volatility is $\sqrt{e^{\sigma^2} - 1} \times e^{\mu+0.5\sigma^2} \approx 0.15$.

The long-term strategic investment in risky stocks, s^{LT}, is set to 80%. All the figures shown in the paper are based on 5000 simulations.

3.2. *Comparison Plans*

In most of the illustrations, I compare a selection of the risk-sharing pension plans to a pure DC plan, to understand better the advantages and disadvantages of the risk-sharing plan. I do not compare the plans to a DB plan, as the latter type of plan typically has a sponsoring employer who makes good any deficit and this makes a like-for-like comparison difficult. The DC plan follows exactly the long-term investment strategy of the risk-sharing plans, i.e., it invests the proportion s^{LT} of its assets in the risky stock, and the remainder in the risk-free asset. The strategy is rebalanced annually to this proportion. The benefit paid to a retiring member is the accumulation of that member's contributions from time 0, accumulated at the actual achieved investment return. This results in a volatile benefit payment to all members over time: the benefit can decrease as well as increase in line with the cumulative investment return. The DC plan is always 100% funded, since the benefit promise is to pay the accumulation of the contributions.

In the preliminary investigation, I also compare the risk-sharing plans to a *benchmark plan*. In the benchmark plan, neither the investment strategy nor the AAF is adjusted for over- or under-funding, that is $a = 0$ and $\beta = 0$. Instead, the AAF equals the expected investment return each year based on the long-term strategic investment strategy s^{LT}. This means that the benchmark plan is not a risk-sharing plan. Assuming that $s^{\mathrm{LT}} \in [0,1]$, then the AAF in year n in the benchmark plan is $\left(1 + r + s^{\mathrm{LT}}(\mathbb{E}(R_n) - r)\right)$. I use this plan as a benchmark plan since it accumulates contributions at a constant rate, up to the time that it runs out of money (although it may not run out of money). It makes it a helpful reference line between the plots, and for this reason I keep it in the further investigation although I do not analyze it any more.

3.3. *Preliminary Investigation*

3.3.1. Simple Membership Profile

As a first look at the risk-sharing plan, I assume a simple membership. Each member pays a contribution of \$1 at time 0, and nothing else. Thus $B_0^{(k)} = 1$ for $k = 1, 2, \ldots, N$ and $C_n^{(k)} = 0$ for $n = 1, \ldots, k-1$ and $k = 2, \ldots, N$. At the start, there are $N := 40$ members in the plan, the first of whom retires at time 1 (i.e., generation 1), the second of whom retires at time 2 (i.e., generation 2), and so on, until the Nth member retires at time N. This assumption is made to enable a straightforward comparison of outcomes between plans. In practice, members would be expected to pay contributions up to their retirement. Each member's contributions are accumulated each year, until they are paid out at the member's retirement date as a single lump sum. The final accumulated value of the contributions that is paid out to each retiring member is called the retirement benefit.

3.3.2. Plans Which Vary Only the Investment Strategy

Figure 1 illustrates quantiles of the (geometric) average AAF for plans which adjust only the investment strategy—through the parameter a—and not the accumulation factors. Rather than showing the accumulated contributions paid at retirement, the average AAF for each year is plotted. For example, if the AAF is 1.02 for year 1, 1.03 for year 2 and 1.05 for year 3 then the average AAF is approximately $1.033 = (1.02 \times 1.03 \times 1.05)^{1/3}$. However, the average AAF of 1.033 is displayed as 0.033 in the figures.

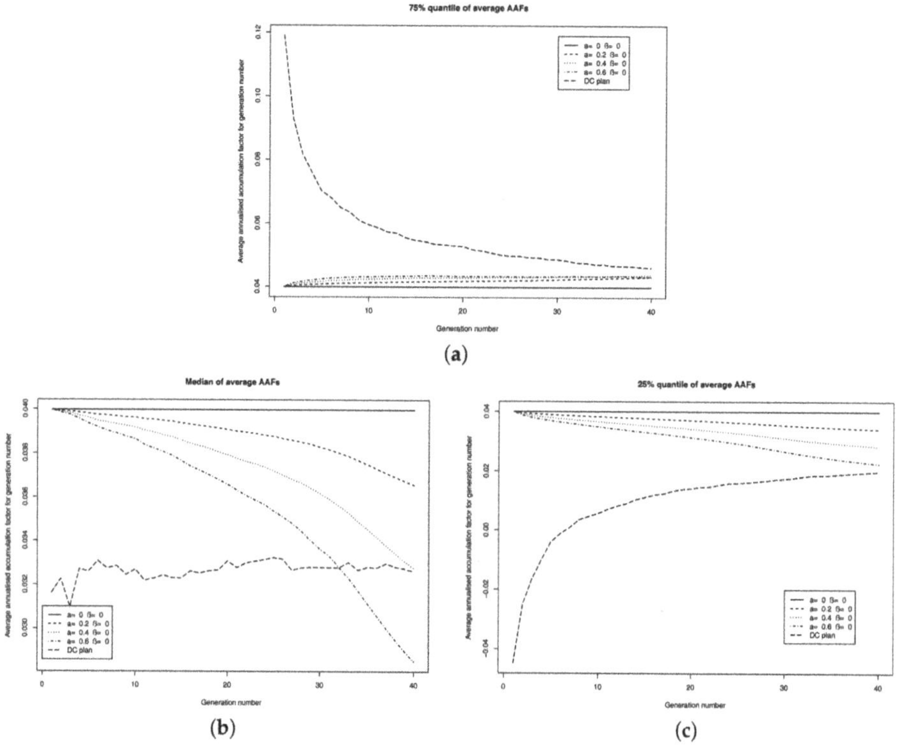

Figure 1. The average AAF for each generation in the model, as the investment risk adjustment (a) is varied and the AAF adjustment (β) is set equal to zero. The target funding level is $\overline{F} = 100\%$. In this simple membership, each of the 40 members starts with \$1 at time 0, and makes no further contribution. (**a**) 75% quantile, $\overline{F} = 100\%$; (**b**) Median, $\overline{F} = 100\%$; (**c**) 25% quantile, $\overline{F} = 100\%$.

Also shown in Figure 1 is a plot for a DC plan. In the DC plan, the proportion s^{LT} of its assets is invested in the risky stock, and the remainder in the risk-free asset. The strategy is rebalanced annually to this proportion. The retirement benefit paid to a member is the accumulation of that member's contributions, accumulated at the actual achieved investment return. The solid black line shows the average AAF for the benchmark plan.

Examining the five plans (the benchmark plan, the DC and the three risk-sharing plans) at the three chosen quantiles, the risk-sharing plans have quite a smooth average AAF. The risk-sharing plans have a lower inter-quartile range of average AAFs than the DC plan. The lower the value of the parameter a in the risk-sharing plans, the lower is the inter-quartile range of the average AAF.

3.3.3. Plans Which Vary Only the AAFs

Next I consider risk-sharing plans which adjust only the AAFs—through the parameter β—and not the investment strategy. The 25%, 50% and 75% quantiles of the (geometric) average AAF is shown in Figure 2. Again, the DC and benchmark plan quantiles are also shown. It is observed than the risk-sharing plans do not have the same smooth average AAF as when the investment strategy is adjusted. As in the latter plans, the risk-sharing plans have a lower inter-quartile range of average

AAFs than the DC plan, although the range is wider. The lower the value of the parameter β in the risk-sharing plans, the lower is the inter-quartile range of the average AAF. The figures suggests that the parameter β, which adjusts the annual accumulation factors, has a lesser effect on the AAFs than the parameter a, which adjusts the investment strategy.

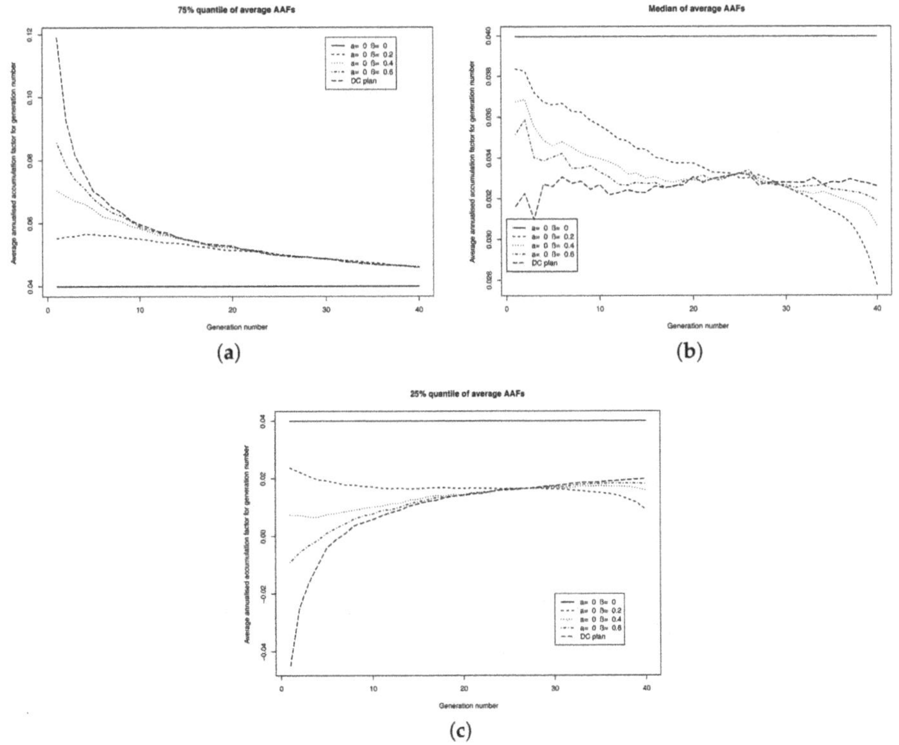

Figure 2. The average AAF for each generation in the model, as the AAF adjustment (β) is varied and the investment risk adjustment (a) is set equal to zero. The target funding level is $\overline{F} = 100\%$. In this simple membership, each of the 40 members starts with \$1 at time 0, and makes no further contribution. (**a**) 75% quantile, $\overline{F} = 100\%$; (**b**) Median, $\overline{F} = 100\%$; (**c**) 25% quantile, $\overline{F} = 100\%$.

3.3.4. Devastation

Although the benchmark plan is promising to pay out a constant average AAF, of around 1.04 per annum (which is displayed as 0.04 in the figures), it may run out of money before the last generation has retired. To capture the catastrophic risk that a plan runs out of money before all members have retired, I introduce a measure of *devastation*. This counts the number of consecutive years in which retiring members receive zero retirement benefits. Doing this across all simulations, I can calculate the probability of two or more consecutive generations of members receiving zero retirement benefits, the probability of three or more consecutive generations receiving zero retirement benefits, and so on. As there is no sponsoring employer for any of the plans considered, then a probability of 30% of two or more generations receiving zero retirement benefits means that there is a 30% chance of the plan running out of money on or after the $(N-2)$th generation, where the Nth generation is the last generation to retire. The devastation measure is zero for the DC plan, since there is no risk-sharing, and it is therefore not shown in the devastation plots.

On the devastation measure, none of the plans in which only the investment strategy is adjusted perform particularly well (Figure 3). For these plans and the benchmark plan, there is a 60%–70% chance of the plan running out of money just before the last generation has retired (shown in Figure 3 as the left-most probabilities plotted for each plan). The risk-sharing plans have a higher probability of this event than the benchmark plan. However, this varies across the retirement times. There is around a 35% chance of all the plans running out of money just before the 31st generation has retired (shown in Figure 3 as the probabilities for 9 consecutive years of zero benefits). For generations retiring earlier than the 31st, the benchmark plan performs worse than the risk-sharing plans. For example, the benchmark plan has a 10% chance of running out of money just before the 25th generation has retired, and the corresponding probability for the considered risk-sharing plans is below 10% (shown in Figure 3 as the probabilities for 15 consecutive years of zero benefits). Risk-sharing plans with a lower value of the parameter β have a probability of running out of money which is closer to that of the benchmark plan.

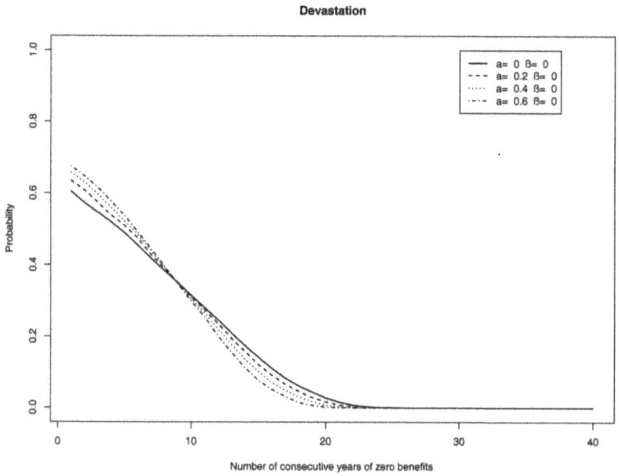

Figure 3. Devastation. The number of consecutive years in which there is no retirement benefit paid to a retiring generation, plotted against the probability. The investment risk adjustment (a) is varied and the AAF adjustment (β) is set equal to zero, and the target funding level $\overline{F} = 100\%$.

Plotting the devastation measure for plans in which only the AAFs are adjusted, Figure 4 is obtained. Here, the difference of the risk-sharing plans from the benchmark plan is dramatic. The chance of the risk-sharing plans running out of money is significantly less than for the benchmark plan. The higher the value of the AAF adjustment β, the lower is this probability. However, it is important to note that although the members may receive something, the amount of their retirement benefits may be small.

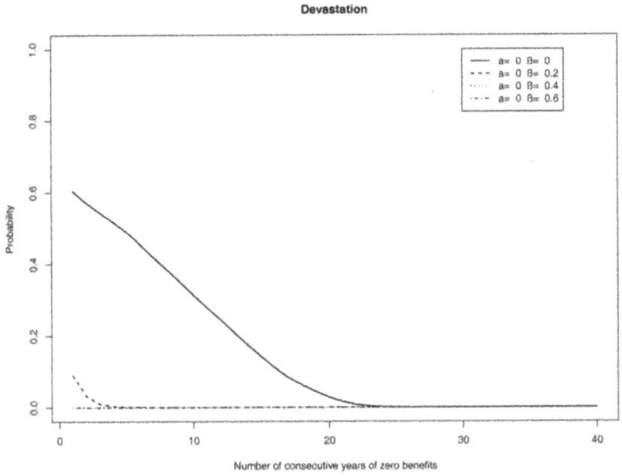

Figure 4. Devastation. The number of consecutive years in which there is no retirement benefit paid to a retiring generation, plotted against the probability. The AAF adjustment (β) is varied and the investment risk adjustment (a) is set equal to zero, and the target funding level $\overline{F} = 100\%$.

3.3.5. Preliminary Findings

This preliminary investigation indicates the impact of the two adjustment factors. The average AAF is most sensitive to the investment strategy adjustment a. Choosing a positive value of a can reduce the inter-generational volatility of the retirement benefit, i.e., maintain a relatively steady increase in the AAF as the generations retire. However, the chance of the plan running out of money is most sensitive to the AAF adjustment β. Choosing a positive value of β can reduce the chance of the plan running out of money. For this reason, in the sequel, I examine plans in which both a and β are positive.

3.4. *Further Investigation*

Here I examine a different selection of the risk-sharing plans under a more realistic membership. In the selection of risk-sharing plans, both the adjustments a and β are positive. I also introduce a measure of *disappointment* that measures the year-on-year decline in the AAFs and their average. Examining the devastation measure is not meaningful for the membership, in which non-retired members make annual contributions. Due to the annual contributions, the plans do not run out of money.

The critical element to examine is the retirement benefit paid to the members, as this is the purpose of the plan. I look at the quantiles of the retirement benefit paid to each generation because this is important to an individual. I do not look at the expected retirement benefit across all generations. A beneficiary does not care if across all generations, the retirement benefit of Plan A is higher than Plan B, if they themselves get a lower benefit under Plan A than under Plan B.

Some questions to ask are: are the AAFs and their average high enough for each generation? Are they stable enough across the generations? Are earlier generations benefiting at the expense of the later generations, or vice versa? Through a numerical investigation, it is seen that the expected answers to these questions depend heavily on the choice of the three *plan parameters*: the investment strategy adjustment a, the AAF adjustment β and the target funding level $\overline{F}$.

3.4.1. Selected Risk-Sharing Pension Plans

I choose three plans which combine adjustments to both the benefits and the investments strategy, but which—for the chosen financial market model—do not result in the plan running out of money before all members have retired. I continue to keep the benchmark plan in, as a benchmark plan. The parameters of the plans are shown in Table 1.

Table 1. Plan parameters for the risk-sharing plans.

Plan Type	Investment Risk Adjustment a	AAF Adjustment β
Benchmark plan	0	0
Risk-sharing	0.2	0.2
Risk-sharing	0.2	0.4
Risk-sharing	0.4	0.2
DC plan	N/A	N/A

3.4.2. Membership Profile

There are $N := 40$ generations at time 0, the first generation retiring at time 1, the second generation at time 2, and so on. The kth generation contributes $\$(N+1-k)$ to the plan as an initial lumpsum payment at time 0, for $k = 1, 2, \ldots, 40$. Additionally, each generation pays an annual lumpsum contribution of \$1 at each integer time before their retirement time. Thus generation 1 pays only a lumpsum of $\$N$ at time 0, and nothing else until their retirement at time 1. Generation 2 pays a lumpsum of $\$(N-1)$ at time 0, another contribution of \$1 at time 1, and nothing else until their retirement at time 2. In the introduced notation, $B_0^{(k)} = N+1-k$ for $k = 1, 2, \ldots, N$, and $C_n^{(k)} = 1$ for $n = 1, \ldots, k-1$, for $k = 2, \ldots, N$. The motivation is to represent the contribution profile of a more realistic membership. Moreover, by fixing the total amount of contributions made by each generation at $\$N$, it makes the measure of disappointment introduced below more meaningful: members who contribute the same amount may feel that they should receive similar benefits.

The notional funding level of each risk-sharing plan is exactly equal to 100% at time 0.

3.4.3. Quantiles of the Average AAF

Figure 5 shows the 25%, 50% (median) and 75% quantiles of the annualized average accumulation factor under the selected risk-sharing plans, the DC plan and the benchmark plan. The target funding level is $\overline{F} = 100\%$ for the risk-sharing plans. It can be seen that up to, roughly, the 25th generation, the average AAF is more stable (i.e., has a lower inter-quartile range) under the risk-sharing plans than the DC plan. Past the 25th generation, the differences in inter-quartile range between the risk-sharing plans and the DC plan is not significant. The median average AAF has a decreasing trend as time increases for the risk-sharing plans, whereas it is flat for the DC plan.

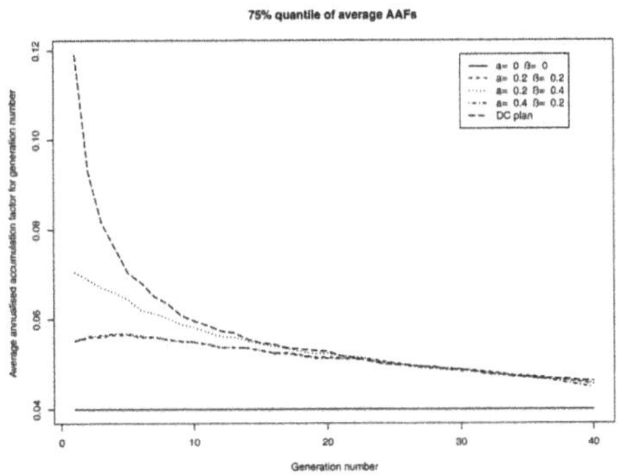

(a)

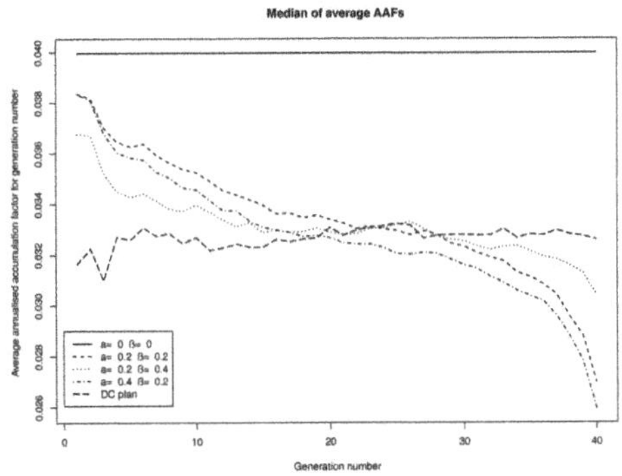

(b)

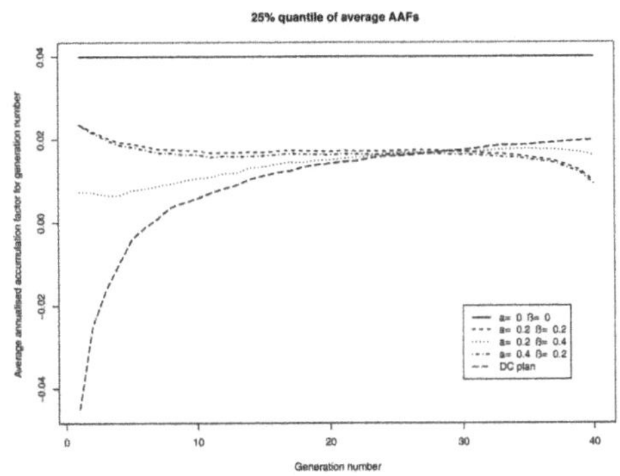

(c)

Figure 5. The annualized average accumulation factor for each generation in the model, for the more realistic membership, as both the investment risk adjustment (a) and the AAF adjustment (β) are varied. The target funding level is $\overline{F} = 100\%$. In this membership profile, the kth generation contributes $\$(40 - k + 1)$ at time 0, and contributes a further \$1 per annum at the end of each year that they are not retired. (**a**) 75% quantile, $\overline{F} = 100\%$; (**b**) Median, $\overline{F} = 100\%$; (**c**) 25% quantile, $\overline{F} = 100\%$.

The widest range of possible retirement benefits is with the DC plan. The earliest generations of the DC plan experience a huge range of possible benefits, although this declines with the investment period.

Increasing the target funding level to $\overline{F} = 120\%$ for the risk-sharing plans, Figure 6 shows the same quantiles. Since the risk-sharing plans are only 100% funded at time 0, they attempt to reach the target funding level through reducing the AAFs (via the adjustment β) and reducing the investment in the risky stock (via the adjustment a). This is observed in the figures, as the average AAF is below one (shown in Figure 6 as negative values, since the figure displays the value of the average AAF minus one) for the earliest retiring generations, and becomes greater than one (shown in Figure 6 as positive values) for the later generations as the target funding level is attained. The average AAF remains more stable (i.e., has a lower inter-quartile range) under the risk-sharing plans than the DC plan, for generations up to, roughly, the 30th.

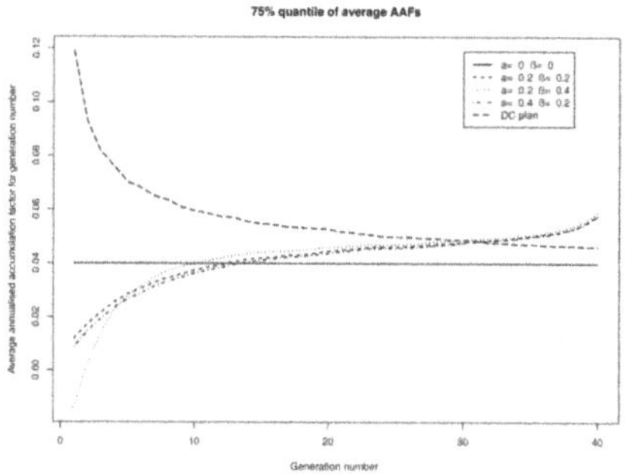

(a)

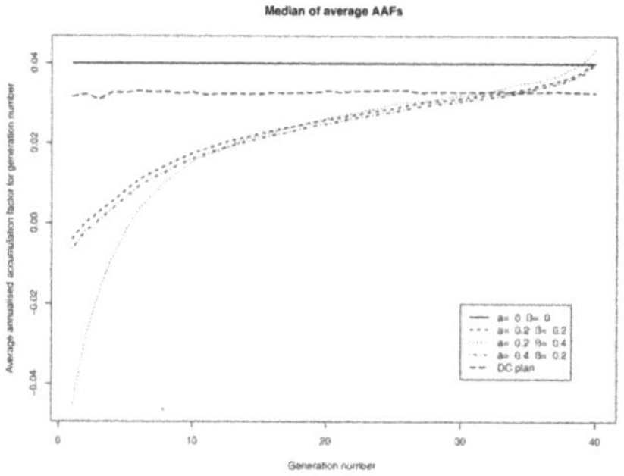

(b)

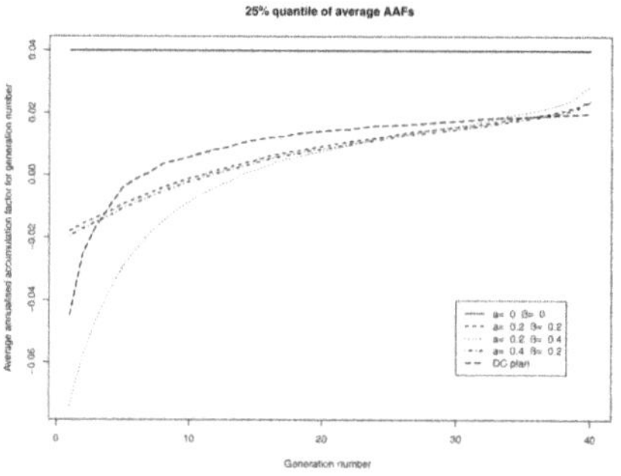

(c)

Figure 6. The annualized average accumulation factor for each generation in the model, for the more realistic membership, as both the investment risk adjustment (a) and the AAF adjustment (β) are varied. The target funding level is $\overline{F} = 120\%$. In this membership profile, the kth generation contributes $\$(40 - k + 1)$ at time 0, and contributes a further $1 per annum at the end of each year that they are not retired. (**a**) 75% quantile, $\overline{F} = 120\%$; (**b**) Median, $\overline{F} = 120\%$; (**c**) 25% quantile, $\overline{F} = 120\%$.

The shift in the median quantile, between Figures 5b and 6b, is interesting. For the higher target funding level $\overline{F} = 120\%$, the median average AAF has an increasing trend as time increases for the risk-sharing plans. This is the opposite trend to the plans with a target funding level $\overline{F} = 100\%$. The conclusion is that the target funding level can be used to shift the investment gains from the latest retiring generations to the earliest retiring generations. The reason for this shift is that the plan attempts to build up a cushion of assets, to reach the target funding level $\overline{F} = 120\%$. This cushion comes at the expense of the earlier generations, who pay for it and hence who are more likely to receive a lower average AAF than the later generations.

The figures demonstrate the flexibility of the risk-sharing plan; the plan parameters allow us to adjust the average AAF quantiles (and hence the amount of retirement benefit) across the generations.

3.4.4. Analyzing Benefit Stability

Here I analyze the stability of the average AAFs across generations for each plan. Rather than looking at means, I try to capture the spread of the possible average AAFs through an inter-quantile range. Setting for generation $n = 1, 2, \ldots, 40$,

$$\begin{aligned} \mathrm{IQR}_n \quad &:= 95\% \text{ average AAF quantile of } n\text{th generation} \\ &\quad -5\% \text{ average AAF quantile of } n\text{th generation}, \end{aligned}$$

Next I calculate the range of $\{\mathrm{IQR}_n\}_{n=1,\ldots,40}$ for each plan, namely

$$\mathrm{IQR\ instability} := \max_{n=1,2,\ldots,40} \{\mathrm{IQR}_n\} - \min_{n=1,2,\ldots,40} \{\mathrm{IQR}_n\}.$$

A plan with low instability should have an average AAF whose 5% to 95% quantile range does not change much between generations. However, this does not tell us whether the values in the range change between generations; a plan can have zero instability but generation 1 faces an average AAF in the range $[0\%, 3\%]$, generation 2 in the range $[1\%, 4\%]$, and so on. The disparity between the values of the average AAF is also important, so that a plan does not give highly negative increases to the earlier generations and highly positive increases to the later generations, or vice versa. To capture the latter, define

$$\begin{aligned} \text{Quantile inequity} \quad := &\max_{n=1,2,\ldots,40} \{95\% \text{ average AAF quantile of } n\text{th generation}\} \\ - &\min_{n=1,2,\ldots,40} \{5\% \text{ average AAF quantile of } n\text{th generation}\}. \end{aligned}$$

The lower the quantile inequity, the lower is the overall range of the average AAFs across all generations. This means that a plan with a low quantile inequity does not have the earlier generations benefiting at the expense of the later generations, or vice versa.

A narrower measure is the median inequity, which looks at the range of the median average AAF across all generations.

$$\begin{aligned} \text{Median inequity} \quad := &\max_{n=1,2,\ldots,40} \{50\% \text{ average AAF quantile of } n\text{th generation}\} \\ - &\min_{n=1,2,\ldots,40} \{50\% \text{ average AAF quantile of } n\text{th generation}\}. \end{aligned}$$

Table 2 shows the values of instability and inequity of the plans, for different target funding levels. Note that the values for the DC plan do not depend on the target funding level.

Table 2. Instability and inequity, across the generations for different target funding levels.

Plan Type	α	β	Target Funding Level $\overline{F} = 100\%$		
			IQR Instability	Qu. Inequity	Median Inequity
Risk-sharing	0.2	0.2	9.4%	10.3%	3.8%
Risk-sharing	0.2	0.4	15.7%	15.7%	3.7%
Risk-sharing	0.4	0.2	9.7%	10.5%	3.8%
DC	N/A	N/A	40.7%	40.7%	3.3%
Plan Type	α	β	**Target Funding Level $\overline{F} = 120\%$**		
			IQR Instability	**Qu. Inequity**	**Median Inequity**
Risk-sharing	0.2	0.2	9.5%	12.1%	4.4%
Risk-sharing	0.2	0.4	14.9%	19.4%	8.9%
Risk-sharing	0.4	0.2	9.5%	12.2%	4.6%
DC	N/A	N/A	40.7%	40.7%	3.3%

The risk-sharing plans have significantly lower values of IQR instability and quantile inequity than the DC plan. Thus, in terms of having a low range of possible average AAFs faced by different generations between the 5% and 95% quantiles, the risk-sharing plans perform well. The lowest measures are seen in the two plans with $\beta = 0.2$. Looking further down the table, the IQR instability measures decline for the risk-sharing plans as the target funding level increases, but this is at the cost of the quantile inequity increasing. Thus while the 5%–95% inter-quantile range declines over all generations, the range of possible values that the average AAF can take increases.

Interestingly, the DC plan has the lowest median average AAF inequity. For the risk-sharing plans, the median inequity rises as the target funding level rises. This is the due to the plans starting with a funding level of 100%, and therefore being under-funded relative to the higher target funding levels considered. Earlier generations are granted lower AAFs as the plan attempts to reach the target funding level. Later generations gain from the lower payments out from the plan's assets and the accumulated investment returns.

3.4.5. Disappointment

Although reducing the accumulated contributions is a integral part of the considered risk-sharing plans, perhaps some plan structures result in a higher chance of reductions in the accumulated value of contributions than others. If reductions occur too often, then it is possible that members will exit the plan. They will compare what they are getting with the recently retired members, and will be unhappy if they get a lower retirement benefit than them [23–26]. I call this *member disappointment*.

Member disappointment is related to disappointment aversion, which was introduced by Gul [27]. Ang et al. [28] develop a portfolio choice framework under disappointment aversion preferences, using a dynamic CRRA problem. Fielding and Stracca [29] analyze both loss and disappointment aversion, and find that stocks may disappoint in the long term.

Here I introduce a way of trying to measure retiring members' disappointment if their average AAF is less than the average AAF for the previous year's retiring generation. To measure member disappointment over two consecutive years, in each simulation I count the number of runs of exactly two consecutive years in which the average AAF is strictly declining. Doing this across all simulations, I calculate the probability of having two consecutive years in which the average AAF is strictly declining. Using the same approach, I calculate the probability of having three consecutive years in which the average AAF is strictly declining. I repeat this for four consecutive years, five consecutive years and so on. The resulting probability can be used to see the frequency of runs of declining average AAFs.

Figures 7 and 8 show the probability of disappointment for the plans, i.e., the probability of a fixed number of years of declining average AAF, for a target funding levels of 100% and 120%, respectively.

Members of the plans with the higher target funding level $\overline{F} = 120\%$ (Figure 8) are less likely to suffer disappointment. Thus the higher target funding level gives more security to the members. In all figures, it is observed that members of the risk-sharing plans are more likely to suffer declining average AAFs than DC plan participants. Therefore, communication of this possibility to members is essential for risk-sharing plans.

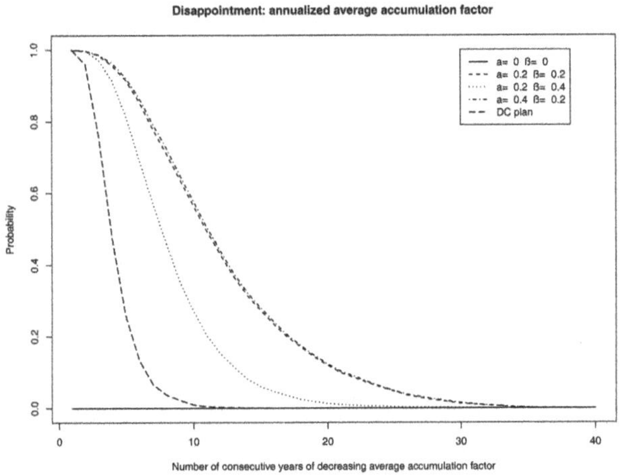

Figure 7. Disappointment for the more realistic membership when the target funding level $\overline{F} = 100\%$. The probability of a declining average AAF plotted against the number of consecutive years that the decline occurs over. Both the investment risk adjustment (a) and the AAF adjustment (β) are varied.

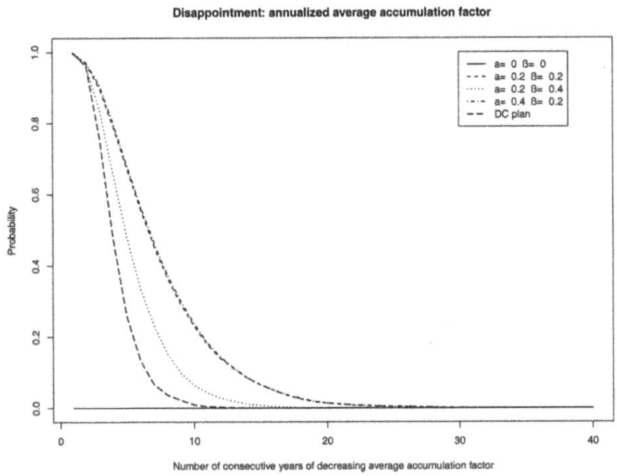

Figure 8. Disappointment for the more realistic membership when the target funding level $\overline{F} = 120\%$. The probability of a declining average AAF plotted against the number of consecutive years that the decline occurs over. Both the investment risk adjustment (a) and the AAF adjustment (β) are varied.

Figures 9 and 10 show the probability of disappointment for the plans, but for the AAF instead of the average of the AAFs. The message is the same, albeit the disappointment measure is very close to that of the DC plan. Disappointment is reduced by increasing the target funding level. This suggests that members who are easily disappointed should be in a plan with a higher target funding level.

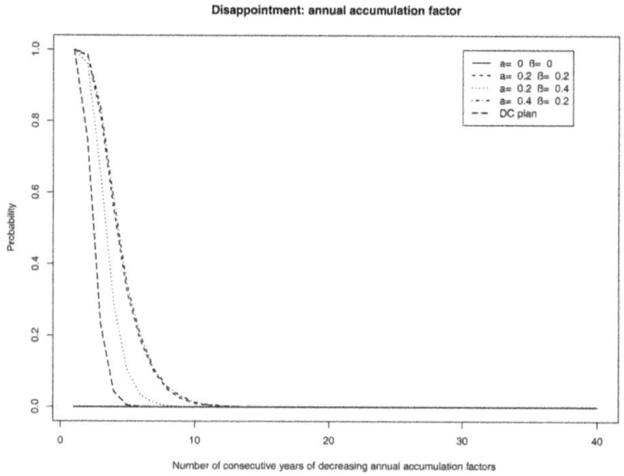

Figure 9. Disappointment for the more realistic membership when the target funding level $\overline{F} = 100\%$. The probability of a declining AAF plotted against the number of consecutive years that the decline occurs over. Both the investment risk adjustment (a) and the AAF adjustment (β) are varied.

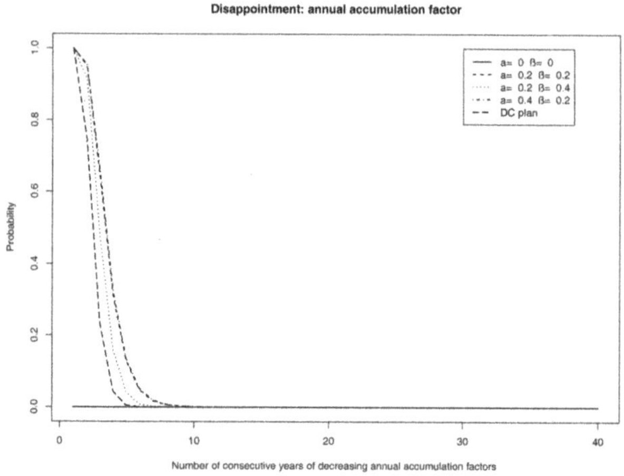

Figure 10. Disappointment for the more realistic membership when the target funding level $\overline{F} = 120\%$. The probability of a declining AAF plotted against the number of consecutive years that the decline occurs over. Both the investment risk adjustment (a) and the AAF adjustment (β) are varied.

4. Conclusions

The risk-sharing plan presented enables its members to receive more stable increases on their contributions than under a DC plan. However, the downside is that members may face year-on-year reductions in the accumulated value of their contributions, which I call disappointment. There is a higher chance of this than under a DC plan, for the chosen financial market model and membership profile. The possibility of members' accumulated contributions declining over time would need to be well-communicated to them. However, as the average accumulation factors on the contributions made in the risk-sharing plan are more stable than under a DC plan, a risk-sharing plan may allow members to plan better for their retirement since they have more certainty about the amount of their retirement benefit.

The chance of year-on-year reductions in the accumulated value of contributions can be reduced by increasing the target funding level. This suggests that members who wish to reduce the chance of reductions should be in a plan with a higher target funding level. However, increasing the target funding level means that earlier generations pay for a cushion of assets from which they may not benefit. Instead, the later retiring generations are more likely to benefit from the cushion, in the form of higher accumulation factors granted on their contributions.

The choice of the plan parameters—which determine by how much to adjust the investment strategy, the accumulation factors and the target funding level—are critical to the sustainability of the plan, and the degree of risk-sharing between generations. Based on the studied plans, I draw the following conclusions. The accumulation factor granted on contributions is most sensitive to the parameter that adjusts the investment strategy. The chance of the plan running out of money is most sensitive to the parameter that adjusts the accumulation factors. The target funding level can be used to shift the level of accumulation factors between generations; a higher target funding level means that earlier generations are granted lower accumulation factors than later generations, and vice versa.

The choice of the plan parameters requires a careful study of the expected membership profile, allowing for a financial market model or models. A preliminary analysis by the author, using the membership profiles analyzed in the paper, suggests that the conclusions continue to hold when the financial model is changed. While this paper analyzes a selection of the plan parameters, any implementation in practice would require further analysis to choose appropriate values for the expected plan membership.

Acknowledgments: The author gratefully acknowledges the financial support of the 2013 Individual Grant received from The Actuarial Foundation. The author thanks the reviewers of the paper, who made valuable comments which helped to greatly improve the paper.

Conflicts of Interest: The author declares no conflict of interest.

References

1. Ramaswamy, S. *The Sustainability of Pension Schemes*; Technical Report; Working Papers No. 368; Bank for International Settlements: Basel, Switzerland, 2012.
2. Franzen, D. *Managing Investment Risk in Defined Benefit Pension Funds*; Technical Report; Organisation for Economic Co-Operation and Development; OECD Working Papers on Insurance and Private Pensions; Number 38; OECD Publishing: Paris, France, 2010.
3. Lusardi, A.; Mitchell, O. Financial literacy around the world: An overview. *J. Pension Econ. Financ.* **2011**, *10*, 497–508. [CrossRef]
4. Greenwald & Associates. *2015 Risks and Process of Retirement Survey*; Technical Report; Society of Actuaries: Schaumburg, IL, USA, January 2016.
5. Ponds, E.; Riel, B. Sharing risk: The Netherlands' new approach to pensions. *J. Pension Econ. Financ.* **2009**, *8*, 91–105. [CrossRef]
6. Cui, J.; de Jong, F.; Ponds, E. Intergenerational risk sharing within funded pension schemes. *J. Pension Econ. Financ.* **2011**, *10*, 1–29. [CrossRef]
7. Gollier, C. Intergenerational risk-sharing and risk-taking of a pension fund. *J. Public Econ.* **2008**, *92*, 1463–1485. [CrossRef]
8. Pugh, C.; Yermo, J. *Funding Regulations and Risk-Sharing*; Technical Report; Organisation for Economic Co-operation and Development; OECD Working Papers on Insurance and Private Pensions; Number 17; OECD Publishing: Paris, France, 2008.
9. Blommestein, H.; Janssen, P.; Kortleve, N.; Yermo, J. *Evaluating the Design of Private Pension Plans: Costs and Benefits of Risk-Sharing*; Technical Report; Organisation for Economic Co-operation and Development; OECD Working Papers on Insurance and Private Pensions; Number 34; OECD Publishing: Paris, France, 2009.
10. Briys, E.; de Varenne, F. On the risk of insurance liabilities: Debunking some common pitfalls. *J. Risk Insur.* **1997**, *64*, 673–694. [CrossRef]
11. Barbarin, J.; Devolder, P. Risk measure and fair valuation of an investment guarantee in life insurance. *Insur. Math. Econ.* **2005**, *37*, 297–323. [CrossRef]

12. Graf, S.; Kling, A.; Ruß, J. Risk analysis and valuation of life insurance contracts: Combining actuarial and financial approaches. *Insur. Math. Econ.* **2011**, *49*, 115–125. [CrossRef]
13. Grosen, A.; Jørgensen, P. Fair valuation of life insurance liabilities: The impact of interest rate guarantees, surrender options, and bonus policies. *Insur. Math. Econ.* **2000**, *26*, 37–57. [CrossRef]
14. Hieber, P.; Korn, R.; Scherer, M. Analyzing the effect of low interest rates on the surplus participation of life insurance policies with different annual interest rate guarantees. *Eur. Actuar. J.* **2015**, *5*, 11–28. [CrossRef]
15. Guillén, M.; Jørgensen, P.; Nielsen, J. Return smoothing mechanism in life and pension insurance. *Insur. Math. Econ.* **2006**, *38*, 229–252. [CrossRef]
16. Baumann, R.; Müller, H. Pension funds as institutions for intertemporal risk transfer. *Insur. Math. Econ.* **2008**, *42*, 1000–1012. [CrossRef]
17. Bohnert, A.; Gatzert, N. Analyzing surplus appropriation schemes in participating life insurance from the insurer's and the policyholder's perspective. *Insur. Math. Econ.* **2012**, *50*, 64–78. [CrossRef]
18. Zemp, A. Risk comparison of different bonus distribution approaches in participating life insurance. *Insur. Math. Econ.* **2011**, *49*, 249–264. [CrossRef]
19. Goecke, O. Pension saving schemes with return smoothing mechanisms. *Insur. Math. Econ.* **2013**, *53*, 678–689. [CrossRef]
20. Galer, R. *"Prudent Person Rule" Standard for the Investment of Pension Fund Assets*; Technical Report; Organisation for Economic Co-Operation and Development; Financial Market Trends; Number 83; OECD Publishing: Paris, France, November 2002.
21. De Jong, F. Pension fund investments and the valuation of liabilities under conditional indexation. *Insur. Math. Econ.* **2008**, *42*, 1–13. [CrossRef]
22. Hardy, M. *Investment Guarantees: Modeling and Risk Management for Equity-Linked Life Insurance*; Wiley Finance: Hoboken, NJ, USA, 2003.
23. Boyce, C.; Brown, G.; Moore, S. Money and happiness: Rank of income, not income, affects life satisfaction. *Psychol. Sci.* **2010**, *21*, 471–475. [CrossRef] [PubMed]
24. Clark, A.; Senik, C. Who compares to whom? The anatomy of income comparisons in Europe. *Econ. J.* **2010**, *120*, 573–594. [CrossRef]
25. Luttmer, E. Neighbors as negatives: Relative earnings and well-being. *Q. J. Econ.* **2005**, *120*, 963–1002. [CrossRef]
26. Wolbring, T.; Keuschnigg, M.; Negele, E. Needs, comparisons, and adaptation: The importance of relative income for life satisfaction. *Eur. Sociol. Rev.* **2013**, *29*, 86–104. [CrossRef]
27. Gul, F. A theory of disappointment aversion. *Econometrica* **1991**, *59*, 667–686. [CrossRef]
28. Ang, A.; Bekaert, G.; Liu, J. Why stocks may disappoint. *J. Financ. Econ.* **2005**, *76*, 471–508. [CrossRef]
29. Fielding, D.; Stracca, L. Myopic loss aversion, disappointment aversion, and the equity premium puzzle. *J. Econ. Behav. Organ.* **2007**, *64*, 250–268. [CrossRef]

risks MDPI

Article

The Shifting Shape of Risk: Endogenous Market Failure for Insurance

Thomas G. Koch

Bureau of Economics, Federal Trade Commission, Washington, DC 20580, USA; tkoch@ftc.gov;
Tel.: +1-512-809-8014

Academic Editor: Luca Regis
Received: 6 July 2016; Accepted: 9 December 2016; Published: 27 January 2017

Abstract: This article considers an economy where risk is insurable, but selection determines the pool of individuals who take it up. First, we demonstrate that the comparative statics of these economies do not necessarily depend on its marginal selection (adverse versus favorable), but rather other characteristics. We then use repeated cross-sections of medical expenditures in the U.S. to understand the role of changes in the medical risk distribution on the fraction of Americans without medical insurance. We find that both the level and the shape of the distribution of risk are important in determining the equilibrium quantity of insurance. Symmetric changes in risk (e.g., shifts in the price of medical care) better explain the shifting insurance rate over time. Asymmetric changes (e.g., associated with a shifting age distribution) are not as important.

Keywords: risk sharing; medical insurance; adverse selection

JEL Classification: D3; I1

1. Introduction

This article considers how the price for insurance and the number of people insured varies when the risk and other characteristics of the population change. We study these relationships, known as comparative statics, for insurance markets that suffer from either adverse or advantageous selection, and then consider the specific case of medical insurance markets.

The comparative statics of medical insurance markets is of interest, as these markets leave millions of Americans uninsured against medical risk. Eighty percent of the private medical insurance in the US is employer-provided[1], and employers are not allowed to discriminate according to relevant demographic and medical information when they price insurance provided to their employees.[2] Policies, such as the income-tax deductability of health insurance, or a "Cadillac tax" on expensive health plans, should induce changes in prices and quantity. I demonstrate that increases in the cost of insurance, such as the "Cadillac tax", may actually increase the amount of insurance, rather than decrease it. The actual price and quantity effects of policies designed to shift either the supply or demand curves in insurance markets may have counter-intuitive effects. For example, many aspects of the Affordable Care Act (ACA), such as the Cadillac tax or ACA plan subsidies, that are designed to decrease or increase the amount of insurance, respectively, may have opposite effects.

In these models, the amount of risk left uninsured due to selection depends upon the distribution of risks—for example, what is the ratio of high-cost to low-cost individuals, and how different in average costs are high- and low-cost individuals. We use repeated cross-sections of medical expenditure

[1] This number is based upon the author's calculations using the MEPS, which is described below.
[2] This is why a menu of contracts is unlikely to solve the adverse selection problem here: any separate pooling they could induce would rely on indirect, and possibly manipulable, correlates with expected cost.

data to infer such ratios, and use them in a model of insurance markets with asymmetric information. I also find that changes to the distribution of medical risk faced by consumers in recent years should have lead to more expensive medical insurance. It should also have lead to more people with medical insurance.

The price of employer-provided medical insurance to cover a single employee has grown five percent a year from 1996 to 2005. The price of family coverage has grown 5.7 percent per year over the same period.[3] At the same time, more Americans have gone without medical insurance. Among the non-poor and non-elderly, the percentage of individuals without private insurance rose 22 percent (18 percent to 22) from 1996 to 2004.[4]

One explanation for higher insurance prices is the well-documented growth in average medical spending (Swartz [1]; Freudenheim [2]). As medical costs grow, the supply curve for medical insurance shifts up, and induces movement along the demand curve. This new equilibrium price is higher, while equilibrium quantity is lower. However, changes in the distribution of medical expenditures (e.g., mean, median, variance, etc.) are the result of changes in the distribution of medical risk. In this case, the demand curve also shifts up. The new equilibrium price is larger, but whether the new equilibrium quantity is larger or smaller is unclear.

This article attempts to disentangle these changes. This study complements the findings of Gruber and Levy [3], which documented similar (though differently measured) changes to the distribution of medical risk. We use changes in the distribution of medical expenditures in the US to infer changes in the distribution of medical risk. We then take these measured differences in the distribution of medical risk into a quantitative model of insurance choice with asymmetric information. We find that measured changes in the distribution of medical risk should have made insurance more expensive and more prevalent. While the former trend is consistent with the data, the latter is not.

This work can help shed light on recent research that considers alternative risk-adjustment factors; that is, what kinds of information could be used to price insurance that would limit the amount of market failure due to adverse selection. Both [4,5] find evidence that age-based health insurance prices may drive some of those age-specific markets to collapse. Here, we identify some of the characteristics of risk pools that make them sustainable.

The lessons from this exercise go beyond the sectoral concerns of medical insurance. If the source of uninsurance in other markets is asymmetric information, then this reminds us that distributions matter. If there is an across-the-board increase in risk, then insurance markets likely would provide more insurance, instead of less, as the demand curve shifts out further than the supply curve because of risk aversion. Furthermore, it introduces the notion that comparative statics do not depend upon the nature of the selection (adverse vs. advantageous). Instead, the comparative statics depend upon the stability of the equilibrium. For example, if wage volatility goes up, it matters whose wage volatility goes up.

This also relates to the market failure as discussed in recent work on insurance against aggregate, catastrophic risk [6–8]. When a natural disaster strikes, it may test the solvency of the risk pool, leading to partial insurance. The risks under study here have idiosyncratic realizations, as opposed to the widespread loss of property due to an earthquake or hurricane. For example, we do not consider how insurance markets might deal with a flu pandemic. Likewise, the tax subsidy of health insurance should mitigate adverse selection, and the indirect nature of the contract (typically via employers, instead of directly to consumers) may also influence the extent of adverse selection.

---

3 The level changes from 1996 to 2005 for these two prices is 1992 to 3227, and 4954 to 8675, as reported by the MEPS-IC. These calculations adjust for changes in the price level, as measured by the Urban CPI.

4 These numbers are calculated from the MEPS-HC, which collects information from a nationally-representative sample of households.

2. A General Framework with Initial Results

Suppose there is a unit measure of risk-averse agents, heterogenous in their financial risk, $\tilde{x}$. Each agent's risk is characterized by $\lambda \in \mathbb{R}$, with conditional expectation $\mathbb{E}\left[\tilde{x}|\lambda\right] \in \mathbb{R}$. Risk types are distributed according to a second distribution, $\lambda \sim \Gamma$. Agents with wealth w and preferences $u(\cdot)$[5] have a willingness to pay for insurance, $\pi(\lambda)$, which is the dollar amount that makes the agent indifferent between paying $\pi(\lambda)$ for insurance, or facing the risk without insurance:

$$u(w - \pi(\lambda)) = \mathbb{E}[u(w - \tilde{x})|\lambda].$$

Risk aversion means that willingness to pay for insurance is greater than expected outcome. An agent purchases insurance if his or her willingness to pay for insurance is larger than its price, $\varpi \in \mathbb{R}$—that is, if $\pi \geq \varpi$, and not otherwise. An inverse demand function, $\pi^{-1}(\varpi)$, provides the risk type(s) associated with a particular level of demand at price ϖ.

The demand curve for insurance is simply the ordering of the individual demands:

$$D(\varpi) = 1 - \Gamma(\pi^{-1}(\varpi)).$$

The demand curve is downward sloping by construction.

We assume that insurance firms provide insurance via price competition. These firms cannot provide risk-type contingent contracts because of asymmetric information. The sources of this asymmetric information may either be based in the microfoundations of the model, or due to legal constraints imposed upon insurers. In the case of the US medical insurance market, the latter case is certainly true—firms that offer their workers medical insurance are not allowed to discriminate the premiums paid for that insurance according to individual criteria such as age, gender, and health status. Given that employer-provided insurance is the dominant source of insurance, it is a reasonable assumption for this question.

Thus, firms offer a full insurance at price ϖ, and agents select into the contract according to their demand. The firm's per-contract profit is:

$$\Pi = \varpi - \mathbb{E}\left[\tilde{x}|\pi(\lambda) \geq \varpi\right].$$

Free entry drives the expected profits of insurance firms to zero. Thus, the supply curve is the average cost of supplying insurance to the first $1 - \Gamma(\pi^{-1}(\varpi))$ agents who select into it. The shape of supply curve is determined by the mechanics of marginal selection at every price. The supply curve may or may not be monotonic, depending upon the expected cost of the each agent, relative to the average cost of the agents up to that agent.

An equilibrium is a price of insurance, ϖ, and set of agents, $\Lambda \subset \Gamma$, who select, or pool, into that insurance contract, that are consistent with price equals average cost. Five equilibria types are possible:

- Downward-sloping demand and upward-sloping supply: in this case, the marginal agents are more expensive than the average agent;
- Downward-sloping demand and supply with, from left to right:
  - demand going from above to below supply;
  - demand going from below to above supply;
  - supply and demand just tangent, with supply above demand; and
  - supply and demand just tangent, with demand above supply.

[5] It will be assumed that marginal utility does not change with the realization of the risk, besides the risk's effect on the agent's consumption level. If the risk changed the agent's marginal utility, then the agent may want consumption levels that are unequal between different outcomes of the realization. While such circumstances may be interesting, state-dependent utility functions are beyond the scope of study here.

The first equilibrium exhibits local favorable selection, as in Jovanovic [9]. This could be due to heterogeneity in risk preferences that was negatively correlated with expected cost. Alternatively, the final four equilibria exhibit local adverse selection. This typology of equilibria is necessary because different types of equilibria have different comparative statics. For the balance of the article, the tangency equilibria will be ignored, as they are not robust to changes in the supply and demand curves—either the equilibrium vanishes (supply and demand no longer cross), or two equilibria emerge from the changes (they further overlap).

Consider the second and third types. Suppose there is an outward shift of demand without a shift in supply—for example, if agents become more risk averse. When demand starts above supply, the new equilibrium supports more insurance at a lower price. The price falls because the selection is locally adverse. However, when supply begins above demand, the shift in the demand curve leads to less insurance at a higher price. These two cases are demonstrated in the sub-figures of Figure 1.

The response to a change in preferences can be characterized according to an equilibrium's stability.

Definition 1. *An equilibrium characterized by its marginal agent λ_m is locally stable, if, for all local $\varepsilon > 0$,*

$$\varpi(\lambda_m + \varepsilon) \geq \pi(\lambda_m + \varepsilon)$$

and

$$\varpi(\lambda_m - \varepsilon) \leq \pi(\lambda_m - \varepsilon).$$

The stability refinement is similar to the trembling-hand refinement of Selten [10], and the stability refinement of Kohlberg and Mertens [11]. This refinement is intuitive—the equilibria in this model are pooling equilibria. The first and second equilibria are stable, while the third is not.

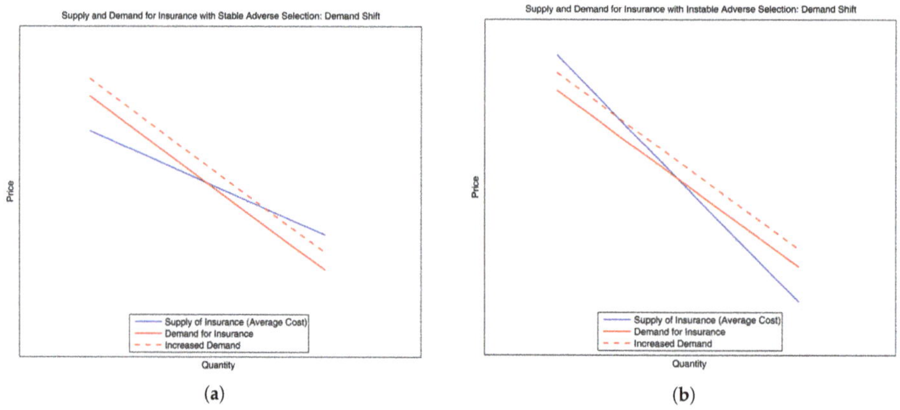

Figure 1. Supply and demand for insurance with asymmetric information and changes in demand.

Changes in preferences are generally difficult to identify, whereas it may be more feasible to identify changes to the distribution of risk, Γ. Changes to the distribution of risk can be classified as symmetric or asymmetric. First, consider asymmetric changes. Such changes have consequences for the average cost (supply) curve, with relatively modest effects on the marginal benefit (demand) curve. Figure 2 presents the three cases of interest—a (stable) equilibrium with favorable selection, and two equilibria exhibiting adverse selection, one stable and the other unstable.

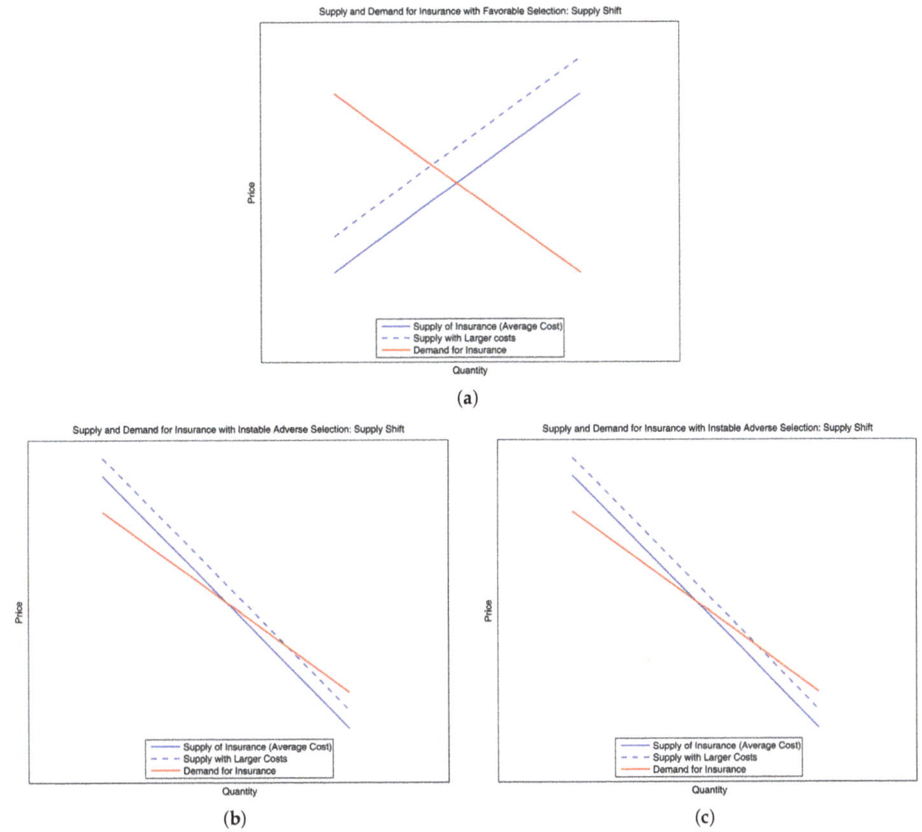

Figure 2. Supply and demand for insurance with asymmetric information and asymmetric changes to cost (i.e., no change in marginal demand).

The comparative statics depend upon the stability of the equilibrium. A shift up in the supply curve without a commensurate shift in the demand curve will lead to less insurance (a smaller pool) if we consider a stable equilibria. However, if we consider unstable equilibria, the opposite is true—a shift up in the supply curve will lead to an increase in the amount of insurance provided in spite of asymmetric information.

The number and stability of equilibria depend upon the micro-foundations of the model—preferences, and risk types and distributions, for example. In order to more clearly understand the relationship between risk and insurance in spite of asymmetric information, more assumptions are required.

3. A Series of Instructive Numerical Examples

Consider an economy with two types of agents who face a Bernoulli risk—they may catch an illness and have to go to the doctor. The cost of a visit, L, is the same for both types, though the healthy differ from the sick in that they face a smaller probability of going to the doctor, $p_h < p_s$. Fraction s of the population is sick, while the rest are healthy. The specific values for these parameters and calculations for each example can be found in Table 1. If preferences for risk can be characterized by CARA, with degree of risk aversion r, each agent's willingness to pay for full insurance is:

$$\pi(p., L; r) = \frac{1}{r} \ln \left(1 - p. + p.e^{rL}\right).$$

Note that $\pi(p, L; r)$ is an increasing function in each of its arguments. Sicker agents are willing to pay more for insurance, $\frac{\partial \pi(p,L;r)}{\partial p} > 0$, and all agents are willing to pay more for full insurance as the cost of a visit grows, $\frac{\partial \pi(p,L;r)}{\partial L} > 0$. It will also be useful to think of each agent's certainty equivalent, $\pi(p., L; r) - p.L$—the amount an agent is willing to pay for insurance above and beyond a fair price.

Table 1. Parameter values for Bernoulli numerical examples in the text.

Example	L	p_s	p_h	s	a^*_{all}	π_h	Adverse Selection?
1	1200	0.5	0.1	0.5	360	316	Yes
2	1500	0.5	0.1	0.5	450	483	No
3	1500	0.8	0.1	0.5	675	483	Yes

The average medical cost in the economy is $a^*_{all} = (sp_s + (1-s)p_h)L$. Note that this value can increase because of increasing cost, L, or increasing probability of illness, $p.$. Suppose that the population is half sick and half healthy ($s = 0.5$). Furthermore, let $L = 1200$, and set the probabilities of illness to $p_s = 0.5$ and $p_h = 0.1$. The average medical cost is now 360, which would be the price of insurance if all agents chose full insurance bought in competitive markets with asymmetric information—the insurers do not provide type-based insurance. However, the healthy may not choose to buy such insurance, as their willingness to pay for insurance is less than its unfair price. This is the case here, using a calibration, $r = 0.0018$—a healthy agent is only willing to pay 316 for insurance. The healthy go uninsured in such a market, while the sick sort into fairly-priced insurance.

Suppose that the price of a doctor's visit rises to $L' = 1500$—a symmetric change in risk. Average medical costs rise to 450. Now note, though, that the healthy agents are willing to pay for unfairly-priced full insurance provided by a competitive market. That is, $\pi(0.1, 1200; 0.002) = 483 > 450$. As the cost of a visit grows, the certainty equivalent of the healthy agent grows faster than the price of insurance. More full insurance was provided because these changes were symmetric—both the healthy and the sick face larger risks.

Now suppose an asymmetric change, $p'_s = 0.8$, keeping the price of a doctors visit at 1500. Average medical costs rise to 675. The healthy are not willing to pay this much for full insurance, as their willingness to pay for insurance does not change. Here, there is a decrease in insurance because the change was asymmetric.

This specification for risk is clearly not useful when considering the U.S. medical insurance market, as it is very coarse and does not allow for much heterogeneity. That said, it does suggest the general principle at work in the following section: following the average medical cost is not enough to determine whether an insurance market with incomplete information will allow for more insurance or less. The change in the distribution of risk that induced the change in the average medical cost is what determines the amount of insurance provided under asymmetric information. We will now apply that general principle to the preferred specification for medical risk.

4. A More General Setting

The model economy has a unit measure of risk-averse agents with utility function $u(\cdot)$. Each agent faces medical expenditures risk, $\widetilde{mx}_i$, and its risk is private information. The risks faced by agents are heterogeneous and are distributed according to Γ. This model was previously used in Koch [12], which contains the details of preference parameter estimation. The private information assumption means that insurers are not able to sort, so all agents face a common price of insurance, ϖ. The purchase of insurance is subsidized at a rate s, which is paid for using lump-sum taxes, τ. Insurance is subsidized at a rate here as it is in the U.S. federal income tax code—here it is a positive subsidy, relative to wage income. The two are equivalent with constant absolute risk aversion. Depending upon type, each agent has a willingness to pay for insurance, π_i, which makes them indifferent between facing the risk associated with with their type, $\widetilde{mx}_i$, and paying for insurance. The decision to purchase insurance, ι_i, is a discrete choice:

$$U_I(w, \widetilde{mx}_i; \varpi, \tau) = \max\left\{ u(w - (1-s)\varpi - \tau), E\left[u(w - \widetilde{mx}_i - \tau)\right] \right\}. \tag{1}$$

If $u(w - (1-s)\varpi - \tau) > E\left[u(w - \widetilde{mx}_i - \tau)\right.$ (i.e., $\pi_i \geq \varpi$), then the agent purchases insurance, and does not otherwise. Because of asymmetric information, agents do not get access to fairly-priced insurance. The distribution of π_i is the demand curve for full insurance.

The market to provide full insurance is competitive, so that the price of insurance is equal to the average realized risk of the insured. Thus, we define an equilibrium to be:

- the insurance choice, ι_i, is the optimal solution to Equation (1);
- insurance price, ϖ, is equal to the average realized risk of the insured; and,
- tax level, τ, is equal to the total cost of the subsidy of medical insurance.

The specification of preferences and risk heterogeneity is chosen to mirror several empirical facts, while also aiding in the computation of equilibria. The cross-sectional distribution of medical expenditures has three main features: a large number of zeros, a monotonically-decreasing partial density, and a fat, Pareto-like tail.

In order to match the three main features of the distribution of medical expenditures, we will use the following specification of individual risk and heterogeneity:

- individual i faces risk according to the exponential distribution, parameterized by λ_i; and,
- these types are distributed according to the Gamma distribution, with parameters α and β.

These two assumptions lead to a cross-sectional (i.e., unconditional) Pareto-type distribution of realized medical risk, with all three characteristics. This specification of uncertainty was originally proposed by Harris [13], though in a different context. Preferences against this risk are assumed to exhibit CARA.

CARA preferences are tractable, especially in this context. The willingness to pay for insurance, given type λ_i, parameter of risk aversion r, and upper bound of risk κ can be written as:

$$\pi(\lambda_i) = \frac{1}{r}\log\left(\frac{\lambda_i - re^{-(\lambda_i - r)\kappa}}{\lambda_i - r}\right).$$

Note that willingness to pay for insurance with CARA preferences is independent of wages or wealth.

It can be shown that this willingness to pay is monotonically decreasing in λ_i. Because of this, equilibria can be characterized by their marginal agent type, λ_m, whose willingness to pay for insurance is equal to its price. The price of medical insurance is equal to the average realized risk of the insured:

$$\begin{aligned}\varpi(\lambda_m) &= \int_0^{\lambda_m} t^{-1} \frac{t^{\alpha} e^{-\frac{t}{\beta}}}{\beta^{\alpha+1}\Gamma(\frac{\lambda_m}{\beta}, \alpha+1)} dt \\ &= \frac{\Gamma(\frac{\lambda_m}{\beta}, \alpha)}{\beta\Gamma(\frac{\lambda_m}{\beta}, \alpha+1)},\end{aligned}$$

where $\Gamma(\cdot,\cdot)$ is the incomplete gamma function.

These specifications also mitigate the problem of multiple equilibria. Figure 3 plots out the supply and demand curves for a set of candidate parameters—the degree of risk aversion, r, upper bound of risk faced by an agent, κ, and the distribution of medical risk, α and β. Preferences and adverse selection (due to asymmetric information) lead to a downward-sloping supply curve. In this case, there are two potential equilibria. Other parameterizations could lead to one equilibrium (the supply and demand curve are just tangent), or no equilibria—the case where no risk sharing is possible.

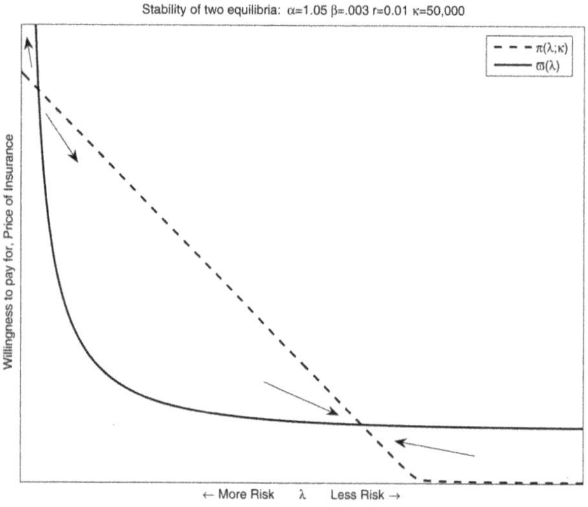

Figure 3. The stability of two equilibria.

Because the movements in insurance rates and prices are steady, it is unlikely that the equilibria we observe is unstable. Figure 3 demonstrates that the equilibrium with more insurance is the stable of the two. Parameter values that lead to a single equilibrium lead to unstable equilibria.

Medical insurance in the U.S. is primarily provided in the context of firms. Thus, the ideal data set would consider risk sharing across individuals within a firm. Unfortunately, such data is not publicly available. Instead, we use data from a nationally representative data set. To the extent that risks faced by workers within a firm look like the general population, this will be a useful examination. If workers could act on the distribution of medical risks within a firm, or firms could fire workers for being poor medical risks, this would be an unreasonable approximation. However, in both cases, such behavior might very well be either infeasible or illegal. Part of the medical risk under consideration here is latent—factors such as family history can impact future expectations—and information about it would thus be difficult to gather reliably. Even for evident medical conditions, it may be against the law for supervisors or co-workers to be informed about the health status of others, let alone act upon it.

Alternatively, one might worry that workers do not have an opportunity to take-up insurance within a firm. Decreases in the overall insurance rate may be due to fewer firms offering insurance, instead of fewer workers taking it up. This model does not account for these sorts of changes. Evidence suggests that these kinds of changes are not important. Stanton [14] finds that the number of workers employed by firms that offered medical insurance rose from 1996 to 2002. The decrease in employer-provided insurance over this period is instead tied to decreases in take-up by employees, and, to a lesser extent, fewer employees being eligible for medical insurance.

Here, we use the Medical Expenditure Panel Survey (MEPS). The MEPS is a series of overlapping two-year panels, with information on annual medical expenditures, charges, and insurance status. The panel aspect of the data is beyond the focus of this article—we use the series of cross sections in the

MEPS, starting in 1996, going to 2004, in order to infer each year's distribution of medical risk—each year's Gamma distribution, its (α_t, β_t) pair. We will later use these values to infer the amount of private insurance possible in the asymmetric-information model.

We restrict the sample to the non-elderly and the non-poor in order to avoid complications due to Medicare and Medicaid. Veterans are also removed, due to access to VA care. In all three cases, publicly-provided insurance can crowd out private insurance. This restriction also avoids potential confusion about private insurance among the elderly (over 65).

Unfortunately, the data do not present a perfect candidate for the insurable (i.e., covered by insurance) realizations of medical risk. One potential measure is the total charges for an individual over a year. Because medical insurance contracts typically have co-payments or deductibles, this is an imprecise measure of the realized insurable medical risk.

This specification of risk has an internally-coherent and tractable way to back out the insurable fraction of total risk. If a fraction $\rho^{-1} < 1$ of an exponential risk is insurable, parameterized by λ, then this fraction of a risk is also an exponential risk. This new risk is parameterized by $\frac{\lambda}{\rho}$. If this fraction ρ is common across agents, then all of the exponential risks are scaled by ρ. A common ρ might come from the fact that these co-insurance rates are used to solve a hidden-action problem, and type privacy does not allow for discrimination. Finally, since β is a scale parameter for the Gamma distribution, the new distribution of insurable risk is also a Gamma distribution, with parameters α and $\frac{\beta}{\rho}$.

The distribution of insurable risk can also be inferred from the distribution of medical expenditures paid by private insurance companies for the privately insured. The first moment of the conditional distribution, the average realized risk of the insured, can be found by integrating the expected realized risk over the types who choose insurance; i.e.,

$$\begin{aligned} E(\widetilde{mx}_i|\iota_i = 1) &= \int_0^{\lambda_m} t^{-1} \frac{t^{\alpha} e^{-\frac{t}{\beta}}}{\beta^{\alpha+1}\Gamma(\frac{\lambda_m}{\beta}, \alpha+1)} dt \\ &= \frac{\Gamma(\frac{\lambda_m}{\beta}, \alpha)}{\beta\Gamma(\frac{\lambda_m}{\beta}, \alpha+1)}. \end{aligned}$$

The average square of realized risk of the insured (i.e., the second non-central conditional moment) is found similarly:

$$\begin{aligned} E(\widetilde{mx}_i^2|\iota_i = 1) &= \int_0^{\lambda_m} 2t^{-2} \frac{t^{\alpha} e^{-\frac{t}{\beta}}}{\beta^{\alpha+1}\Gamma(\frac{\lambda_m}{\beta}, \alpha+1)} dt \\ &= \frac{2\Gamma(\frac{\lambda_m}{\beta}, \alpha-1)}{\beta^2\Gamma(\frac{\lambda_m}{\beta}, \alpha+1)}. \end{aligned}$$

These are two unique moments that identify the two parameters of the risk distribution, (α, β).

That said, the amount paid for treatment by a private insurance company is unlikely to be the amount billed to the uninsured. Insurance companies buy a large volume of medical goods and services throughout a year, and frequently bargain with with medical providers over the cost of treatment. This bargaining power is not available to the individual uninsured patient. The resolution here is the same as for charges—assume a common proportional mark-up from the expenditures paid for by private medical insurance companies. This new marked-up distribution of risk is also a Gamma distribution, with parameters α and $\frac{\beta}{\rho}$. The balance of this article will use both methods—marking up from private medical expenditures, and marking down from total charges. Both series tell the same story.

It may be useful to characterize changes in α and β. As the discussions of mark-up and mark-down above suggest, changes in β are easier to interpret. Since β is a scale parameter, a decrease in β scales up the medical risk faced by every agent an equal amount.

The parameter α is best characterized by a distribution's kurtosis. A distribution's kurtosis is the ratio of its fourth moment to the square of its second moment (variance). As discussed in Balanda and MacGillivray [15], kurtosis is synonymous with "peakedness" and "tail weight." Two distributions may have the same variance, but kurtosis measures whether that variance is due to a large amount of moderate dispersion or a moderate amount of large dispersion. Flatter distributions have lower kurtosis.

Changes in kurtosis are central to the ability of insurance markets to spread risk across types. The variance of risk types may increase. If this increase is because many types became a little more different, then it is unlikely that many will newly refuse to buy the same insurance. However, if a few of the agents became very different from the rest, then cross-type risk sharing becomes less likely.

The kurtosis for a gamma distribution is $\frac{6}{\alpha}$. Thus, as α decreases, the risk types are becoming more and more disparate, and market failure becomes more pervasive. The sickest members of the population are becoming relatively more sick than the rest of the population. We will refer to this effect as the *kurtosis effect*—as α increases, risk types become more similar, and insurance becomes more widespread. When κ is large, the kurtosis effect dominates.

However, the calibrated value of κ is only \$5600. This reflects the many ways in which uninsured individuals can seek and receive free or uncompensated care. Hospitals reported providing an average of \$20 billion per year in uncompensated and charity care (American Hospital Association [16]). The charity portion of care reflects the not-for-profit and humanitarian missions of many hospitals. Uncompensated care is typically provided in emergency rooms, where hospitals are required to provide care independent of insurance status or ability to pay. In either case, this provides an upper bound risk faced by an uninsured individual, and it has consequences for an agent's willingness to pay for insurance (i.e., in distribution, the demand curve for insurance). The calibrated value for CARA risk aversion, $r = 0.0018$, is in the range of risk preferences estimated by Cohen and Einav [17].

The subsidy rate, s, has important implications for the calibration. Because ninety percent of the privately insured get medical insurance from their employer, and the cost of that insurance is not taxed as wage income would be, the subsidy rate is the marginal tax rate faced by the individual. Marginal tax rates are important, because they provide extra incentive to have insurance, and increase the insurance rate. This model corresponds to a competitive labor market where workers are compensated with their productivity, and only their compensation can come in the form of taxed wages or untaxed medical insurance.

Saez [18] provides the average marginal tax rates for the US. These calculations stop at the year 2000. The marginal tax rate for the year 2001 and later will be the average value for the years 1996 to 2000.

When α decreases, the marginal agent faces a larger risk, and her willingness to pay for insurance increases. However, when that agent faces only a fraction of the realized risk (i.e., κ is small), the marginal agent's willingness to pay for insurance does not increase more than the increase in the price of insurance. Here, the price of insurance is increasing because everyone who has insurance is also becoming more expensive. The kurtosis effect is dominated by the price effect of decreasing α.

Recall the claim in Swartz [1] that increases in the average cost of care led to the increased price of insurance, and therefore fewer people had medical insurance. If the increase in average medical expenditure is due to a common increase in medical risk (β goes down), then the insurance rate may increase. As everyone's medical risk grows, so does their certainty equivalent—how much above and beyond a fair price each agent is willing to pay for insurance. Larger certainty equivalents allow for more risk sharing across types. If the increase in medical expenditure is the result of a change in the shape of the distribution of medical risk, then the outcome is ambiguous—either the price effect or the kurtosis effect may dominate.

As described in Table 2, the changes inferred from 1996 to 2004 are a mixture of the two. Over this period, we might derive these changes as coming from two sources: an increasing price of medical goods and services (falling β); and an increasing incidence of costly medical conditions (falling α). This latter trend is consistent with the aging American population and the increased incidence of obesity, each associated with costly medical conditions.

The mark-up rate for a given year is exactly identified as the ratio of the price of insurance and the average medical expenditure paid for insurance on behalf of the insured, both from the data. The mark-down rate from total charges for a particular year is found by matching the model's price of insurance to that found in the data. These estimates are presented in Table 2. The price of insurance used here is the average price of single-coverage employer-provided medical (hospital and doctor) insurance in the US, as reported in the MEPS. Since the risk is reported on the individual level, the price of the corresponding coverage is considered as well. As mentioned in the introduction, the price of single-coverage and family-coverage employer-provided insurance grew at similar rates. Over this period, family coverage (covering two or more individuals) was steadily two-and-a-half times as expensive as single coverage. The implicit assumption is that there are constant returns to scale when it comes to family insurance plans versus single coverage, and there is no differential selection across them.

Table 2. Parameter values that vary by year; see text for explanation of subsidy rate for years since 2000.

Year	Charges			Expenditures			Subsidy
	α_{year}	β_{year}	ρ_{year}	α_{year}	β_{year}	ρ_{year}	
1996	1.091	5.30×10^{-4}	0.9706	1.0453	0.0010	1.8046	0.2475
1997	1.107	5.17×10^{-4}	0.968	1.1557	0.0011	2.0931	0.2533
1998	1.087	4.70×10^{-4}	0.9079	1.1645	0.0011	2.1757	0.2556
1999	1.128	4.57×10^{-4}	0.988	1.1479	0.0010	2.1994	0.2584
2000	1.156	3.95×10^{-4}	1.0028	1.1203	0.0010	2.2978	0.2613
2001	1.132	3.51×10^{-4}	0.9145	1.166	0.0008	2.118	0.2522 *
2002	1.141	3.21×10^{-4}	0.9293	1.1838	0.0008	2.2149	0.2522 *
2003	1.049	3.01×10^{-4}	0.84	1.0547	0.0008	1.9889	0.2522 *
2004	1.067	2.72×10^{-4}	0.8126	1.1096	0.0007	2.0232	0.2522 *

Figure 4a,b plot the insurance rate predicted by the model against the rate observed in the data. The two trends are within four percentage points of one another until 2001, the year of significant tax reform legislation. Since this tax reform decreased the marginal tax rates faced by households, this may explain why the model predicts increasing insurance rates, while the data finds insurance rates dropping slightly since 2000.

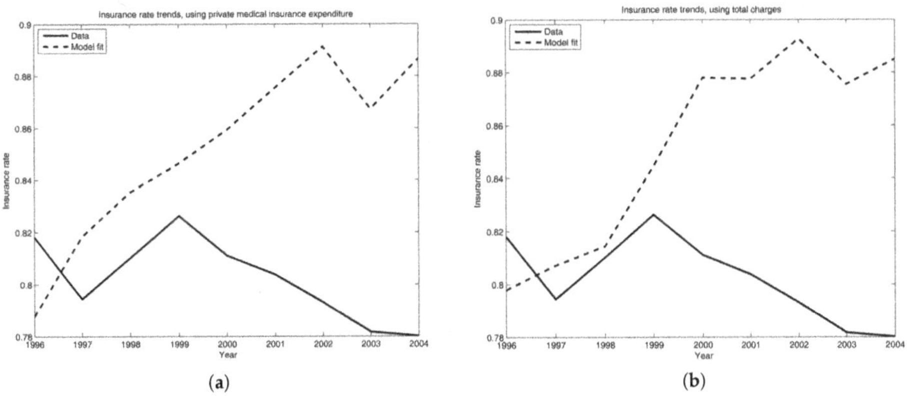

Figure 4. Predicted trends are consistent across methods.

Figure 5a,b assess the relative importance of changes in the level of risk (β) and the shape of risk (α). They each plot two counterfactual insurance rates—the first, if the shape of the distribution of risk stayed the same, but the level of risk changed as described in Table 2 (i.e., α_{1996} for all years, β_t for all t); the second, if the level of risk did not change, but the shape of the distribution of risk changed as described in the same table (i.e., β_{1996} for all years, α_t for all t).

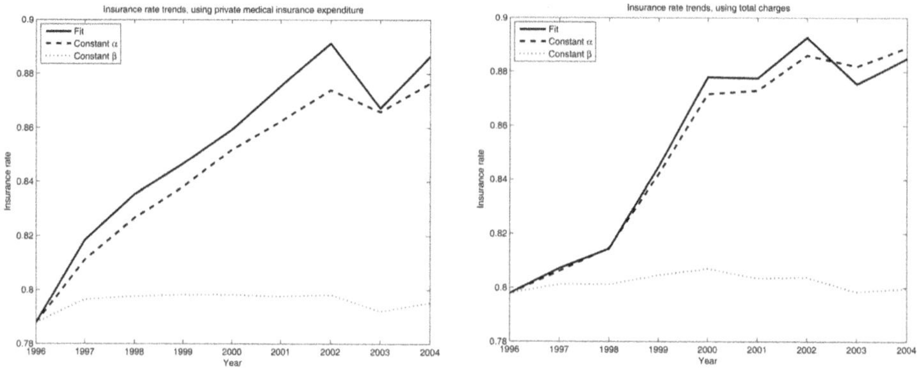

(**a**) (**b**)

Figure 5. Changes in levels dominate changes in shape.

Changes common to the medical risk of all agents are driving the insurance rate trends predicted by the model. Inferred changes in the shape in the distribution of medical risk (i.e., changes in α) play a very small roll in the predicted trends. Thus, in this period, changes due to the shifting age distribution or obesity have very little explanatory power. Instead, the model suggests a focus on changes common to all agents, such as moving prices for medical goods and services.

5. Conclusions

A competitive insurance market's capacity to provide insurance in spite of asymmetric information depends upon the distribution of risk. When an economy faces greater average risk, the amount of uninsured risk may vary, but depends crucially upon what kind of change took place. An observed increase in average medical costs could be due to either a common increase in the risk faced by all; or, it could reflect the change in risk faced by some agents. In the former case, there is more opportunity for risk sharing across types. In the latter, uninsurance is more frequent because the risk types are more disparate.

Changes in the cross-sectional distribution of medical risk suggest that there have been changes to both the level and the shape in the distribution of medical risk. The changes in the medical insurance rate predicted here are due primarily to the former. This emphasizes the role of changing medical prices for the rate of and price for insurance. It meanwhile suggests that changes due to shifting demographics, such as age and obesity, have had little effect on the number of people with medical insurance.

Conflicts of Interest: The views expressed in this article are those of the author. They do not necessarily represent those of the Federal Trade Commission, and the work was not prepared as part of the author's work for the FTC.

References

1. Swartz, K. *Reinsuring Health: Why More Middle-Class People Are Uninsured and What Government Can Do*; Russell Sage Foundation Publications: New York, NY, USA, 2006.

2. Freudenheim, M. *Cost of Health Insurance Rises Again, but at a Slightly Slower Rate*; New York Times: New York, NY, USA, 2007.
3. Gruber, J.; Levy, H. The Evolution of Medical Spending Risk. *J. Econ. Perspect.* **2009**, *23*, 25–48.
4. Handel, B.R.; Hendel, I.; Whinston, M.D. Equilibria in Health Exchanges: Adverse Selection vs. Reclassification Risk. *Econometrica* **2015**, *83*, 1261–1313.
5. Koch, T.G. One pool to insure them all? Age, risk and the price (s) of medical insurance. *Int. J. Ind. Organ.* **2014b**, *35*, 1–11.
6. Charpentier, A.; le Maux, B. Natural catastrophe insurance: How should the government intervene? *J. Public Econ.* **2014**, *115*, 1–17.
7. Cummins, J.D. Should the government provide insurance for catastrophes. *Fed. Reserve Bank St. Louis Rev.* **2006**, *88*, 337–379.
8. Kousky, C.; Cooke, R. Explaining the failure to insure catastrophic risks. *Geneva Pap. Risk Insur. Issues Pract.* **2012**, *37*, 206–227.
9. Jovanovic, B. Favorable Selection with Asymmetric Information. *Q. J. Econ.* **1982**, *97*, 535–39.
10. Selten, R. Re-examination of the perfectness concept for equilibrium points in extensive games. *Int. J. Game Theory* **1975**, *4*, 25–55.
11. Kohlberg, E.; Mertens, J.-F. On the Strategic Stability of Equilibria. *Econometrica* **1986**, *54*, 1003–1037.
12. Koch, T.G. Bankruptcy, medical insurance, and a law with unintended consequences. *Health Econ.* **2014**, *23*, 1326–1339.
13. Harris, C.M. The Pareto Distribution as a Queue Service Discipline. *Oper. Res.* **1968**, *16*, 307–313.
14. Stanton, M.W. *Employer-Sponsored Health Insurance: Trends in Cost and Access*; Research in Action 17; Agency for Healthcare Research and Quality: Rockville, MD, USA, 2004.
15. Balanda, K.P.; MacGillivray, H.L. Kurtosis: A Critical Review. *Am. Stat.* **1988**, *42*, 111–119.
16. American Hospital Association. *Uncompensated Hospital Care Cost Fact Sheet*; American Hospital Association: Washington, DC, USA, 2014.
17. Cohen, A.; Einav, L. Estimating Risk Preferences from Deductible Choice. *Am. Econ. Rev.* **2007**, *97*, 745–788.
18. Saez, E. *Reported Incomes and Marginal Tax Rates, 1960–2000: Evidence and Policy Implications*; NBER Working Papers 10273; National Bureau of Economic Research, Inc.: Cambridge, MA, USA, 2004.

risks

MDPI

Article

Compositions of Conditional Risk Measures and Solvency Capital

Pierre Devolder and Adrien Lebègue *

Institut de Statistique, Biostatistique et Sciences Actuarielles, Université catholique de Louvain, Voie du Roman Pays 20 bte L1.04.01, B-1348 Louvain-la-Neuve, Belgium; pierre.devolder@uclouvain.be
* Correspondence: adrien.lebegue@uclouvain.be

Academic Editor: Luca Regis
Received: 14 November 2016; Accepted: 9 December 2016; Published: 16 December 2016

Abstract: In this paper, we consider compositions of conditional risk measures in order to obtain time-consistent dynamic risk measures and determine the solvency capital of a life insurer selling pension liabilities or a pension fund with a single cash-flow at maturity. We first recall the notion of conditional, dynamic and time-consistent risk measures. We link the latter with its iterated property, which gives us a way to construct time-consistent dynamic risk measures from a backward iteration scheme with the composition of conditional risk measures. We then consider particular cases with the conditional version of the value at risk, tail value at risk and conditional expectation measures. We finally give an application of these measures with the determination of the solvency capital of a pension liability, which offers a fixed guaranteed rate without any intermediate cash-flow. We assume that the company is fully hedged against the mortality and underwriting risks.

Keywords: dynamic risk measures; time consistency; iterated risk measures; pension liability; solvency capital

---

1. Introduction

The determination of the economic capital of a life insurer or pension fund has become of paramount importance over the past decade due to the recent financial crisis in the banking sector. The management and measurement of risk is of great interest, as can be seen from the recent Basel II and III regulatory frameworks for banks and Solvency II for the European insurance sector. These new regulations are designed to be risk sensitive. The Solvency II regulation recognizes that the insurer faces different kinds of risks, like market and longevity risks, while the previous regulation (Solvency I) is factor based. These regulations use risk measures as introduced in [1–3] in order to quantify the riskiness of financial positions and to provide a criterion to determine their acceptability. For instance, the new Solvency II framework requires a value at risk (VaR) measure to determine the solvency capital requirement, while the Swiss Solvency Test uses the tail value at risk (TVaR) measure for its target capital. These measures consider a real-valued random variable describing a future financial value and measure its risk at the beginning of the time period. Under the Solvency II and the Swiss Solvency Test regulations, the length of the time period is equal to one year, i.e., these frameworks consider the evolution of their own funds of the insurance undertaking over one year. However, life insurers and pension funds hold also long-term products, such as pension liabilities, which are the topic of this paper.

In this paper, we consider pension liabilities, and we study risk measures that consider the long-term characteristic of these products. We focus here on the market risk, especially the equity risk. We also assume that the company is fully hedged against the mortality and underwriting risks.

An important drawback of the classic static risk measures is that they do not take into account the information disclosed through time. These measures only consider the end-points of the time period.

If we deal with liabilities with a maturity of one year, then these risk measures are adapted as we work with a time horizon equal to the accounting horizon. Because we consider pension liabilities with a long-term horizon, this information could be meaningful in the computation of the solvency capital through time, especially on a yearly basis, as is the case for accounting purposes. That is why we consider dynamic risk measures as studied in [3–6]. The information is modeled by a filtration, and this filtration is incorporated in the computation of the capital each year.

A first example of a dynamic risk measure could be the recalculated version of the static risk measures. We could for instance recalculate the solvency capital each year according to a static risk measure by incorporating the information available. However, this approach only incorporates past information, and for well-known measures, such as the VaR or TVaR measures, this could lead to time inconsistency, i.e., a position that was acceptable could become undesirable in any scenario. Therefore, we require a particularly useful property for dynamic risk measures, which is called time consistency. This property tells us that if we prefer a position tomorrow in almost every state of the world, then we already prefer it today. It is well known that the recalculated versions of the VaR and TVaR measures are not time consistent (see [7,8]).

It has been proven that a time-consistent dynamic risk measure is closely linked to a backward iteration scheme [9]. We then consider this property to construct time-consistent risk measures through the iteration of conditional risk measures. This approach has been considered for the determination of the solvency capital of life insurance products in [10–12]. Nevertheless, it appears that the solvency capital obtained can be very expensive if we do not take care of the confidence level of each conditional VaR and TVaR measures involved in the iteration scheme. This is linked to a result obtained in [13], which tells us that, under certain hypotheses, if we consider a great number of iterations, the risk measure obtained is close to either the conditional expectation of the risk or its essential supremum.

In order to overcome this difficulty, we consider the iterations of different conditional risk measures with a yearly time step fitting the accounting point of view. We also build these measures in such a way that they are coherent with the Solvency II or Swiss Solvency Test frameworks, meaning that for the last year of the product, the measures we introduce here correspond to the one used in these frameworks.

This paper then introduces a new way to compute the solvency capital in life insurance, in order to take into account simultaneously the following three constraints

- to be in line with Solvency II on a one-year horizon;
- to be time consistent;
- to incorporate in the risk measurement the maturity of the product.

The paper is organized as follows. We set the mathematical framework in Section 2. Then, we recall the definition of conditional and dynamic risk measures in Section 3, of time consistency and iterated risk measures in Section 4 and present some compositions of conditional risk measures in order to determine the solvency capital in Section 5. We then compute the solvency capital in Section 6 and finally give a numerical illustration in Section 7.

2. Framework

Throughout the paper, we consider a complete atomless probability space $(\Omega, \mathcal{F}, \mathbb{P})$. We write $\mathbb{N}^* = \mathbb{N} \setminus \{0\}$. We fix $T \in \mathbb{N}^*$ seen as the maturity of a pension liability and define $\mathbb{T} = \{0, \dots, T-1\}$ as the set of intermediate dates. We also consider a filtration:

$$\mathbb{F} = (\mathcal{F}_t)_{t \in \mathbb{T} \cup \{T\}},$$

such that $\mathcal{F}_0 = \{\emptyset, \Omega\}$ and $\mathcal{F}_T = \mathcal{F}$. All inequalities and equalities between random variables (r.v.'s) are meant to hold $\mathbb{P}$-almost surely ($\mathbb{P}$-a.s.) if not stated otherwise. Let $t \in \mathbb{T} \cup \{T\}$. We define $\mathrm{L}^1(\Omega, \mathcal{F}_t, \mathbb{P})$ as the space of all real-valued $\mathcal{F}_t$-measurable r.v.'s X, such that $\mathbb{E}[|X|] < +\infty$, where two r.v.'s are identified if they coincide a.s. We consider an equivalence class $X \in \mathrm{L}^1(\Omega, \mathcal{F}_t, \mathbb{P})$ as a r.v., and we understand X as a financial amount at date t of date t money. We also identify $\mathrm{L}^1(\Omega, \mathcal{F}_0, \mathbb{P})$ with $\mathbb{R}$.

3. Conditional and Dynamic Risk Measures

We consider dynamic risk measures in order to determine the solvency capital of a pension liability. The solvency capital is the amount the company has to put aside, in addition to the initial value of its portfolio, in order to be solvent. The idea behind dynamic risk measures is to consider the amount of information available through time. In our setting, this amount of information is modeled by the filtration $\mathbb{F}$.

Let $t \in \mathbb{T}$. We consider a reference instrument $\iota_{t,T} \in \mathrm{L}^1(\Omega, \mathcal{F}_T, \mathbb{P})$, as introduced in [1] in the static case. The amount $\iota_{t,T}$ is the value at time T of one unit of currency invested in this reference instrument between time t and T. The solvency capital computed at date t is then invested in this financial instrument $\iota_{t,T}$ from date t to the maturity T. We assume that $\iota_{t,T}(\omega) > 0$ for all $\omega \in \Omega$. This reference instrument could be a risk-free zero-coupon bond, and the value at time T would be:

$$\iota_{t,T} = \frac{1}{P(t,T)},$$

where $P(t,T)$ is the price of a risk-free zero-coupon bond at time t with maturity T and paying one unit of currency.

We first recall the definition of a conditional risk measure. In the following, we understand $X \in \mathrm{L}^1(\Omega, \mathcal{F}_T, \mathbb{P})$ as a profit r.v., which means that if $X(\omega) < 0$, then the company faces a loss at maturity T under scenario $\omega \in \Omega$; otherwise, it makes a profit.

Definition 1. *A conditional risk measure ρ_t on $\mathrm{L}^1(\Omega, \mathcal{F}_T, \mathbb{P})$ with a reference instrument $\iota_{t,T}$ is a function:*

$$\rho_t : \mathrm{L}^1(\Omega, \mathcal{F}_T, \mathbb{P}) \longrightarrow \mathrm{L}^1(\Omega, \mathcal{F}_t, \mathbb{P}),$$

such that it satisfies the following properties, for $X, Y \in \mathrm{L}^1(\Omega, \mathcal{F}_T, \mathbb{P})$,

- *(monotonicity) $X \leq Y$ implies $\rho_t(X) \geq \rho_t(Y)$;*
- *(conditional cash invariance) for all $m_t \in \mathrm{L}^1(\Omega, \mathcal{F}_t, \mathbb{P})$,*

$$\rho_t(X + m_t \iota_{t,T}) = \rho_t(X) - m_t;$$

- *(normalization) $\rho_t(0) = 0$.*

We can also define convex and coherent conditional risk measures as in the classic static setting.

Definition 2. *A conditional risk measure ρ_t on $\mathrm{L}^1(\Omega, \mathcal{F}_T, \mathbb{P})$ is called convex if for $X, Y \in \mathrm{L}^1(\Omega, \mathcal{F}_T, \mathbb{P})$ and $\lambda \in \mathrm{L}^1(\Omega, \mathcal{F}_t, \mathbb{P})$, $0 \leq \lambda \leq 1$,*

$$\rho_t\left(\lambda X + (1-\lambda)Y\right) \leq \lambda \rho_t(X) + (1-\lambda)\rho_t(Y).$$

Furthermore, ρ_t is called coherent if it is convex and, for $X \in \mathrm{L}^1(\Omega, \mathcal{F}_T, \mathbb{P})$ and $\lambda \in \mathrm{L}^1(\Omega, \mathcal{F}_t, \mathbb{P})$, $\lambda \geq 0$,

$$\rho_t(\lambda X) = \lambda \rho_t(X).$$

A dynamic risk measure is simply a sequence of conditional risk measures.

Definition 3. *A dynamic risk measure:*

$$\rho = (\rho_t)_{t \in \mathbb{T}}$$

on $\mathrm{L}^1(\Omega, \mathcal{F}_T, \mathbb{P})$ *is a sequence of conditional risk measures* ρ_t *on* $\mathrm{L}^1(\Omega, \mathcal{F}_T, \mathbb{P})$ *(with the reference instrument* $\iota_{t,T}$*), for* $t \in \mathbb{T}$*. It is called convex (resp.* coherent*) if* ρ_t *is convex (resp. coherent) for all* $t \in \mathbb{T}$.

Remark 1. *We refer the reader to [3–6] for a detailed study of this kind of measure.*

For $X \in \mathrm{L}^1(\Omega, \mathcal{F}_T, \mathbb{P})$ seen as a final net worth at date T of a life insurer or pension fund and $t \in \mathbb{T}$, the amount $\rho_t(X)$ (which is an r.v.) can be seen as a solvency capital at date t of date t money for the final net worth X, which is invested in the reference instrument $\iota_{t,T}$ over the period $[t, T]$, i.e.,

$$\rho_t\left(X + \rho_t(X)\iota_{t,T}\right) = 0,$$

by the conditional cash invariance property, where we recall that this equality holds in the $\mathbb{P}$-a.s. sense.

4. Time Consistency and Iterated Risk Measures

A time-consistent risk measure tells us that if we prefer a position tomorrow, in almost all states of nature, then we already prefer it today (see [4,5], for instance).

Definition 4. *A dynamic risk measure* ρ *on* $\mathrm{L}^1(\Omega, \mathcal{F}_T, \mathbb{P})$ *is called time consistent if:*

$$\rho_{t+1}(X) \leq \rho_{t+1}(Y),$$

implies:

$$\rho_t(X) \leq \rho_t(Y),$$

for all $t \in \mathbb{T}, t \neq T-1$ *and* $X, Y \in \mathrm{L}^1(\Omega, \mathcal{F}_T, \mathbb{P})$.

Example 1. *In order to understand why this property is important, in particular in the field of a pension liability, we consider two r.v.'s X and Y described in Figure 1. While in Section 2, we consider an atomless probability space, we set here for the purpose of the example a discrete probability space* $(\Omega, \mathcal{F}, \mathbb{P})$.

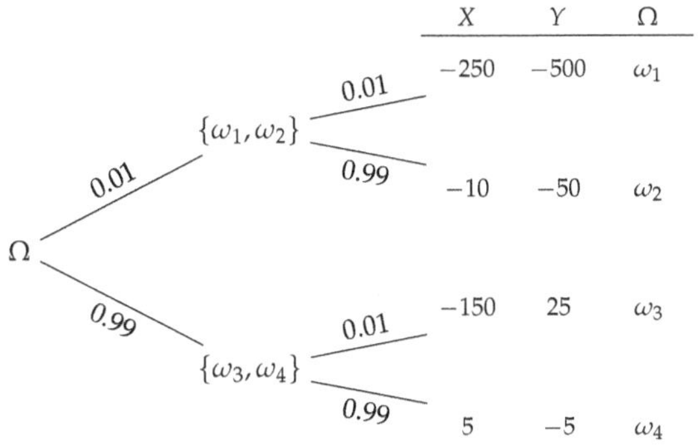

Figure 1. Distributions of X and Y (Example 1).

The set of states of nature Ω *is given by:*

$$\Omega = \{\omega_1, \omega_2, \omega_3, \omega_4\},$$

with the σ*-algebra* $\mathcal{F}$ *given by:*

$$\mathcal{F} = \mathcal{P}(\Omega),$$

and a probability measure $\mathbb{P}$ given by:

$$\begin{aligned}
\mathbb{P}[\{\omega_1\}] &= 0.01 \times 0.01 = 0.0001 \\
\mathbb{P}[\{\omega_2\}] &= 0.01 \times 0.99 = 0.0099 \\
\mathbb{P}[\{\omega_3\}] &= 0.99 \times 0.01 = 0.0099 \\
\mathbb{P}[\{\omega_4\}] &= 0.99 \times 0.99 = 0.9801.
\end{aligned}$$

We consider two periods, i.e., we set $T = 2$. We then define a filtration $\mathbb{F} = (\mathcal{F}_t)_{t\in\{0,1,2\}}$ with:

$$\begin{aligned}
&\mathcal{F}_0 = \{\emptyset, \Omega\} \\
&\mathcal{F}_1 = \sigma\left(\{\omega_1, \omega_2\}, \{\omega_3, \omega_4\}\right) \\
&\mathcal{F}_2 = \mathcal{F}.
\end{aligned}$$

This filtration means that at time $t = 1$, we know if we are at node $\{\omega_1, \omega_2\}$ or $\{\omega_3, \omega_4\}$, i.e., at time $t = 1$, we know that two scenarios are possible, either ω_1 and ω_2 or ω_3 and ω_4. We also compute that:

$$\begin{aligned}
\mathbb{P}[\{\omega_1\}|\{\omega_1, \omega_2\}] &= 0.01 \\
\mathbb{P}[\{\omega_2\}|\{\omega_1, \omega_2\}] &= 0.99 \\
\mathbb{P}[\{\omega_3\}|\{\omega_3, \omega_4\}] &= 0.01 \\
\mathbb{P}[\{\omega_4\}|\{\omega_3, \omega_4\}] &= 0.99.
\end{aligned}$$

We see X and Y as two possible outcomes (strategies) for our life insurer or pension fund at time $T = 2$. For instance, if we follow the strategy of X, we see that at time $t = 1$, if we are at node $\{\omega_1, \omega_2\}$, the probability of facing a loss of 250 is 1%. We emphasize that when X or Y are positive, the company faces a profit, while it faces a loss when X or Y are negative. That is why the amount of the loss is 250, while X takes as a value -250. We assume here that $\iota_{0,2} = \iota_{1,2} = 1$, so that we neglect the time value of money for this example.

We consider the VaR measure with a level of 99% in order to make a choice between X and Y. We first compute the VaR measure with a confidence level of 99% at time $t = 0$ (see [1,3]),

$$\begin{aligned}
\mathrm{VaR}_0^{0.99}(X) &= -\inf\{x \in \mathbb{R} : \mathbb{P}[X \le x] > 0.01\} \\
&= 10\,,
\end{aligned}$$

and:

$$\mathrm{VaR}_0^{0.99}(Y) = 5\,,$$

which means that at time $t = 0$, we prefer Y over X, because:

$$\mathrm{VaR}_0^{0.99}(X) > \mathrm{VaR}_0^{0.99}(Y)\,.$$

However, at time $t = 1$, we compute that, if we are at node $\{\omega_1, \omega_2\}$,

$$\begin{aligned}
\mathrm{VaR}_1^{0.99}(X)\Big|\,\{\omega_1, \omega_2\} &= -\inf\{x \in \mathbb{R} : \mathbb{P}[X \le x|\{\omega_1, \omega_2\}] > 0.01\} \\
&= 10\,,
\end{aligned}$$

and:

$$\mathrm{VaR}_1^{0.99}(Y)\Big|\,\{\omega_1, \omega_2\} = 50\,;$$

and, at node $\{\omega_3, \omega_4\}$,

$$\mathrm{VaR}_1^{0.99}(X)\Big| \{\omega_3, \omega_4\} = -\inf\{x \in \mathbb{R} : \mathbb{P}[X \leq x | \{\omega_3, \omega_4\}] > 0.01\}$$
$$= -5\,,$$

and:

$$\mathrm{VaR}_1^{0.99}(Y)\Big| \{\omega_3, \omega_4\} = 5\,,$$

which means that at time $t = 1$, *we now prefer* X *over* Y, *because:*

$$\mathrm{VaR}_1^{0.99}(X) < \mathrm{VaR}_1^{0.99}(Y)\,,$$

while we chose Y *at time* $t = 0$ *(see Figure 2 for a summary). It is clear that at time* $t = 1$, *the strategy* Y *appears riskier than strategy* X. *If the dynamic (recalculated) version of the VaR measure was time consistent, we would not have faced such an inconsistent behavior over time. That is why we believe that a time-consistent measure is needed.*

Figure 2. Evolution of the VaR between times $t = 0$ and 1 (Example 1). **Left**: evolution for X. **Right**: evolution for Y.

For instance, let us consider the conditional expectation. We compute that:

$$\mathbb{E}[-X] = -3.29 < 5.2 = \mathbb{E}[-Y]\,,$$

so that we prefer X *over* Y *at time* $t = 0$. *Then, at time* $t = 1$, *we compute that:*

$$\mathbb{E}\left[-X | \{\omega_1, \omega_2\}\right] = 12.4 < 54.5 = \mathbb{E}\left[-Y | \{\omega_1, \omega_2\}\right]\,,$$

and:

$$\mathbb{E}\left[-X | \{\omega_3, \omega_4\}\right] = -3.45 < 4.7 = \mathbb{E}\left[-Y | \{\omega_3, \omega_4\}\right]\,,$$

which means that at time $t = 1$, *we still prefer* X *over* Y *(see Figure 3 for a summary). According to this measure, the choice of* X *is constant over time, because this measure is time consistent.*

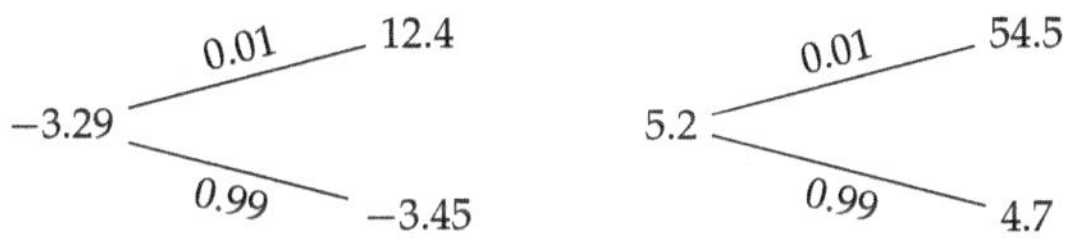

Figure 3. Evolution of the expectation between times $t = 0$ and 1 (Example 1). **Left**: evolution for X. **Right**: evolution for Y.

Remark 2. *We also refer to [11] for another example and [8] for an example with an atomless probability space.*

Time-consistent risk measures are closely-linked to iterated risk measures.

Definition 5. *A dynamic risk measure ρ on $\mathrm{L}^1(\Omega, \mathcal{F}_T, \mathbb{P})$ is called iterated if:*

$$\rho_t(X) = \rho_t\left(-\rho_{t+1}(X)\iota_{t+1,T}\right),$$

for $t \in \mathbb{T}$, $t \neq T-1$ and $X \in \mathrm{L}^1(\Omega, \mathcal{F}_T, \mathbb{P})$.

Theorem A1 of Appendix A tells us that time-consistent and iterated risk measures are equivalent and then that a time-consistent risk measure can be computed following a backward iteration scheme. Furthermore, it also gives us a way to construct time-consistent risk measures following this backward iteration scheme. This is formalized in Corollary 1. Section 5 aims at designing suitable time-consistent risk measures by means of this result.

Corollary 1. *Let γ be a dynamic risk measure on $\mathrm{L}^1(\Omega, \mathcal{F}_T, \mathbb{P})$ that is not time consistent. Then, the dynamic risk measure ρ on $\mathrm{L}^1(\Omega, \mathcal{F}_T, \mathbb{P})$ given by:*

$$\rho_{T-1}(X) = \gamma_{T-1}(X),$$

and:

$$\rho_t(X) = \gamma_t\left(-\rho_{t+1}(X)\iota_{t+1,T}\right),$$

for all $t \in \mathbb{T}$, $t \neq T-1$, is time consistent. Furthermore, if γ is convex (resp. coherent), then ρ is also convex (resp. coherent).

5. Compositions of Conditional Risk Measures

While classic static risk measures have been considered to determine the solvency capital of a financial institution (see, for instance, [1,3]), we would now like to consider dynamic risk measures and, more precisely, time-consistent dynamic risk measures in order to determine the solvency capital of a life insurer or pension fund. A first study of this approach can be found in [10–12], where they consider iterated versions of the conditional VaR or TVaR measures. However, it appears clear that the levels of the solvency capital are quite expensive (about equal to the present value of the liability for long maturities in some cases).

This observation is related to ([13] [Theorem 1.10]). Following this result, they assume a certain class of dynamic risk measures, i.e., law-invariant, and a great number of iterations, i.e., they consider $\mathbb{T} = \mathbb{N}$, which means that a countably infinite number of steps is considered. Then, under these hypotheses, the dynamic risk measure obtained is given by a sequence of conditional entropic risk measures. In particular, if the dynamic measure is assumed coherent, then the solvency capital would be given by either the expected value of the final net worth or its largest possible value, its essential supremum.

The difference between the approach of ([13] [Theorem 1.10]) and the one we present here lies in the number of iterations. We consider here T iterations, i.e., a finite number of steps $t \in \mathbb{T}$ (see Corollary 1), while in ([13] [Theorem 1.10]) they consider an infinite (but still countable) number of iterations, i.e., $t \in \mathbb{N}$. However, depending on the choice of the dynamic risk measure and on the actual final net worth considered, a great number of iterations T could converge towards ([13] [Theorem 1.10]), which is the case in [10–12].

The idea behind this section is to consider a yearly basis for the computation of the solvency capital and to be careful of the confidence level considered within each iteration. If we reduce the time step (for instance, with a weekly or daily basis, without considering its practicability), then we will tend toward the previous observation because, due to the long-term characteristic of our pension products (typically 45 years), we would obtain a great number of iterations (about 2340 with a weekly-step over 45 years). This yearly time step is based on an accounting point of view and allows us to develop some time-consistent risk measures that could fit the Solvency II or Swiss Solvency Test frameworks in the last year of the product.

In Section 5.1, we consider the composition of conditional VaR measures, while in Section 5.2, we consider the case with conditional TVaR measures. Finally, in Section 5.3, we construct a time-consistent measure from the composition of either a conditional VaR measure or a conditional TVaR measure and conditional expectations.

5.1. Composition of VaRs

We begin this section with the definition of a conditional VaR measure (see [3]).

Definition 6. *Let $t \in \mathbb{T}$ and $\alpha \in (0,1)$. The conditional VaR measure on $\mathrm{L}^1(\Omega, \mathcal{F}_T, \mathbb{P})$ with the confidence level α is defined by:*

$$\mathrm{VaR}_t^\alpha(X) = -\operatorname{ess\,inf}\left\{V \in \mathrm{L}^1(\Omega, \mathcal{F}_t, \mathbb{P}) : \mathbb{P}\left[X \leq V\iota_{t,T}|\mathcal{F}_t\right] > 1-\alpha \text{ a.s.}\right\},$$

for $X \in \mathrm{L}^1(\Omega, \mathcal{F}_T, \mathbb{P})$, where ess inf *stands for the essential infimum as defined in [3].*

We are now able to define the dynamic generalization of the classic static VaR measure, the recalculated VaR measure, which is simply the sequence of conditional VaR measures.

Definition 7. *The recalculated VaR measure on $\mathrm{L}^1(\Omega, \mathcal{F}_T, \mathbb{P})$ with a confidence level $\alpha \in (0,1)$ is defined by the sequence:*

$$\mathrm{VaR}^\alpha = (\mathrm{VaR}_t^\alpha)_{t\in\mathbb{T}}\,.$$

This dynamic risk measure does not fulfill the useful property of time consistency and is even not convex.

Proposition 1. *Let $\alpha \in (0,1)$. The dynamic risk measure VaR^α on $\mathrm{L}^1(\Omega, \mathcal{F}_T, \mathbb{P})$ is neither convex nor time consistent.*

Proof. For the convexity, take for instance $t = 0$, and for the time consistency, see ([3] [Example 11.13]). □

Let $\boldsymbol{\alpha} \in (0,1)^T$, i.e.,

$$\boldsymbol{\alpha} = (\alpha_1, \ldots, \alpha_T)\,,$$

with $\alpha_i \in (0,1)$ for $i \in \{1, \ldots, T\}$. We define an iterated measure according to this vector, by means of conditional VaR measures. This vector is a vector of confidence levels, which could be different. The iterated measure is then a composition of different conditional (VaR) measures.

Definition 8. *Let $\boldsymbol{\alpha} \in (0,1)^T$. For $X \in \mathrm{L}^1(\Omega, \mathcal{F}_T, \mathbb{P})$, the iterated VaR (IVaR) measure on $\mathrm{L}^1(\Omega, \mathcal{F}_T, \mathbb{P})$ is given by,*

$$\mathrm{IVaR}_{T-1}^{\boldsymbol{\alpha}}(X) = \mathrm{VaR}_{T-1}^{\alpha_1}(X),$$

and:

$$\mathrm{IVaR}_t^{\boldsymbol{\alpha}}(X) = \mathrm{VaR}_t^{\alpha_{T-t}}\left(-\mathrm{IVaR}_{t+1}^{\boldsymbol{\alpha}}(X)\iota_{t+1,T}\right),$$

for $t \in \mathbb{T}, t \neq T-1$.

Remark 3. *It is clear that this measure is a dynamic risk measure that is time consistent, because the sequence:*

$$\left(\mathrm{VaR}_t^{\alpha_{T-t}}\right)_{t\in\mathbb{T}}$$

defines a dynamic risk measure, and Corollary 1 allows us to conclude.

Remark 4. *For a given $\alpha \in (0,1)$ and $\alpha_i = \alpha$, for all $i \in \{1,\ldots,T\}$, this case has been considered in [8,12]. However, it appears in [12] that this dynamic measure gives expensive solvency capital. This is due to ([13] [Theorem 1.10]) and the observation made at the beginning of this section. Instead of considering the same α within each iteration, we propose here to make it dependent on the date $t \in \mathbb{T}$ of valuation.*

Remark 5. *If we set $\alpha_1 = 99.5\%$, then this time-consistent dynamic risk measure is consistent with the Solvency II framework. For a product with a time to maturity of one year or, more generally, for the last year of a product, we get back the SIIframework, since we then only consider a VaR at a level of 99.5% over one year.*

5.2. Composition of TVaRs

We can also consider the case of the iterated TVaR measure, which will give us a coherent and time-consistent risk measure. We recall the definition of the conditional TVaR measure (see ([3] [Proposition 11.9])).

Definition 9. *Let $t \in \mathbb{T}$ and $\alpha \in (0,1)$. For $X \in \mathrm{L}^1(\Omega,\mathcal{F}_T,\mathbb{P})$, the conditional TVaR measure on $\mathrm{L}^1(\Omega,\mathcal{F}_T,\mathbb{P})$ with the confidence level α is defined by,*

$$\mathrm{TVaR}_t^{\alpha}(X) = \mathrm{VaR}_t^{\alpha}(X) + \frac{1}{1-\alpha}\mathbb{E}\left[\left(\frac{X}{\iota_{t,T}} + \mathrm{VaR}_t^{\alpha}(X)\right)_- \middle| \mathscr{F}_t\right],$$

where $(\cdot)_- = -\min(\cdot,0)$.

Its corresponding dynamic risk measure is not time consistent.

Definition 10. *The recalculated TVaR measure on $\mathrm{L}^1(\Omega,\mathcal{F}_T,\mathbb{P})$ with a confidence level $\alpha \in (0,1)$ is defined by the sequence:*

$$\mathrm{TVaR}^{\alpha} = (\mathrm{TVaR}_t^{\alpha})_{t\in\mathbb{T}}.$$

Proposition 2. *Let $\alpha \in (0,1)$. The dynamic risk measure TVaR^{α} on $\mathrm{L}^1(\Omega,\mathcal{F}_T,\mathbb{P})$ is coherent, but not time consistent.*

Proof. It is clearly coherent from the classic properties of the conditional expectation. Concerning the time consistency, we refer to ([3] [Example 11.13]). □

Again, we consider Corollary 1 in order to construct a time-consistent version.

Definition 11. *Let $\boldsymbol{\alpha} \in (0,1)^T$. The iterated TVaR (ITVaR) measure on $\mathrm{L}^1(\Omega,\mathcal{F}_T,\mathbb{P})$ is given by, for $X \in \mathrm{L}^1(\Omega,\mathcal{F}_T,\mathbb{P})$,*

$$\mathrm{ITVaR}_{T-1}^{\boldsymbol{\alpha}}(X) = \mathrm{TVaR}_{T-1}^{\alpha_1}(X),$$

and:

$$\mathrm{ITVaR}_t^{\boldsymbol{\alpha}}(X) = \mathrm{TVaR}_t^{\alpha_{T-t}}\left(-\mathrm{ITVaR}_{t+1}^{\boldsymbol{\alpha}}(X)\iota_{t+1,T}\right),$$

for $t \in \mathbb{T}, t \neq T-1$.

Remark 6. *Following Remark 5, if we set $\alpha_1 = 99\%$, then this time-consistent dynamic risk measure is also consistent with the Swiss Solvency Test.*

5.3. Composition with Conditional Expectations

In this section, we define a time-consistent dynamic measure as the composition of either a conditional VaR measure or a conditional TVaR measure and conditional expectations. We start by giving the definition of a conditional expectation measure.

Definition 12. *Let $t \in \mathbb{T}$. The conditional expectation measure* E_t *on* $\mathrm{L}^1(\Omega, \mathcal{F}_T, \mathbb{P})$ *is defined by,*

$$\mathrm{E}_t(X) = \mathbb{E}\left[-\frac{X}{\iota_{t,T}} \middle| \mathcal{F}_t \right],$$

for $X \in \mathrm{L}^1(\Omega, \mathcal{F}_T, \mathbb{P})$.

We now give the definition of the composition of a conditional VaR measure and conditional expectation measures. We construct it by means of Corollary 1, and we call it the expected VaR measure. With the first iteration, we consider a usual conditional VaR measure, then through the following steps, we consider its expected value.

Definition 13. *Let $\alpha \in (0,1)$. The expected VaR (EVaR) measure* EVaR^α *on* $\mathrm{L}^1(\Omega, \mathcal{F}_T, \mathbb{P})$ *with the confidence level α is given by:*

$$\mathrm{EVaR}^\alpha_{T-1}(X) = \mathrm{VaR}^\alpha_{T-1}(X),$$

and:

$$\mathrm{EVaR}^\alpha_t(X) = \mathrm{E}_t\left(-\mathrm{EVaR}^\alpha_{t+1}(X)\iota_{t+1,T}\right),$$

for $t \in \mathbb{T}, t \neq T-1$ and $X \in \mathrm{L}^1(\Omega, \mathcal{F}_T, \mathbb{P})$.

Remark 7. *Again, following Remark 5, if we set $\alpha = 99.5\%$, this time consistent dynamic risk measure is consistent with the Solvency II framework. The first iteration is the same as with the IVaR measure. However, the difference between the IVaR and EVaR measures is in the following steps, where we consider now the conditional expected measure.*

We also consider the expected TVaR measure.

Definition 14. *Let $\alpha \in (0,1)$. The expected TVaR (ETVaR) measure* ETVaR^α *on* $\mathrm{L}^1(\Omega, \mathcal{F}_T, \mathbb{P})$ *with the confidence level α is given by:*

$$\mathrm{ETVaR}^\alpha_{T-1}(X) = \mathrm{TVaR}^\alpha_{T-1}(X),$$

and:

$$\mathrm{ETVaR}^\alpha_t(X) = \mathrm{E}_t\left(-\mathrm{ETVaR}^\alpha_{t+1}(X)\iota_{t+1,T}\right),$$

for $t \in \mathbb{T}, t \neq T-1$ and $X \in \mathrm{L}^1(\Omega, \mathcal{F}_T, \mathbb{P})$.

We see that this definition is a particular case of Definition 11. If we consider the vector $\boldsymbol{\alpha} \in (0,1)^T$ in Definition 11 with:

$$\alpha_i = \begin{cases} \alpha & \text{if } i = 1 \\ 0 & \text{if } i > 1 \end{cases},$$

then we get back Definition 14.

Remark 8. *We emphasize that the order considered in Definitions 13 and 14 is important. In the first step, we consider the conditional VaR or TVaR measure, and then, we use the conditional expectation for the subsequent steps. This means that for the last year of the product, or equivalently, when the time to maturity is equal to one, we get back the classic VaR or TVaR.*

However, if we chose the conditional expectation for $t = 1, \ldots, T-1$ and used the VaR or TVaR for $t = 0$, then we would get a completely different time-consistent measure. For the last year of the product, the capital would be given by the conditional expectation only and not by a VaR or TVaR. This is due to the fact that each year t, when we recompute the solvency capital, we do not consider anymore the measure used at time $t-1$.

6. Solvency Computation

The purpose of this section is to study the impact of the equity risk on the solvency capital computed by means of the measures previously defined. The inclusion of the interest rate and longevity risks has been considered in [14] with static risk measures. However, the inclusion of these risks in our dynamic setting would require the use of numerical techniques in order to compute the solvency capital, while the framework that we consider here allows us to obtain closed-form formulae. For instance, considering a simple Vasicek model for the short-term interest rate would gives us differences between log-normally-distributed random variables.

In Section 6.1, we set the pension liability of the life insurer or pension fund. We define its assets in Section 6.2, its final net worth in Section 6.3 and consider its solvency capital in Section 6.4.

6.1. Liabilities

We consider a life insurer or pension fund that offers a fixed guaranteed rate $r_G \in \mathbb{R}$ over a time horizon $T \in \mathbb{N}^*$. We assume that the company is fully hedged against the mortality and underwriting risks. Then, the liability at maturity is given by:

$$L_T = \pi_0 e^{r_G T},$$

where $\pi_0 \in \mathbb{R}$ is the initial unique contribution paid for the affiliate.

Remark 9. *This corresponds to a defined contribution with a minimum guaranteed rate or a cash-balance plan. However, we could have considered a defined benefit (DB) plan, as well. Results in Propositions 3, 4 and 5 are sufficiently general to allow easy adaptations when liabilities and interest rate are deterministic.*

6.2. Assets

We assume a financial market modeled by a Black–Scholes–Merton model [15,16] with $r \in \mathbb{R}$ the constant risk-free interest rate, a bank account and a stock. The contribution π_0 is invested in a portfolio A over the period $[0, T]$ made up of these assets and which follows a constant proportion allocation strategy, i.e., its stochastic differential equation (SDE) is given by, for $t \in [0, T]$,

$$\mathrm{d}A_t = (\theta\mu + (1-\theta)r)\, A_t\, \mathrm{d}t\, + \theta\sigma A_t\, \mathrm{d}W_t,$$

where $\theta \in [0,1]$ is the deterministic proportion of the portfolio invested in the stock, W is a standard Brownian motion, $A_0 = \pi_0$, $\mu, \sigma \in \mathbb{R}$ and $\sigma > 0$. Therefore, at any time $t \in [0, T]$, a proportion θ of the portfolio A_t is invested in the stock, and a proportion $1-\theta$ is invested in the bank account. We then have:

$$A_t = \pi_0 \exp\left[\left(\theta\mu + (1-\theta)r - \frac{\theta^2\sigma^2}{2}\right) t + \theta\sigma W_t\right], \tag{1}$$

for all $t \in [0, T]$.

As the term structure is flat and known with certainty, the price at time $t \in [0, T]$ of a zero-coupon bond paying one unit of currency at maturity $s \in [0, T], t \leq s$, is given by:

$$P(t, s) = e^{-r(s-t)}.$$

6.3. *Final Net Worth*

The final net worth (at maturity T) of the pension liability is simply given by the difference between its final assets and liabilities, i.e., given by the r.v.:

$$\mathrm{FNW}_T = A_T - L_T.$$

For $\omega \in \Omega$, the company faces a loss at maturity under scenario ω if:

$$\mathrm{FNW}_T(\omega) < 0,$$

otherwise, it is solvent.

6.4. *Solvency Capital*

We define the solvency capital as the amount the company has to put aside, in addition to the initial value of its portfolio, in order to be solvent at maturity according to a particular measure. This amount at time $t \in \mathbb{T}$ is invested in a product $\iota_{t,T}$ over the period $[t, T]$. We consider here:

$$\iota_{t,T} = \frac{1}{P(t, T)},$$

which means that the solvency capital at time t is invested in a zero-coupon bond between dates t and T. This choice for the reference instrument can be considered as prudent. For instance, we could have decided to invest the solvency capital in the portfolio of assets, i.e.,

$$\iota_{t,T} = \frac{A_T}{A_t},$$

which is clearly riskier. This approach has been considered in [12] where it is observed that the solvency capital computed according to this investment strategy is higher than the prudent approach of a risk-free zero-coupon bond.

The solvency capital given by the iterated VaR and TVaR measures (see Definitions 8 and 11) is computed as follows.

Proposition 3. *Let $\boldsymbol{\alpha} \in (0, 1)^T$. We compute that:*

$$\begin{aligned}&\mathrm{IVaR}_t^{\boldsymbol{\alpha}}(\mathrm{FNW}_T)\\&\quad = L_T P(t, T) - P(t, T) A_t \exp\left[\left(\theta\mu + (1-\theta) r - \frac{\theta^2\sigma^2}{2}\right)(T - t) + \theta\sigma \sum_{i=1}^{T-t} \Phi^{-1}(1 - \alpha_i)\right], \end{aligned} \qquad (2)$$

and:

$$\mathrm{ITVaR}_t^{\boldsymbol{\alpha}}(\mathrm{FNW}_T) = L_T P(t, T) - P(t, T) A_t \exp\left[(\theta\mu + (1-\theta) r)(T - t)\right] \prod_{i=1}^{T-t} \left[\frac{\Phi\left(\Phi^{-1}(1 - \alpha_i) - \theta\sigma\right)}{1 - \alpha_i}\right],$$

for $t \in \mathbb{T}$, *where* Φ *denotes the cumulative distribution function of a standard normal r.v., i.e., for* $y \in \mathbb{R}$,

$$\Phi(y) = \frac{1}{\sqrt{2\pi}} \int_{-\infty}^{y} e^{-\frac{x^2}{2}} \, dx \,,$$

and Φ^{-1} *its inverse.*

Proof. See Appendix B. □

Remark 10. *For both the iterated VaR and TVaR measures, we observe that the solvency capital is a decreasing function of* μ, *while it is increasing with* σ. *Furthermore, for the iterated VaR, the first derivative with respect to* μ *is a decreasing function, meaning that the speed of decrease will increase with* μ, *while the first derivate with respect to* σ *is an increasing function.*

We also consider the solvency capital given by the expected VaR and TVaR measures (see Definitions 13 and 14).

Proposition 4. *Let* $\alpha \in (0,1)$. *We compute that:*

$$\mathrm{EVaR}_t^{\alpha}(\mathrm{FNW}_T) = L_T P(t,T) - P(t,T) A_t \exp\left[(\theta\mu + (1-\theta)r)(T-t) - \frac{\theta^2\sigma^2}{2} + \theta\sigma\Phi^{-1}(1-\alpha) \right],$$

and:

$$\mathrm{ETVaR}_t^{\alpha}(\mathrm{FNW}_T) = L_T P(t,T) - P(t,T) A_t \exp\left[(\theta\mu + (1-\theta)r)(T-t) \right] \frac{\Phi\left(\Phi^{-1}(1-\alpha) - \theta\sigma\right)}{1-\alpha},$$

for $t \in \mathbb{T}$.

Proof. Similar to the proof of Proposition 3. □

If we compare Propositions 3 and 4, we see that the iterated VaR (resp. TVaR) considers a sequence of bad events, while the expected VaR (resp. TVaR) only considers one bad event affecting the last year of the product (the first iteration). The expected VaR (resp. TVaR) incorporates a security margin in the first iteration, for the last year of the product. However, the iterated VaR (resp. TVaR) can incorporate a security margin in each iteration, according to the confidence level considered at each step. For instance, we could consider a linearly-decreasing margin when the number of iterations increases (see examples below). We could then consider the expected VaR or TVaR as a lower bound for the solvency capital.

Finally, we compare this solvency capital with that obtained by means of the recalculated risk measures.

Proposition 5. *Let* $\alpha \in (0,1)$. *We compute that:*

$$\mathrm{VaR}_0^{\alpha}(\mathrm{FNW}_T) = L_T P(0,T) - P(0,T) A_0 \exp\left[\left(\theta\mu + (1-\theta)r - \frac{\theta^2\sigma^2}{2} \right) T + \theta\sigma\sqrt{T}\Phi^{-1}(1-\alpha) \right],$$

and:

$$\mathrm{TVaR}_0^{\alpha}(\mathrm{FNW}_T) = L_T P(0,T) - P(0,T) A_0 \exp\left[(\theta\mu + (1-\theta)r) T \right] \frac{\Phi\left(\Phi^{-1}(1-\alpha) - \theta\sigma\sqrt{T}\right)}{1-\alpha}.$$

Proof. We only consider one step in the proof of Proposition 3. □

7. Numerical Illustration

In this section, we consider different values for $\boldsymbol{\alpha} \in (0,1)^T$ and $\alpha \in (0,1)$ in order to compute the solvency capital. We only compare the initial values of the solvency capital, i.e., $t = 0$.

We assume that $T \in \{1,\ldots,45\}$, $\theta = 40\%$, so that 40% of the portfolio is invested in the stock, that the guaranteed interest rate is equal to the risk free rate, i.e., $r_G = r$, and that $\pi_0 = 1000$ €. Concerning the financial market, the stock has been calibrated on daily log returns of the Belgian BEL20 index from 2 April 1991 to 31 December 2013 by means of the maximum likelihood estimation (MLE) method (see Table 1). We also set the constant interest rate to 1.5%.

Table 1. Parameters of the GBMobtained by the MLE method with the corresponding standard errors between brackets.

μ	σ
0.05564 (0.03827)	0.18415 (0.00172)

In order to be consistent with either a Solvency II or a Swiss Solvency Test approach, we will consider:

$$\alpha^{(\text{SII})} = 0.995\,,$$

when working with VaR measures and:

$$\alpha^{(\text{SST})} = 0.99\,,$$

for TVaR measures.

We first define the confidence levels in the case of the recalculated measures of Proposition 5. We follow the maturity approach as introduced in [10] and set:

$$\alpha^1 = \left(\alpha^{(\text{SII})}\right)^T,$$

and:

$$\alpha^2 = \left(\alpha^{(\text{SST})}\right)^T.$$

We also consider four definitions for the vector $\boldsymbol{\alpha} \in (0,1)^T$ for the VaR and TVaR cases. We write for the j-th definition, $j \in \{1,\cdots,4\}$,

$$\boldsymbol{\alpha}^{(\text{SII}),j} = \left(\alpha_i^{(\text{SII}),j}\right)_{i\in\{1,\ldots,T\}},$$

when dealing with VaR measures and:

$$\boldsymbol{\alpha}^{(\text{SST}),j} = \left(\alpha_i^{(\text{SST}),j}\right)_{i\in\{1,\ldots,T\}},$$

for TVaR measures. We give an illustration of these definitions in Figure 4 for the SII case.

The first one is the constant case, which is also studied in [12],

$$\alpha_i^{(\text{SII}),1} = \alpha^{(\text{SII})}\,,$$

and:

$$\alpha_i^{(\text{SST}),1} = \alpha^{(\text{SST})}\,,$$

for $i \in \{1,\ldots,T\}$.

For the three others definitions, we consider an integer $K > 0$. We see this parameter as the maturity after which we consider that a product is a long-term product, for instance $K = 8$ years.

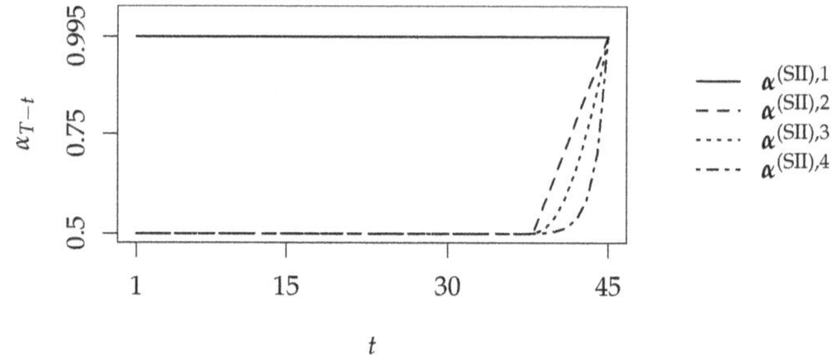

Figure 4. Different choices for the confidence vector, for a maturity $T = 45$ and a long-term threshold $K = 8$.

The second definition follows a linear increase when the time to maturity is decreasing, i.e., when i decreases,

$$\alpha_i^{(SII),2} = \begin{cases} \alpha^{(SII)} - \frac{\alpha^{(SII)}-0.5}{K-1}(i-1) & \text{if } i < K \\ 0.5 & \text{if } i \geq K \end{cases},$$

and:

$$\alpha_i^{(SST),2} = \begin{cases} \alpha^{(SST)} - \frac{\alpha^{(SST)}-1}{K-1}(i-1) & \text{if } i < K \\ 0 & \text{if } i \geq K \end{cases},$$

for $i \in \{1, \ldots, T\}$. We see that the confidence parameter decreases linearly towards either 50% or 0% within K years and afterwards stays constant. We chose 50% for the measures based on the VaR in order to obtain either the mean of the solvency capital if its distribution is symmetric or its median if not. With 0% for the measures based on the TVaR, we obtain directly the mean of the solvency capital. These choices are linked with the EVaR and ETVaR measures where the decrease is instantaneous ($K = 1$). In other words, for a time to maturity greater than K years, the parameter stays constant while it starts increasing towards either 99.5% or 99% when the time to maturity decreases.

Now, instead of considering a linear increase in terms of time to maturity, we could consider a square or an exponential increase, which is the aim of the two others definitions. We then have, for the square increase,

$$\alpha_i^{(SII),3} = \begin{cases} 1 - \frac{0.5-\alpha^{(SII)}}{(K-1)^2}\left(i^2 - 2Ki + K^2 + 0.5\frac{(K-1)^2}{0.5-\alpha^{(SII)}}\right) & \text{if } i < K \\ 0.5 & \text{if } i \geq K \end{cases},$$

$$\alpha_i^{(SST),3} = \begin{cases} 1 + \frac{\alpha^{(SST)}}{(K-1)^2}\left(i^2 - 2Ki + K^2 - 100\%\frac{(K-1)^2}{\alpha^{(SST)}}\right) & \text{if } i < K \\ 0 & \text{if } i \geq K \end{cases},$$

and for the exponential increase,

$$\alpha_i^{(SII),4} = \begin{cases} 0.5 + \left(\alpha^{(SII)}-0.5\right)\left(\frac{0.5-s^{(SII)}}{\alpha^{(SII)}-0.5}\right)^{\frac{i-1}{K-1}} & \text{if } i < K \\ 0.5 & \text{if } i \geq K \end{cases},$$

$$\alpha_i^{(SST),4} = \begin{cases} \alpha^{(SST)}\left(\frac{1-s^{(SST)}}{\alpha^{(SST)}}\right)^{\frac{i-1}{K-1}} & \text{if } i < K \\ 0 \text{ if } i \geq K \end{cases},$$

for $t \in \mathbb{T}$, where $0 < s^{(\mathrm{SII})} < \alpha^{(\mathrm{SII})}$ and $0 < s^{(\mathrm{SST})} < \alpha^{(\mathrm{SST})}$ are some adjustment parameter for the smoothness around K, typically $s^{(\mathrm{SII})}$ close to $\alpha^{(\mathrm{SII})}$ and $s^{(\mathrm{SST})}$ close to $\alpha^{(\mathrm{SST})}$.

We now study the level of the initial solvency capital according to the previous definitions of the confidence vectors. In Figure 5, we consider the solvency capital at time $t = 0$ given by Propositions 3, 4 and 5, for $T \in \{1, \ldots, 45\}$ and $K = 8$. We only consider the positive part. We observe that for the constant case, i.e., $\boldsymbol{\alpha}^{(\mathrm{SII}),1}$ and $\boldsymbol{\alpha}^{(\mathrm{SST}),1}$, the level of the solvency capital significantly increases with the maturity of the product. As already mentioned, it has been observed in [11,12]. The level of the solvency capital converges towards 100% of the initial value of the portfolio, i.e., towards the present value of the liability, which is here its supremum.

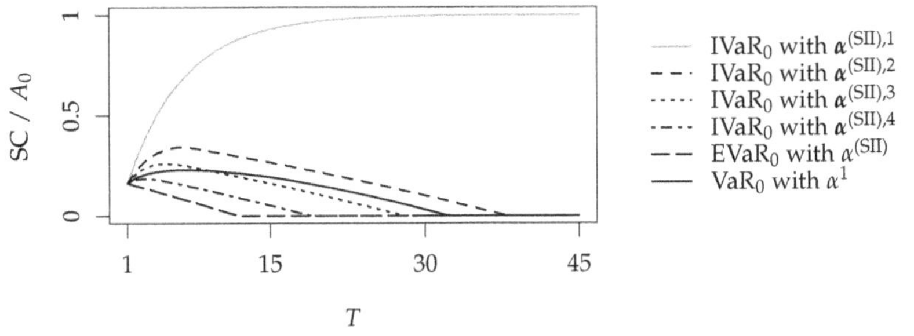

Figure 5. Computation of the solvency capital in the proportion of the initial value of the portfolio, for maturities $T \in \{1, \ldots, 45\}$ and a long-term threshold $K = 8$.

However, for the three others definitions of the confidence level, we remark that the solvency capital level increases for short maturities, while it decreases for long maturities. This decrease in the level is higher when the decrease of the confidence level increases as well, as expected. For instance, the solvency capital under the exponential function $\boldsymbol{\alpha}^{(\mathrm{SII}),4}$ declines more quickly than the solvency capital under the square function $\boldsymbol{\alpha}^{(\mathrm{SII}),3}$. We also observe a similar increasing and decreasing shape with the recalculated VaR and TVaR measures. This shape is very similar to the one given by the maturity approach of [10]. However, the main advantage is that the measure that we consider now is time consistent.

Concerning the EVaR measures, we see that we could consider it as the lower bound for the solvency capital level. This solvency capital is simply the expectation of the solvency capital needed for the last year of the product. It is the best estimate of the capital needed for the last year and does not include any security margin, except for the last year.

The difficulty we face now is the determination of a reasonable or relevant confidence level function. We could obtain any shape of the curve of the solvency capital with a particular choice of the confidence function. A way of solving this would be to consider an easy understandable function, such as the linear increase, e.g., starting K years before the maturity, we increase the confidence level from a fixed amount each year towards a classic level, such as the Solvency II or the Swiss Solvency Test levels.

Finally, according to Remark 10, we also observe in Figure 6 that the solvency capital increases when μ decreases and σ increases, while it decreases when μ increases and σ decreases.

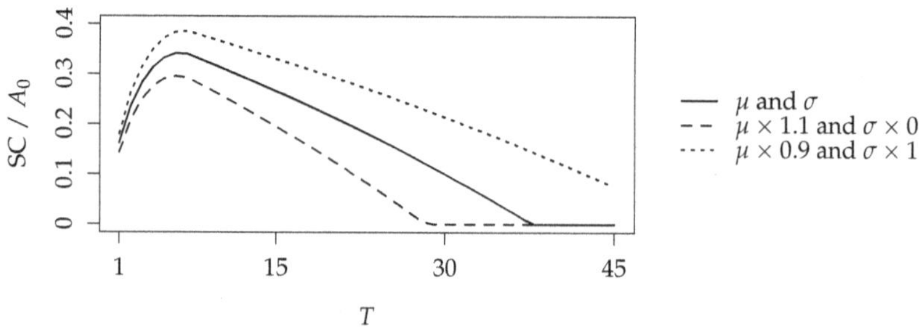

Figure 6. Computation of the solvency capital in the proportion of the initial value of the portfolio according to the iterated VaR measure with $\alpha^{(\mathrm{SII}),2}$ and with different values for μ and σ, for maturities $T \in \{1, \ldots, 45\}$ and a long-term threshold $K = 8$.

8. Conclusions

In this paper, we presented different constructions of time-consistent dynamic risk measures in order to determine the solvency capital of a life insurer or pension fund by taking into account the information disclosed through time. These dynamic risk measures are built such that they are coherent with the Solvency II or Swiss Solvency Test regulatory frameworks in the last year of the product.

We saw that according to the choice of the conditional risk measures considered for the iteration scheme and, in particular, according to the choice of the confidence levels for each iteration, different shapes for the solvency capital can be obtained. Several confidence levels that seem convenient have been proposed in order to benefit from the long-term characteristic of these products.

We also introduced a time-consistent measure where the first iteration is a VaR or TVaR measure, and the subsequent iterations make use of the conditional expectation. This measure is a kind of best estimate of the capital needed for the last year of the product and is particularly intuitive and elegant.

Finally, an important step forward will be to consider the case of multiple cash flows and to include more risks, such as the interest rate and mortality risks.

Acknowledgments: We would like to thank the referees of an earlier version of this paper for useful remarks and suggestions. We also acknowledge the financial support from the Pensionvaluation and solvency AGInsurance Chair.

Author Contributions: Both authors have contributed equally to this paper.

Conflicts of Interest: The authors declare no conflict of interest. The founding sponsors had no role in the design of the study; in the collection, analyses or interpretation of data; in the writing of the manuscript; nor in the decision to publish the results.

Appendix A. Link between Time-Consistent and Iterated Measures

We recall here the equivalence between time-consistent and iterated risk measures (see [4]).

Theorem A1. *Let ρ be a dynamic risk measure on $\mathrm{L}^1(\Omega, \mathcal{F}_T, \mathbb{P})$. The following conditions are equivalent:*

(a) *ρ is time consistent;*

(b) *if:*

$$\rho_{t+1}(X) = \rho_{t+1}(Y),$$

then:

$$\rho_t(X) = \rho_t(Y),$$

for all $t \in \mathbb{T}, t \neq T-1$ and $X, Y \in \mathrm{L}^1(\Omega, \mathcal{F}_T, \mathbb{P})$;

(c) *ρ is iterated.*

Proof. We first prove (a) implies (b). Let $t \in \mathbb{T}, t \neq T-1$ and $X, Y \in L^1(\Omega, \mathcal{F}_T, \mathbb{P})$. If:

$$\rho_{t+1}(X) = \rho_{t+1}(Y),$$

then by time consistency, we have either:

$$\rho_t(X) \leq \rho_t(Y),$$

or:

$$\rho_t(X) \geq \rho_t(Y),$$

and the first conclusion holds.

We now prove (b) implies (c). Let $t \in \mathbb{T}, t \neq T-1$ and $X \in L^1(\Omega, \mathcal{F}_T, \mathbb{P})$. By conditional cash invariance and normalization of the conditional risk measure, we compute that:

$$\rho_{t+1}\left(-\rho_{t+1}(X)\iota_{t+1,T}\right) = \rho_{t+1}(X),$$

and by (b) with:

$$Y = -\rho_{t+1}(X)\iota_{t+1,T},$$

ρ is iterated.

Finally, we see that (c) implies (a). Let $t \in \mathbb{T}, t \neq T-1$ and $X, Y \in L^1(\Omega, \mathcal{F}_T, \mathbb{P})$. If:

$$\rho_{t+1}(X) \leq \rho_{t+1}(Y),$$

then by the assumption of recursiveness and the monotonicity of the conditional risk measure, we have:

$$\begin{aligned}\rho_t(X) &= \rho_t\left(-\rho_{t+1}(X)\iota_{t+1,T}\right) \\ &\leq \rho_t\left(-\rho_{t+1}(Y)\iota_{t+1,T}\right) \\ &= \rho_t(Y),\end{aligned}$$

and the proof is complete. □

Appendix B. Proof of Proposition 3

The demonstration requires the following lemma; see ([17] [Lemma A.108]), for a proof of this result.

Lemma B1. *Let $X, Y \in L^1(\Omega, \mathcal{F}_T, \mathbb{P})$ and $\mathcal{G} \subseteq \mathcal{F}_T$ be a σ-algebra, such that X is independent of $\mathcal{G}$ and Y is $\mathcal{G}$-measurable. Then, for every $\mathcal{B}(\mathbb{R}^2)$-measurable bounded (or non-negative) function:*

$$h : \mathbb{R}^2 \longrightarrow \mathbb{R},$$

we have that:

$$\mathbb{E}\left[h(X,Y)|\mathcal{G}\right] = g(Y),$$

where $\mathcal{B}(\mathbb{R}^2)$ is the Borel σ-algebra on $\mathbb{R}^2$ and:

$$g(y) = \mathbb{E}\left[h(X,y)\right],$$

for $y \in \mathbb{R}$.

We only consider the case of the IVaR measure, and we start the proof with $t = T-1$. We find that:

$$\begin{aligned}\mathrm{IVaR}^{\alpha}_{T-1}(\mathrm{FNW}_T) &= \mathrm{VaR}^{\alpha_1}_{T-1}(A_T - L_T) \\ &= \mathrm{VaR}^{\alpha_1}_{T-1}(A_T) + L_T P(T-1,T),\end{aligned}$$

by conditional cash invariance. Let $V \in \mathrm{L}^1(\Omega, \mathcal{F}_{T-1}, \mathbb{P})$. We compute that, by Equation (1),

$$\begin{aligned}&\mathbb{P}\left[A_T P(T-1,T) \leq V \middle| \mathcal{F}_{T-1}\right] \\ &= \mathbb{P}\left[A_{T-1}\frac{A_T}{A_{T-1}}P(T-1,T) \leq V \middle| \mathcal{F}_{T-1}\right] \\ &= \mathbb{P}\left[A_{T-1}\exp\left[\theta\mu + (1-\theta)r - \frac{\theta^2\sigma^2}{2} + \theta\sigma\left(W_T - W_{T-1}\right)\right]P(T-1,T) \leq V \middle| \mathcal{F}_{T-1}\right] \\ &= \mathbb{P}\left[Z \leq \frac{1}{\theta\sigma}\left[\ln V - \ln A_{T-1} - \ln P(T-1,T) - \left(\theta\mu + (1-\theta)r - \frac{\theta^2\sigma^2}{2}\right)\right] \middle| \mathcal{F}_{T-1}\right],\end{aligned}$$

with Z a standard normal r.v. independent of $\mathcal{F}_{T-1}$ and the r.v. V must satisfy the condition $V > 0$. According to Lemma B1 with $X = Z$,

$$Y = \frac{1}{\theta\sigma}\left[\ln V - \ln A_{T-1} - \ln P(T-1,T) - \left(\theta\mu + (1-\theta)r - \frac{\theta^2\sigma^2}{2}\right)\right],$$

and:

$$h(x,y) = \chi_{\{x \leq y\}},$$

for $x, y \in \mathbb{R}$, where χ stands for the indicator function, we find that:

$$\begin{aligned}&\mathbb{P}\left[A_T P(T-1,T) \leq V \middle| \mathcal{F}_{T-1}\right] \\ &= \Phi\left(\frac{1}{\theta\sigma}\left[\ln V - \ln A_{T-1} - \ln P(T-1,T) - \left(\theta\mu + (1-\theta)r - \frac{\theta^2\sigma^2}{2}\right)\right]\right).\end{aligned}$$

Due to the continuous and strictly increasing properties of the cumulative distribution function Φ, it is invertible and:

$$\mathbb{P}\left[A_T P(T-1,T) \leq V \middle| \mathcal{F}_{T-1}\right] > \alpha_1,$$

is equivalent to:

$$\frac{1}{\theta\sigma}\left[\ln V - \ln A_{T-1} - \ln P(T-1,T) - \left(\theta\mu + (1-\theta)r - \frac{\theta^2\sigma^2}{2}\right)\right] > \Phi^{-1}(\alpha_1).$$

We find that $V \in \mathrm{L}^1(\Omega, \mathcal{F}_{T-1}, \mathbb{P})$ must also satisfy:

$$V > P(T-1,T)A_{T-1}\exp\left[\theta\mu + (1-\theta)r - \frac{\theta^2\sigma^2}{2} + \theta\sigma\Phi^{-1}(\alpha_1)\right],$$

and the case $t = T-1$ follows.

We assume now that the result is true for $t \in \mathbb{T}, t \neq 0$, and we show that it is also true for $t-1$. We have that, by Equation (2),

$$\begin{aligned}
&\mathrm{IVaR}_{t-1}^{\alpha}(\mathrm{FNW}_T) \\
&= \mathrm{VaR}_{t-1}^{\alpha_{T-t+1}}\left(-\mathrm{IVaR}_t^{\alpha}(\mathrm{FNW}_T)\frac{1}{P(t,T)}\right) \\
&= \mathrm{VaR}_{t-1}^{\alpha_{T-t+1}}\left(A_t \exp\left[\left(\theta\mu + (1-\theta)r - \frac{\theta^2\sigma^2}{2}\right)(T-t) + \theta\sigma\sum_{i=1}^{T-t}\Phi^{-1}(\alpha_i)\right]\right) + L_T P(t-1,T).
\end{aligned}$$

Let $V \in \mathrm{L}^1(\Omega, \mathcal{F}_{t-1}, \mathbb{P})$. We then find that,

$$\begin{aligned}
&\mathbb{P}\left[A_t \exp\left[\left(\theta\mu + (1-\theta)r - \frac{\theta^2\sigma^2}{2}\right)(T-t) + \theta\sigma\sum_{i=1}^{T-t}\Phi^{-1}(\alpha_i)\right] P(t-1,T) \leq V \middle| \mathcal{F}_{t-1}\right] \\
&= \mathbb{P}\left[Z \leq \frac{1}{\theta\sigma}\left[\ln V - \ln A_{t-1} - \ln P(t-1,T) - \left(\theta\mu + (1-\theta)r - \frac{\theta^2\sigma^2}{2}\right)(T-(t-1))\right.\right. \\
&\quad \left.\left. - \theta\sigma\sum_{i=1}^{T-t}\Phi^{-1}(\alpha_i)\right] \middle| \mathcal{F}_{t-1}\right],
\end{aligned}$$

where again Z is a standard normal r.v. independent of $\mathcal{F}_{t-1}$, and the r.v. $V \in \mathrm{L}^1(\Omega, \mathcal{F}_{t-1}, \mathbb{P})$ must satisfy the condition $V > 0$. According to Lemma B1 and the properties of the cumulative distribution function Φ, the first result follows from the same reasoning as the first part of the proof.

The second part of the result follows from the same reasoning adapted to the TVaR measure.

References

1. Artzner, P.; Delbaen, F.; Eber, J.M.; Heath, D. Coherent measures of risk. *Math. Financ.* **1999**, *9*, 203–228.
2. Frittelli, M.; Rosazza Gianin, E. Putting order in risk measures. *J. Bank. Financ.* **2002**, *26*, 1473–1486.
3. Föllmer, H.; Schied, A. *Stochastic Finance: An Introduction in Discrete Time*, 3rd ed.; De Gruyter Graduate; Walter de Gruyter: Berlin, Germany, 2011.
4. Acciaio, B.; Penner, I. Dynamic Risk Measures. In *Advanced Mathematical Methods for Finance*; Di Nunno, G., Øksendal, B., Eds.; Springer: Berlin/Heidelberg, Germany, 2011; Chapter 1, pp. 1–34.
5. Detlefsen, K.; Scandolo, G. Conditional and dynamic convex risk measures. *Financ. Stoch.* **2005**, *9*, 539–561.
6. Pflug, G.C.; Römisch, W. *Modeling, Measuring and Managing Risk*; World Scientific Publishing Co. Pte. Ltd.: Toh Tuck Link, Singapore, 2007.
7. Artzner, P.; Delbaen, F.; Eber, J.M.; Heath, D.; Ku, H. Coherent multiperiod risk adjusted values and Bellman's principle. *Ann. Oper. Res.* **2007**, *152*, 5–22.
8. Cheridito, P.; Stadje, M. Time-inconsistency of VaR and time-consistent alternatives. *Financ. Res. Lett.* **2009**, *6*, 40–46.
9. Cheridito, P.; Kupper, M. Composition of time-consistent dynamic monetary risk measures in discrete time. *Int. J. Theor. Appl. Financ.* **2011**, *14*, 137–162.
10. Devolder, P. Revised version of: Solvency requirement for a long-term guarantee: Risk measures versus probability of ruin. *Eur. Actuar. J.* **2011**, *1*, 199–214.
11. Hardy, M.R.; Wirch, J.L. The iterated CTE: A dynamic risk measure. *N. Am. Actuar. J.* **2004**, *8*, 62–75.
12. Devolder, P.; Lebègue, A. Iterated VaR or CTE measures: A false good idea? *Scand. Actuar. J.* **2016**, 1–32, doi:10.1080/03461238.2015.1126343.
13. Kupper, M.; Schachermayer, W. Representation results for law invariant time consistent functions. *Math. Financ. Econ.* **2009**, *2*, 189–210.
14. Devolder, P.; Lebègue, A. Risk measures versus ruin theory for the calculation of solvency capital for long-term life insurances. *Depend. Model.* **2016**, in press.

15. Black, F.; Scholes, M.S. The pricing of options and corporate liabilities. *J. Political Econ.* **1973**, *81*, 637–654.
16. Merton, R.C. Theory of rational option pricing. *Bell J. Econ. Manag. Sci.* **1973**, *4*, 141–183.
17. Pascucci, A. *PDE and Martingale Methods in Option Pricing*; Bocconi & Springer Series; Springer: Milan, Italy, 2011; Volume 2.

risks

MDPI

Article

The Effects of Largest Claim and Excess of Loss Reinsurance on a Company's Ruin Time and Valuation

Yuguang Fan [1,3], Philip S. Griffin [2], Ross Maller [3,*], Alexander Szimayer [4] and Tiandong Wang [5]

1. ARC Centre of Excellence for Mathematical and Statistical Frontiers, School of Mathematics and Statistics, The University of Melbourne, Parkville, VIC 3010, Australia; yuguang.fan@anu.edu.au
2. Department of Mathematics, Syracuse University, Syracuse, NY 13244-1150, USA; psgriffi@syr.edu
3. Research School of Finance, Actuarial Studies and Statistics, Australian National University, Canberra, ACT 0200, Australia
4. School of Economics and Social Science, Universität Hamburg, Von-Melle-Park 5, 20146 Hamburg, Germany; alexander.szimayer@wiso.uni-hamburg.de
5. School of Operations Research and Information Engineering, Cornell University, Ithaca, NY 14853, USA; tw398@cornell.edu

* Correspondence: ross.maller@anu.edu.au

Academic Editor: Luca Regis
Received: 21 November 2016; Accepted: 28 December 2016; Published: 6 January 2017

Abstract: We compare two types of reinsurance: excess of loss (EOL) and largest claim reinsurance (LCR), each of which transfers the payment of part, or all, of one or more large claims from the primary insurance company (the cedant) to a reinsurer. The primary insurer's point of view is documented in terms of assessment of risk and payment of reinsurance premium. A utility indifference rationale based on the expected future dividend stream is used to value the company with and without reinsurance. Assuming the classical compound Poisson risk model with choices of claim size distributions (classified as heavy, medium and light-tailed cases), simulations are used to illustrate the impact of the EOL and LCR treaties on the company's ruin probability, ruin time and value as determined by the dividend discounting model. We find that LCR is at least as effective as EOL in averting ruin in comparable finite time horizon settings. In instances where the ruin probability for LCR is smaller than for EOL, the dividend discount model shows that the cedant is able to pay a larger portion of the dividend for LCR reinsurance than for EOL while still maintaining company value. Both methods reduce risk considerably as compared with no reinsurance, in a variety of situations, as measured by the standard deviation of the company value. A further interesting finding is that heaviness of tails alone is not necessarily the decisive factor in the possible ruin of a company; small and moderate sized claims can also play a significant role in this.

Keywords: largest claims reinsurance; excess of loss reinsurance; ruin probability; ruin time; compound Poisson risk model; heavy tails; Lévy insurance risk process

1. Introduction

The classical insurance risk model for a company employs a compound Poisson process with negative drift as the claims surplus process, and measures the lifetime of the company as the time taken for the value of the process to exceed the initial capital of the firm; the "ruin time". Originally developed under a light tailed Cramér condition, in recent decades a wider spectrum of claim distributions—light, medium and heavy tailed—has been analysed, and, more generally, a Lévy process has been used in place of the compound Poisson process.

A need for heavy tailed insurance risk models has been stressed, for example, by [1–3], and in this context, special interest lies in the possibility of reinsurance, whereby the company can hedge its risk of suffering extremely large claims. A reinsurance scheme increases its potential lifetime, thereby reducing the company's risk of default. However, reinsurance treaties come at a cost, and pricing of those contracts and the consequent impact on the company's overall value need to be considered.

In this paper we investigate how reinsurance can extend the lifetime of the company and reduce the probability of ruin, with attention not just to heavy tailed claim distributions, but also to a variety of other possible distributional tail behaviours. Reinsurance works by transferring responsibility for some portion of the claims in a specified time period from the primary insurance company (the cedant) to the reinsurer. Two types of reinsurance which guard against the possibility of extremely large claims are excess of loss (EOL), and largest claim reinsurance (LCR). Each of these transfers the payment of part, or all, of one or more of the largest claims from the cedant to a reinsurer. A considerable amount of work has been done on these and related methods, usually taking the point of view of the reinsurer. Here, by contrast, we concentrate on the properties of the resulting reduced process from the point of view of the cedant and consider the relative merits of each type.

To illustrate the effects, we analyse compound Poisson models for an insurance risk process incorporating an EOL or LCR aspect, or neither, computing ruin times and probabilities of ruin both in finite and infinite time scenarios. Using a dividend discounting model, we also determine the maximal amount the cedant is able to divert from dividend payments to the reinsurance premium, without reducing company value.

To cover the spectrum of possibilities, as claims distributions we consider subexponential (including Pareto) distributions, as typifying heavy tailed situations, convolution equivalent distributions (such as the Inverse Gaussian) for medium, and distributions satisfying a Cramér condition (we use a Gamma distribution), for light tailed cases. In this way, much insight into the behaviour of the ruin time and associated quantities, such as the shortfall at ruin, can be gained.

The paper is organised as follows. The EOL and LCR reinsurance models are reviewed in Section 2. Section 3 outlines our methods, with the compound Poisson model in Section 3.1, and the tail regimes we consider in Section 3.2. Section 4 gives the results of the simulations, separately for LCR (Section 4.1) and EOL reinsurance (Section 4.2). Section 4.3 compares results across the distributions for both kinds of reinsurance. In Section 5 we set out the dividend discounting model which is our basis for valuation of the cedant company, and use it to find the amount of the dividend the cedant is able to transfer to reinsurance without reducing the value of the company. This value is then simulated under the various regimes and conditions and comparisons made between the EOL and LCR strategies. Section 6 contains a summary discussion of our results with suggestions for future research. In an Appendix we state some useful results concerning Laplace transforms of passage times which can be used to check on some aspects of the simulations, or provide bounds for quantities of interest.

2. Reinsurance Models

A primary incentive for an insurance company to enter a reinsurance contract is to gain some degree of certainty over its cash flows. There are of course many ways in which risks can be transferred from cedant company to reinsurer. We briefly outline the two methods of reinsurance we will consider.

Excess of Loss Reinsurance: Under this scheme, a retention amount L is pre-determined and the amount of any claim in excess of L is liable for the reinsurer. This scheme in effect truncates all claims at the level L, and the modified aggregate claims process is then simply the sum of the truncated claims. Analysis, both theoretical and practical, is relatively straightforward.

A potential problem with this procedure, however, is the moral hazard it may give rise to. Moral hazard refers to changes in the cedant's behaviour that may occur after having taken out reinsurance; it may lead to less cautious behaviour and consequently to an increase in the potential magnitude and/or probability of a large loss. The work of [4,5], for example, discusses the issues involved in this, and how their effects may be disentangled empirically.

Largest Claims Reinsurance: There are various alternatives to using a fixed retention level, usually based on making the insurer liable for a proportion of the total loss in some way. Here we examine the LCR treaty: having set a fixed follow-up time t, we delete from the process the largest claim occurring up to and including that time. Defined in this way, the scheme incorporates a retrospective feature akin to the construction of a "lookback" option as understood in finance [1].

The reduced process constitutes a "trimmed" process, in which some part of, or all of, one or more of the largest claims has been deleted. Changes in the ruin probabilities and the expected ruin times of the cedant due to the trimming are then of particular interest.

Ruin: "Ruin" occurs if the modified claim surplus process, starting from 0, exceeds the initial capital level u. The ruin time and consequent quantities are then calculated on the modified risk process. In Figure 1, we provide graphical realisations of the LCR reinsurance scheme for one particular claim distribution, a Pareto$(1,2)$ (precise definitions of distributions are given in Section 3.2). The black points in Figure 1 indicate individual claims arriving sequentially in time and the red segments represent the amounts that will be covered by reinsurance.

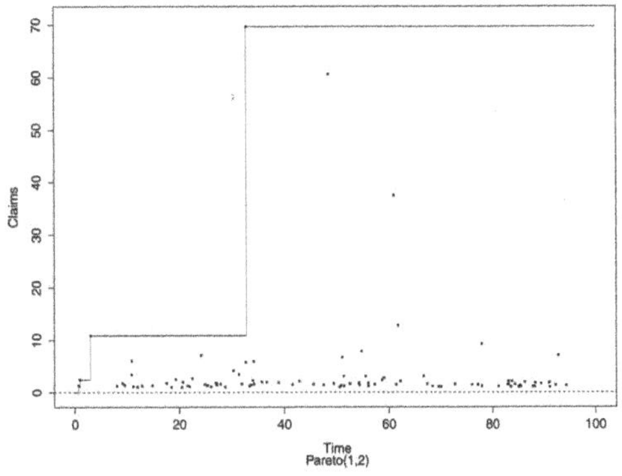

Figure 1. A schematic illustration of the largest claim reinsurance (LCR) reinsurance scheme with a Pareto(1,2) claim distribution. Black dots indicate claim amounts and red lines are the successive amounts liable for the reinsurance company.

Translating this scheme into the sample path of the cedant's insurance risk process, we then have the illustration in Figure 2, where the black line stands for the original risk process and the red line is the process adjusted for LCR reinsurance. Figure 2 also includes a sample path for EOL reinsurance, as the green line. In general, the ruin time with reinsurance will exceed or equal that without, for

1 The LCR procedure can be made prospective by implementing it as a forward looking dynamic procedure in real time, from the cedant's point of view. Designate as time zero the time at which the reinsurance is taken out. At this time, the cedant company's assets amount to $u > 0$, say. The first claim arriving after time 0 is referred to the reinsurer and not debited to the cedant. Subsequent claims smaller than the initial claim are paid by the cedant until a claim larger than the first (the previous largest) arrives. The difference between these two claims is referred to the reinsurer and not debited to the cedant. The process continues in this way so that at time t, the accumulated amount referred to the reinsurer equals the largest claim up till that time. This procedure has the same effect as referring the largest claim up till time t retrospectively to the reinsurer.

each sample path, and the question we address here is how to measure this effect with regard to the company's viability.

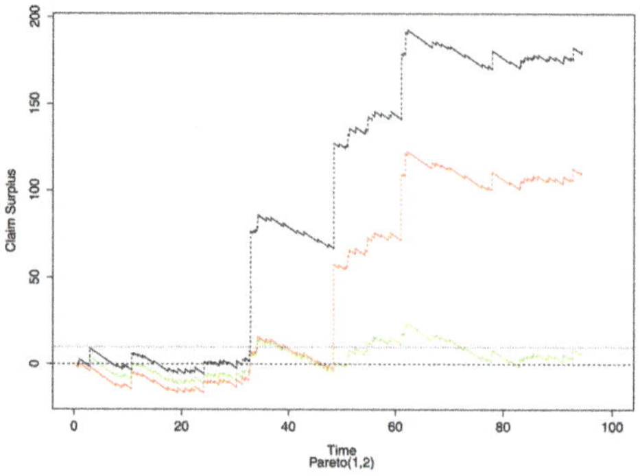

Figure 2. Sample paths of the insurance risk processes without reinsurance (black line), with LCR reinsurance (red line), and with EOL reinsurance (green line), for a Pareto(1,2) claim distribution. The company's initial reserve is $u = 10$, the safety loading is $\theta = 0.1$, expected claim size is μ = 2, claim arrival rate is $\lambda = 1$, and each time unit is 0.01 year = 3.65 days. For comparability between the two schemes, the retention level L for the EOL scheme is chosen so that the expected values of the LCR and EOL aggregate claims are equal at maturity time $T = 5000$.

3. Methods

In this section we briefly set out notation for the compound Poisson process model we will use, and describe the simulations to be carried out.

3.1. Compound Poisson Process Methodology

Our results are formulated in terms of the familiar Cramér-Lundberg compound Poisson process model. In this, the claim surplus process takes the form

$$C_t = \sum_{i=1}^{N_t} \xi_i - ct, \; t \geq 0, \tag{1}$$

where c is the premium rate, the ξ_i are independent positive random variables all having the same claim size distribution function $F(x)$ on $[0, \infty)$ with $F(0) = 0$, and N_t is a Poisson process with intensity λ, independent of the ξ_i. (A sum of the form $\sum_{i=1}^{0}$ is taken as 0, and $N_0 := 0$.) The premium rate c is chosen to satisfy the net profit condition

$$c = (1 + \theta)\lambda\mu, \tag{2}$$

where $\theta > 0$ is a prespecified safety loading factor and μ is the expectation of a random variable generated from F, assumed finite. Ruin occurs if C_t exceeds the initial capital level $u > 0$, for some $t > 0$. The net profit condition ensures that expected income outweighs expected claims, thus precluding the possible case of almost sure ruin; but ruin will occur with positive probability.

In order to describe the reinsured claim surplus process, consider the claims occurring as a point process in time. After reinsurance, the claim surplus process, denoted by C_t^R, can be written at time $t \geq 0$ as

$$C_t^R = C_t - R_t, \tag{3}$$

where in the case of an EOL treaty

$$R_t = \sum_{i=1}^{N_t} (\xi_i - L)\mathbf{1}_{\{\xi_i > L\}}, \tag{4}$$

for some $L > 0$, while for the LCR treaty

$$R_t = \max_{1 \le i \le N_t} \xi_i. \tag{5}$$

($\mathbf{1}_A$ denotes the indicator of an event A, and a maximum of the form $\max_{1 \le i \le 0}$ is taken as 0). In the EOL version, R_t is the accumulated amount of claims exceeding the cutoff level L up till time t, which is referred to the reinsurer hence subtracted from the claim surplus process in (3). In the LCR version, C_t^R is represented as the dynamically trimmed risk process with the largest jump occurring so far omitted at each point in time. In either case, ruin occurs for the reinsured company if C_t^R exceeds the initial capital level u, for some $t > 0$.

3.2. Tail Regimes

Our analysis is divided into three different cases based on the heaviness of the tails of the claims distribution. Thus we consider light (Cramér), medium-heavy (convolution equivalent) and heavy (subexponential) scenarios. For detailed background concerning these models, we refer to [6–8], as well as the references therein. Illustrations of practical applications using convolution equivalent models are in [9,10], Here we only provide a list of basic definitions and the assumptions involved in each regime. In order to make the models comparable, we choose parameters in each case such that $\mathbf{E}\xi_1 = 2$.

(i) **Cramér case:** There exists a finite positive constant ν_0 such that the claim distribution F satisfies

$$\lambda(m_{\nu_0}(F) - 1) = c\nu_0, \tag{6}$$

where $m_\nu(F) = \int_{[0,\infty)} e^{\nu x} \mathrm{d}F(x)$ is the moment generating function (mgf) of F, assumed finite for $\nu = \nu_0$. These are relatively "light-tailed" (exponentially small) distributions. As a typical example in our simulations we choose F to be a Gamma$(2,1)$ distribution with density

$$f(x) = xe^{-x}, \qquad x \ge 0. \tag{7}$$

(ii) **Convolution equivalent case:** The claims distribution function F is said to be *convolution equivalent with index* $\alpha > 0$, if its tail $\overline{F}(x) := 1 - F(x)$, $x > 0$, satisfies

$$\lim_{x\to\infty} \frac{\overline{F}(x-y)}{\overline{F}(x)} = e^{\alpha y} \text{ and } \lim_{x\to\infty} \frac{\overline{F^{2\times}}(x)}{\overline{F}(x)} = 2m_\alpha(F) < \infty, \tag{8}$$

where $F^{2\times}$ is the convolution, $F^{2\times} = F \times F$. The distribution function F has the properties

$$m_\alpha(F) < \infty \quad \text{and} \quad m_{\alpha+\varepsilon}(F) = \infty \quad \text{for} \quad \forall \varepsilon > 0. \tag{9}$$

These distributions have "medium-heavy" tails in the sense that a convolution equivalent distribution of index α has a finite exponential moment of order α, but any larger order moment is infinite. Typical examples are distributions with tails of the form

$$\overline{F}(x) \sim \frac{ce^{-\alpha x}}{x^\rho}, \quad \text{as } x \to \infty, \tag{10}$$

for some $c > 0$, $\alpha > 0$, $\rho > 1$. One important example of a class of distributions which are convolution equivalent is the Inverse Gaussian family with densities parametrised as in Chapter 2.2 of [11]:

$$f(x; a, b) = \sqrt{\frac{b}{2\pi}} x^{-3/2} \exp\left(-\frac{b(x-a)^2}{2a^2 x}\right), \quad x > 0. \tag{11}$$

Here $a > 0$ is the mean parameter and $b > 0$ is called the scale parameter. We denote such a distribution as $IG(a, b)$. In our simulations we choose $a = 2$ and $b = 1.5$.

(iii) **Subexponential case:** When (8) is satisfied with $\alpha = 0$, F is said to have a *subexponential* tail. Typical examples are the Pareto distributions. In our simulations we used a Pareto$(1, 2)$ distribution with (power law) tail of the form

$$\overline{F}(x) = \frac{1}{x^2}, \quad x \geq 1. \tag{12}$$

These distributions have very heavy tails, giving rise to occasional extremely large jumps.

With the parameters as specified above, these three regimes are mutually exclusive; see [8].

3.3. Simulation Methodology

Our focus is on illustrating notionally how reinsurance affects the ruin time of the company, rather than on definitive numerical comparisons, so we adopt a straightforward approach to the simulations which is adequate for our purposes. Specifically, we generate a number $N = 100,000$ sample paths and keep track of whether and when they exceed the predetermined reserve level u at some time during a time interval $[0, T]$, $T > 0$. This allows estimation of the ruin probabilities $P(\tau_u \leq T)$ and $P(\tau_u^R \leq T)$ for the risk processes with and without reinsurance. We also estimate the conditional expected values of these ruin times. The ruin times are defined formally as

$$\tau_u = \inf\{t > 0 : C_t > u\}, \quad \text{and} \quad \tau_u^R = \inf\{t > 0 : C_t^R > u\}. \tag{13}$$

Simulated sample paths may be categorised as follows.

(a) Neither C_t nor C_t^R transits above u in $[0, T]$. Suppose there are n_1 such paths among the N.
(b) C_t transits above u in $[0, T]$ but C_t^R does not. Suppose there are n_2 such paths among the N.
(c) C_t^R transits above u in $[0, T]$ and hence C_t does also. There are $n_3 = N - n_1 - n_2$ such paths among the N.

The ruin probabilities $\mathbf{P}(\tau_u \leq T)$ and $\mathbf{P}(\tau_u^R \leq T)$ were estimated by calculating the proportion of all paths which exceeded the reserve level u during $[0, T]$. Standard errors of the probability estimates were calculated using the binomial variance $\hat{P}(1 - \hat{P})/N$, where $\hat{P}$ was the corresponding estimated probability.

In calculating ruin times, we restrict ourselves to paths of Type (c). These are the only paths for which we can determine both τ_u and τ_u^R, and lead to a useful comparison between them in the form of estimates for $\mathbf{E}(\tau_u^R | \tau_u^R \leq T)$ and $\mathbf{E}(\tau_u | \tau_u^R \leq T)$. For these paths we record the times of first passage above u for each of C_t and C_t^R, denoted by $\tau_{u,T,1}, \cdots, \tau_{u,T,n_3}$ and $\tau_{u,T,1}^R, \cdots, \tau_{u,T,n_3}^R$ respectively, and then estimate $\mathbf{E}(\tau_u^R | \tau_u^R \leq T)$ and $\mathbf{E}(\tau_u | \tau_u^R \leq T)$ by

$$\hat{\tau}_{u,T}^R = \frac{\sum_{i=1}^{n_3} \tau_{u,T,i}^R}{n_3} \tag{14}$$

and

$$\widehat{\tau}_{u,T} = \frac{\sum_{i=1}^{n_3} \tau_{u,T,i}}{n_3}. \quad (15)$$

For each of the n_3 paths of Type (c) we have $\tau_{u,T,i} \leq \tau^R_{u,T,i}$, implying of course that $\widehat{\tau}_{u,T} \leq \widehat{\tau}^R_{u,T}$.

For the simulations in the next section we need to make choices for the parameters T, θ, μ, λ and u. We discuss these choices in more detail in Section 5.2, but for the present purposes, we set them as follows: expectation of claims distributions $\mu = 2$; claim arrival rate is $\lambda = 1$; safety loading $\theta = 0.1$. Initial reserve takes values $u = 10, 30, 50, 70, 100$ and time spans are $T = 100, 500, 1000$. Each time unit is 0.01 year = 3.65 days.

4. Results

In this section, we report on simulations for the classical compound Poisson risk model in which the claim surplus process takes the form specified in (1) and the reinsured process is as in (3). We inspected the impact of EOL and LCR reinsurances in the three different tail regimes by varying the claim size distributions. In all examples, we chose the claim arrival rate as $\lambda = 1$ and the safety loading as $\theta = 0.1$. For a variety of combinations of initial capital u and follow-up time T, we recorded the estimated original and the reinsured ruin probabilities, and the estimated ruin times.

4.1. *Largest Claim Reinsurance*

For the case of LCR we denote the claims surplus process in (3) by C^M and the ruin time in (13) by τ_u^M. We chose a Pareto$(1, 2)$ distribution for the simulations in the heavy-tailed case. This choice of parameters parallels that of [12], who calculated the ultimate ruin probabilities for these particular Cramér-Lundberg risk models. So we can benchmark our results against theirs to check on the accuracy of our simulations.

The results are summarised in Table 1. Comparing Columns 3 and 4 in Table 1, we see that the estimated ruin probability $\widehat{\mathbf{P}}(\tau_u < T)$ drops substantially to $\widehat{\mathbf{P}}(\tau_u^M < T)$ after reinsurance. Correspondingly, significant increases in the expected conditional lifetime of the company with reinsurance are observed (compare Columns 5 and 6). Column 7 gives the percentage change in the conditional ruin times due to reinsurance. As expected, the effect tends to diminish when u is increased, but remains substantial even for $u = 100$. The probabilities in Columns 3 and 4 of Table 1, and in similar tables below, are estimated correct to 2 decimal places (standard error less than 10^{-2}). Numbers in the $T = \infty$ rows in Table 1 are calculated from Algorithm III in [12].

We next investigate the impact of reinsurance on the Cramér-Lundberg model with light or medium-heavy tailed claim distributions. The specific examples chosen are Gamma$(2, 1)$ (light tailed) and IG$(2, 1.5)$ (medium-heavy tailed). For consistency, we chose the expectations of the claims distributions to be $\mu = 2$ (the same as in the Pareto case), and all other parameters (claim arrival rate $\lambda = 1$, safety loading $\theta = 0.1$, initial reserves u and time spans T) also the same.

Table 1. LCR reinsurance for Pareto(1,2) distributed claims. The safety loading is $\theta = 0.1$, expected claim size is $\mu = 2$, claim arrival rate is $\lambda = 1$, and each time unit is 0.01 years. Simulations are done with $N = 100,000$ sample paths. The $T = \infty$ case refers to the results obtained from Algorithm III in [12].

u	T	$\widehat{\mathrm{P}}(\tau_u < T)$	$\widehat{\mathrm{P}}(\tau_u^M < T)$	$\hat{\tau}_{u,T}$	$\hat{\tau}_{u,T}^M$	% Changes
10	100	0.43	0.14	19.06	37.03	93.34
	500	0.53	0.20	38.14	85.45	124.02
	1000	0.55	0.21	44.75	104.35	133.19
	∞	0.56 ± 0.03	-	-	-	-
30	100	0.14	0.02	35.78	58.97	64.84
	500	0.26	0.06	90.65	164.25	81.19
	1000	0.28	0.06	113.18	214.20	89.25
	∞	0.32 ± 0.02	-	-	-	-
50	100	0.06	0.00	44.64	66.40	55.74
	500	0.14	0.02	129.20	215.24	66.59
	1000	0.17	0.03	172.73	303.81	75.89
	∞	0.20 ± 0.02	-	-	-	-
70	100	0.03	0.00	45.66	73.67	61.37
	500	0.09	0.01	157.07	263.60	67.82
	1000	0.11	0.01	221.55	380.55	71.77
	∞	0.14 ± 0.02	-	-	-	-
100	100	0.01	0.00	37.32	75.64	102.71
	500	0.05	0.00	180.25	300.30	66.60
	1000	0.06	0.00	258.22	450.58	74.50
	∞	0.081 ± 0.017	-	-	-	-

Graphical illustrations are in Figures 3 and 4. Relatively smaller claim sizes occur in these two cases (compare the vertical scales of these two plots with that of Figure 1), and as a result the impact of reinsurance is not as dramatic as it is for the heavy-tailed cases. A similar conclusion can be drawn from the numerical results in Tables 2 and 3.

In both the Gamma and Inverse Gaussian cases, improvements in ruin probabilities after reinsurance are significant, especially for u small, but proportionally not as substantial as for the Pareto.

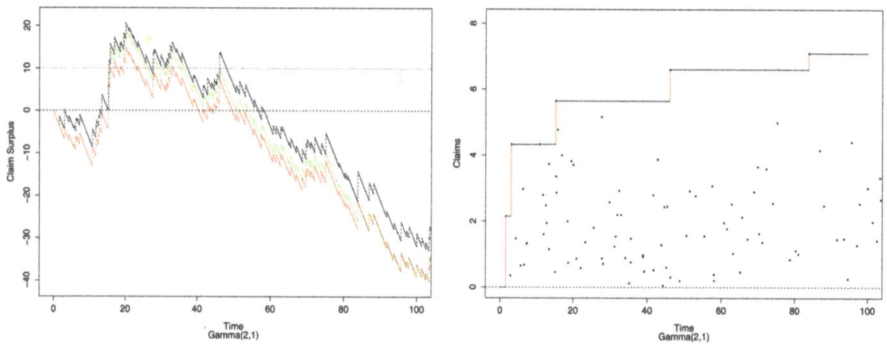

Figure 3. Sample paths of the insurance risk processes without reinsurance (black line), with LCR reinsurance (red line), and with excess of loss (EOL) reinsurance (green line), for a Gamma(2, 1) claim distribution. The safety loading is $\theta = 0.1$, expected claim size is $\mu = 2$, claim arrival rate is $\lambda = 1$, and each time unit is 0.01 years. L for the EOL scheme is chosen so that the expected values of the LCR and EOL claim distributions are equal at maturity time $T = 5000$.

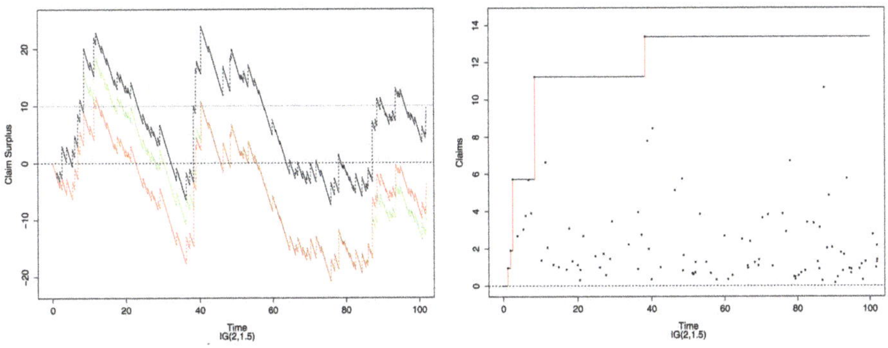

Figure 4. Sample paths of the insurance risk processes without reinsurance (black line), with LCR reinsurance (red line), and with EOL reinsurance (green line), for an IG(2, 1.5) claim distribution. The safety loading is $\theta = 0.1$, expected claim size is $\mu = 2$, claim arrival rate is $\lambda = 1$, and each time unit is 0.01 years. L for the EOL scheme is chosen so that the expected values of the LCR and EOL claim distributions are equal at maturity time $T = 5000$.

Table 2. LCR reinsurance for Gamma(2, 1) distributed claims. The safety loading is $\theta = 0.1$, expected claim size is $\mu = 2$, claim arrival rate is $\lambda = 1$, and each time unit is 0.01 years. Simulations are done with $N = 100,000$ sample paths.

u	T	$\widehat{\mathbb{P}}(\tau_u < T)$	$\widehat{\mathbb{P}}(\tau_u^M < T)$	$\widehat{\tau}_{u,T}$	$\widehat{\tau}_{u,T}^M$	**% Changes**
	100	0.43	0.25	22.22	34.91	57.11
10	500	0.49	0.32	44.35	70.81	61.18
	1000	0.50	0.32	47.79	77.57	63.39
	100	0.08	0.04	47.95	59.49	24.08
30	500	0.14	0.08	115.46	145.61	26.11
	1000	0.15	0.09	135.16	170.45	26.11
	100	0.01	0.00	62.13	72.35	16.45
50	500	0.04	0.02	177.90	208.29	17.08
	1000	0.04	0.02	214.04	254.08	18.71
	100	0.00	0.00	68.07	79.12	16.24
70	500	0.01	0.01	233.81	264.30	13.04
	1000	0.01	0.01	292.09	327.81	12.23
	100	0.00	0.00	-	-	-
100	500	0.00	0.00	315.52	347.89	10.26
	1000	0.00	0.00	393.28	438.94	11.61

Table 3. LCR reinsurance for IG(2, 1.5) distributed claims. The safety loading is $\theta = 0.1$, expected claim size is $\mu = 2$, claim arrival rate is $\lambda = 1$, and each time unit is 0.01 years. Simulations are done with $N = 100,000$ sample paths.

u	T	$\widehat{\mathbf{P}}(\tau_u < T)$	$\widehat{\mathbf{P}}(\tau_u^M < T)$	$\widehat{\tau}_{u,T}$	$\widehat{\tau}_{u,T}^M$	% Changes
	100	0.51	0.24	18.63	35.88	92.61
10	500	0.59	0.33	40.69	83.27	104.67
	1000	0.60	0.34	47.97	100.35	109.18
	100	0.16	0.05	38.97	56.63	45.33
30	500	0.27	0.13	101.28	153.44	51.51
	1000	0.28	0.14	122.80	189.76	54.53
	100	0.04	0.01	52.30	68.41	30.81
50	500	0.12	0.05	150.57	205.16	36.25
	1000	0.13	0.06	197.59	272.25	37.79
	100	0.01	0.00	61.72	78.22	26.73
70	500	0.05	0.02	197.71	253.26	28.10
	1000	0.06	0.03	261.72	339.91	29.88
	100	0.00	0.00	54.87	64.62	17.77
100	500	0.01	0.00	250.91	303.45	20.94
	1000	0.02	0.01	368.16	455.16	23.63

4.2. Excess of Loss Reinsurance

In this section we examine the EOL reinsurance scheme. We denote the corresponding claims surplus process by C^L and the ruin time by τ_u^L. Under this treaty, the reinsurer pays the total amount of any claim in excess of some pre-determined retention level L. For the results in the present section, in order to afford some degree of comparability with the LCR scheme, we chose L such that

$$\mathbf{E}(C_T^L) = \mathbf{E}(C_T^M),$$

For any $t > 0$ we have

$$\mathbf{E}(C_t^M) = \mathbf{E}(C_t) - \mathbf{E}\left(\max_{1\le i\le N_t} \xi_i\right),$$

and

$$\mathbf{E}(C_t^L) = \mathbf{E}(C_t) - \mathbf{E}\left(\sum_{i=1}^{N_t} (\xi_i - L)\mathbf{1}_{\{\xi_i > L\}}\right),$$

so for comparability we need to solve the equation

$$\mathbf{E}\left(\max_{1\le i\le N_t} \xi_i\right) = \mathbf{E}\left(\sum_{i=1}^{N_t} (\xi_i - L)\mathbf{1}_{\{\xi_i > L\}}\right) \tag{16}$$

for $L = L(t)$. The left-hand side of (16) is equal to

$$\begin{aligned}
\mathbf{E}\left(\max_{1\le i\le N_t} \xi_i\right) &= \sum_{n=0}^{\infty} \mathbf{E}\left(\max_{1\le i\le n} \xi_i\right) \frac{e^{-\lambda t}(\lambda t)^n}{n!} \\
&= \sum_{n=0}^{\infty} \int_0^{\infty} \mathbf{P}\left(\max_{1\le i\le n} \xi_i > x\right) \mathrm{d}x \times \frac{e^{-\lambda t}(\lambda t)^n}{n!} \\
&= \int_0^{\infty} \mathrm{d}x \sum_{n=0}^{\infty} (1 - F^n(x)) \times \frac{e^{-\lambda t}(\lambda t)^n}{n!} \\
&= \int_0^{\infty} (1 - e^{-\lambda t \overline{F}(x)})\mathrm{d}x,
\end{aligned}$$

where $\overline{F}(x) = 1 - F(x)$ is the tail of the distribution of the ξ_i. The right-hand side of (16) is equal to

$$\mathbf{E}\left(\sum_{i=1}^{N_t}(\xi_i - L)\mathbf{1}_{\{\xi_i > L\}}\right) = \sum_{n=0}^{\infty} \frac{e^{-\lambda t}(\lambda t)^n}{n!} n\mathbf{E}((\xi_1 - L)\mathbf{1}_{\{\xi_1 > L\}}) = \lambda t \int_L^{\infty}(x - L)\mathrm{d}F(x).$$

Choosing $t = T$ and $\lambda = 1$, L is required to solve

$$\int_L^{\infty}(x - L)\mathrm{d}F(x) = \int_L^{\infty}\overline{F}(x)\mathrm{d}x = \frac{1}{T}\int_0^{\infty}(1 - e^{-T\overline{F}(x)})\mathrm{d}x. \tag{17}$$

This is easily done in the R package, which we used for the simulations also. Once having selected L in this way, we used the same approach as before to estimate ruin probabilities and ruin times. The results are displayed in Tables 4–6.

In these tables we abuse notation slightly and continue to use $\widehat{\tau}_{u,T}$ as the estimated conditional ruin time for the plain risk process, noting, however, that in the present case the conditioning is on the event $\tau_u^L \leq T$ and not on $\tau_u^M \leq T$ as in Tables 1–3. This is the reason for the differing values of $\widehat{\tau}_{u,T}$ in Tables 4–6 as opposed to Tables 1–3.

Tables 4–6 contain an extra column "No Effect" as compared to Tables 1–3. The extra column records the proportion of paths for which ruin occurs but the ruin times are the same for the original sample path C_t as for the reinsured path C_t^L. In these cases the reinsurance scheme does not avoid ruin. There are two ways in which this can happen. One is that ruin occurs but reinsurance is not invoked at all; that is, there was no claim larger than L before ruin. The second scenario is that even though reinsurance was invoked at some time or times before ruin, nevertheless the jump causing ruin has magnitude less than L. There is no saving effect from the EOL scheme in these cases.

Table 4. EOL reinsurance for Pareto(2, 1) distributed claims. The safety loading is $\theta = 0.1$, expected claim size is $\mu = 2$, claim arrival rate is $\lambda = 1$, and each time unit is 0.01 years. Simulations are done with $N = 100{,}000$ sample paths. Retention level L is the solution to (17). For $T = 100$, $L(T) = 5.64$; for $T = 500$, $L(T) = 12.62$; for $T = 1000$, $L(T) = 17.84$.

u	T	$\widehat{\mathrm{P}}(\tau_u < T)$	$\widehat{\mathrm{P}}(\tau_u^L < T)$	$\widehat{\tau}_{u,T}$	$\widehat{\tau}_{u,T}^L$	% Changes	No Effect
	100	0.43	0.20	15.88	21.36	34.55	0.08
10	500	0.53	0.39	31.50	36.55	16.03	0.30
	1000	0.55	0.44	38.93	43.54	11.84	0.38
	100	0.14	0.01	33.48	49.71	48.47	0.00
30	500	0.26	0.08	71.37	92.83	30.08	0.03
	1000	0.28	0.12	87.85	106.86	21.63	0.07
	100	0.06	0.00	45.22	67.26	48.76	0.00
50	500	0.14	0.02	107.64	145.85	35.50	0.00
	1000	0.17	0.03	134.88	172.85	28.15	0.01
	100	0.03	0.00	70.52	79.83	13.20	0.00
70	500	0.09	0.00	144.90	195.31	34.79	0.00
	1000	0.11	0.01	182.04	243.62	33.82	0.00
	100	0.01	0.00	-	-	-	0.00
100	500	0.05	0.00	181.23	281.15	55.13	0.00
	1000	0.06	0.00	235.18	318.21	35.31	0.00

Table 5. EOL reinsurance for Gamma$(2,1)$ distributed claims. The safety loading is $\theta = 0.1$, expected claim size is $\mu = 2$, claim arrival rate is $\lambda = 1$, and each time unit is 0.01 years. Simulations are done with $N = 100,000$ sample paths. Retention level L is the solution to (17). For $T = 100$, $L(T) = 4.49$; for $T = 500$, $L(T) = 6.10$; for $T = 1000$, $L(T) = 6.79$.

u	T	$\widehat{P}(\tau_u < T)$	$\widehat{P}(\tau_u^L < T)$	$\hat{\tau}_{u,T}$	$\hat{\tau}_{u,T}^L$	**% Changes**	**No Effect**
	100	0.43	0.32	20.02	24.34	21.55	0.13
10	500	0.49	0.45	40.67	44.52	9.45	0.32
	1000	0.50	0.47	45.80	48.49	5.85	0.38
	100	0.08	0.03	44.45	53.24	19.77	0.00
30	500	0.14	0.11	106.87	116.82	9.31	0.04
	1000	0.15	0.13	127.08	135.13	6.33	0.07
	100	0.01	0.00	57.85	68.12	17.74	0.00
50	500	0.04	0.03	165.39	181.42	9.69	0.01
	1000	0.04	0.03	200.86	214.19	6.64	0.01
	100	0.00	0.00	66.66	80.33	20.52	0.00
70	500	0.01	0.01	219.09	239.44	9.29	0.00
	1000	0.01	0.01	279.28	294.17	5.33	0.00
	100	0.00	0.00	-	-	-	0.00
100	500	0.00	0.00	306.48	334.20	9.04	0.00
	1000	0.00	0.00	385.12	410.96	6.71	0.00

Table 6. EOL reinsurance for IG$(2,1.5)$ distributed claims. The safety loading is $\theta = 0.1$, expected claim size is $\mu = 2$, claim arrival rate is $\lambda = 1$, and each time unit is 0.01 years. Simulations are done with $N = 100,000$ sample paths. Retention level L is the solution to (17). For $T = 100$, $L(T) = 6.89$; for $T = 500$, $L(T) = 11.27$; for $T = 1000$, $L(T) = 13.39$.

u	T	$\widehat{P}(\tau_u < T)$	$\widehat{P}(\tau_u^L < T)$	$\hat{\tau}_{u,T}$	$\hat{\tau}_{u,T}^L$	**% Changes**	**No Effect**
	100	0.51	0.33	15.99	21.11	32.05	0.15
10	500	0.59	0.52	35.92	41.51	15.55	0.39
	1000	0.60	0.56	44.17	48.64	10.10	0.47
	100	0.16	0.04	35.16	47.97	36.44	0.00
30	500	0.27	0.18	89.10	106.78	19.85	0.07
	1000	0.28	0.22	109.79	124.45	13.35	0.12
	100	0.04	0.00	46.48	63.63	36.89	0.00
50	500	0.12	0.06	133.06	159.35	19.76	0.01
	1000	0.13	0.09	175.11	199.22	13.77	0.03
	100	0.01	0.00	55.19	71.45	29.44	0.00
70	500	0.05	0.02	177.18	211.36	19.29	0.00
	1000	0.06	0.03	233.06	267.53	14.79	0.01
	100	0.00	0.00	-	-	-	0.00
100	500	0.01	0.00	227.50	272.16	19.63	0.00
	1000	0.02	0.00	333.10	384.93	15.56	0.00

Improvements under EOL reinsurance are more substantial when the claims have a heavier tailed distribution (the Pareto$(1,2)$ case) as opposed to the medium-heavy and light tailed cases, where decreases in ruin probabilities and increases in conditional ruin times are comparatively minor. Comparing the results in Tables 4–6 to those in Tables 1–3 correspondingly, we see that when $u \leq 30$ the LCR treaty gives larger percentage improvements in the ruin probabilities over all three tail regimes, but this superiority diminishes as u grows. The same is true of the conditional lifetimes. The EOL method appears to perform markedly better than no reinsurance only when there are heavy tailed claims, whereas the LCR treaty shows consistent improvements over all three classes of claim distributions.

4.3. Comparisons Across Distributions

The simulations also allow us to make interesting comparisons across distributions, that is, between the Pareto, Inverse Gaussian and Gamma distributed cases. Intuitively our initial expectation might be that heavier tailed claims distributions would tend to lead to higher ruin probabilities than lighter tailed ones. Seemingly perplexing at first, then, might be that the ruin probability with or without reinsurance is, for small reserve levels ($u \leq 30$), larger for Inverse Gaussian claims than for Pareto-type claims, despite the fact that the Inverse Gaussian has much lighter tails than the power law distributions. This is true for both LCR (compare Columns 3 and 4 in Table 1 with Columns 3 and 4 in Table 3) and for EOL (compare Columns 3 and 4 in Table 4 with Columns 3 and 4 in Table 6), to varying degrees.

The explanation for this is that in general ruin probabilities and are not closely correlated with "heaviness" of tails, at least for moderate values of u. Ruin can occur by the accumulation of many small or medium sized jumps as well as by occasional huge jumps. When the claim size distribution follows Pareto$(1,2)$, we see in Figure 1 that most claims have relatively small sizes, roughly in the range 1 to 4. Eventually, though, as in Figure 1, a huge claim (having magnitude near 60 in the figure), will arrive. Thus, in a heavy tailed situation, the ruinous jump is very likely to be due to the largest claim. However ruin may occur by the accumulation of many smaller jumps. In Figure 4, for the Inverse Gaussian, we see this effect; there are many small and moderate sized claims which can accumulate to give ruin. The effect tends to be more noticeable when the initial reserve is small.

Figure 5 plots the tails of the three distributions used in the simulations. The tail of the Pareto$(1,2)$ is undoubtedly much bigger than for the other two distributions (not obvious in this figure, but apparent if the x–axis is extended further to the right). Correspondingly, there is less probability mass at small and medium sized claims than for the Gamma and Inverse Gaussian. The Gamma distribution has distinctly higher probability mass around relatively small (<5) claim sizes. In the medium size range (5–15), the Inverse Gaussian provides many substantial claims whose sum can contribute to ruin for a small reserve, more so than for a heavy tailed distribution.

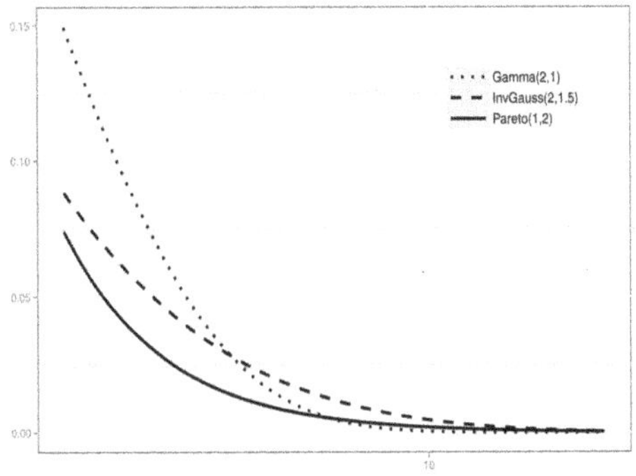

Figure 5. Tails of the three claim distributions involved in our simulations.

The table entries for $\hat{\tau}_{u,T}$ or $\hat{\tau}_{u,T}^{R}$ (with $R = M$ or L) are expected ruin times *conditional on ruin occurring by time* T for the reinsured processes, and consequently are not particularly meaningful across distributions. The percentage changes however are of some interest. In this case improvements due to reinsurance are greater for the Pareto than for the Inverse Gaussian, as evidenced by the values of the percentage-wise increases (Column 7) in all tables.

5. Cost of Reinsurance

Reinsurance treaties are undertaken to reduce risk, but there is a cost attached. In the present section we employ a dividend discount model to determine the available means by which the company is able to pay for reinsurance without reducing the firm's value, and how this affects risk as measured by the standard deviation of the company value.

5.1. Reinsurance Premium and Dividend Adjustment

We assume the company's current value is given by its future potential dividend stream, discounted to present value. Let ρ be the time value of money and assume that dividends are paid at constant rate d until the cedant's default, if this occurs. Then the claim surplus process in (1) must be modified to reflect the dividend payment:

$$Y_t := C_t + dt = \sum_{i=1}^{N_t} \xi_i - (c-d)t,\ t > 0. \tag{18}$$

The insurance company will require a specified safety loading θ to be in effect after the dividend is paid, so the net profit condition (2) is modified to

$$c - d = (1+\theta)\lambda\mu. \tag{19}$$

In (18), Y does not depend directly on c and d, only on $c-d$ through the value of θ. Since our main interest is in the cost of reinsurance, we will take c and d as given. In practice their values will be dependent on policyholders' willingness to pay and the choice of safety loading θ. Note also that the values of c in (1) and (18) must differ if $d > 0$ and the same safety loading is used in both cases.

The ruin time of the company is now given by $\tau_u = \inf\{t : Y_t > u\}$, for an initial capital level $u > 0$, and the cumulative dividend income by

$$I_u = d\int_0^{\tau_u} e^{-\rho t}\,\mathrm{d}t = \frac{d}{\rho}(1 - e^{-\rho\tau_u}). \tag{20}$$

The company is subsequently valued at

$$V_u = \mathbf{E}(I_u) = \frac{d}{\rho}\left(1 - \mathbf{E}(e^{-\rho\tau_u}; \tau_u < \infty)\right). \tag{21}$$

Now suppose a reinsurance scheme is incorporated, for which the cedant pays the reinsurer a premium which is constant in time at rate r. As a result of the consequent change in risk profile of the insurer, policyholders may be willing to pay an increased premium $c^* \geq c$, while shareholders will accept a reduced dividend $d^* \leq d$. The reinsured claim surplus process is then given by

$$Y_t^* = \sum_{i=1}^{N_t} \xi_i - (c^* - r - d^*)t - R_t,\ t > 0, \tag{22}$$

where the nondecreasing process R represents the reduction in claims due to reinsurance. This is given by (4) in the case of an EOL treaty, and by (5) for the LCR treaty. The reinsured claim surplus process has ruin time $\tau_u^* = \inf\{t : Y_t^* > u\}$, and the dividend income Equation (20) and the valuation Equation (21) are then modified by replacing d and τ_u with d^* and τ_u^* respectively. Thus

$$V_u^* = \mathbf{E}(I_u^*) = \mathbf{E}\left(d^*\int_0^{\tau_u^*} e^{-\rho t}\,\mathrm{d}t\right) = \frac{d^*}{\rho}\left(1 - \mathbf{E}(e^{-\rho\tau_u^*}; \tau_u^* < \infty)\right). \tag{23}$$

Since the aim of reinsurance is to prevent, or at least delay ruin, it is natural to require that $\tau_u^* \geq \tau_u$ for all $u > 0$. For the LCR and EOL reinsurance schemes, this can only be guaranteed if $c^* - r - d^* \geq c - d$, and so we make this assumption. Thus for a given new premium rate c^* and dividend rate d^*, the largest reinsurance premium the cedant would consider paying is $r = c^* - c + d - d^*$. When this condition holds, (22) becomes

$$Y_t^* = \sum_{i=1}^{N_t} \xi_i - (c-d)t - R_t := Y_t', \tag{24}$$

which does not depend on c^* or on d^*, and the valuation Equation (23) becomes

$$V_u^* = \frac{d^*}{\rho}\left(1 - \mathbf{E}(e^{-\rho\tau_u'}; \tau_u' < \infty)\right), \tag{25}$$

where $\tau_u' = \inf\{t : Y_t' > u\}$ does not depend on c^* or on d^*. In particular, reducing d^* reduces V_u^*.

Adopting a "utility indifference" rationale ([13,14]) whereby the reinsurance contract is beneficial for the cedant if its utility with reinsurance exceeds that without, and "utility" is taken to be the net present value of dividend income received, acceptable reinsurance contracts must satisfy $V_u^* \geq V_u$. So to find the maximal reinsurance premium r_{max} that the cedant is willing to pay for a reinsurance treaty R, we should maximize $r = c^* - c + d - d^*$ over all $d^* \in [0, d]$ for which $V_u^* \geq V_u$.

Since V_u^* is increasing in d^*, it follows immediately from (21) and (25) that the maximizing value of d^* is given by

$$d_{max}^*(u) = d\,\frac{1 - \mathbf{E}(e^{-\rho\tau_u}; \tau_u < \infty)}{1 - \mathbf{E}(e^{-\rho\tau_u'}; \tau_u' < \infty)}, \tag{26}$$

and the corresponding maximal reinsurance premium by

$$r_{max}(u) = c^* - c + d - d_{max}^*(u) = c^* - c + d\,\frac{\mathbf{E}(e^{-\rho\tau_u}; \tau_u < \infty) - \mathbf{E}(e^{-\rho\tau_u'}; \tau_u' < \infty)}{1 - \mathbf{E}(e^{-\rho\tau_u'}; \tau_u' < \infty)}. \tag{27}$$

One interesting aspect of (27) is that the factor

$$v_\theta(u) := \frac{\mathbf{E}(e^{-\rho\tau_u}; \tau_u < \infty) - \mathbf{E}(e^{-\rho\tau_u'}; \tau_u' < \infty)}{1 - \mathbf{E}(e^{-\rho\tau_u'}; \tau_u' < \infty)} \in (0,1) \tag{28}$$

depends on u and θ only, and not on d, and so represents the proportion of the dividend that may be used to pay the reinsurance premium for a given safety loading. Thus if the reinsurer demands a premium which does not exceed $dv_\theta(u)$, then, without reducing the value of the firm, the premium can be paid for entirely with a reduction in dividend. However if the insurance premium is in excess of $dv_\theta(u)$, then the insurance company will be forced to turn to policyholders to pay part of the cost if a reduction in the value of the firm is to be avoided.

The calculation of d_{max}, r_{max} and $v_\theta(u)$ amounts to the evaluation of the Laplace transforms of τ_u and τ_u', where τ_u' represents the ruin time under whichever type of reinsurance is being considered. For LCR, $\tau_u' = \tau_u^M$, and for EOL, $\tau_u' = \tau_u^L$ as specified in Sections 4.1 and 4.2. Currently there are no known theoretical results for the Laplace transform of τ_u^M, and it would be of interest and useful to derive them [2].

[2] Indeed, from a theoretical perspective, very little appears to be known about the effects of trimming on an insurance risk process and the subsequent ruin quantities. A series of approximate premium calculations for LCR treaties has been made in the literature; see, for example, [15,16], and [17–20], and their references.

In general the Laplace transforms need to be approximated by some means. We did this by using the simulations to directly estimate $\mathbf{E}e^{-\rho(\tau_u \wedge T)}$ for large T, and then observing that

$$0 \leq \mathbf{E}e^{-\rho(\tau_u \wedge T)} - \mathbf{E}(e^{-\rho\tau_u}; \tau_u < \infty) \leq e^{-\rho T}. \tag{29}$$

This applies equally well to τ_u'. As a check on this, and to decide on the number of simulations needed for sufficient accuracy, we also used Proposition A1 in the Appendix, which shows that

$$\mathbf{E}(e^{-\rho\tau_u}; \tau_u < \infty) = \mathbf{P}(\overline{Y}_{\mathbf{e}_\rho} > u) \tag{30}$$

where $\overline{Y}_t = \sup_{0 \leq s \leq t} Y_s$ and $\mathbf{e}_\rho$ is an independent exponential random variable with mean $1/\rho$. The right hand side of (30) can be estimated by simulating the paths of Y. (30) also holds if Y and τ_u are replaced by Y' and τ_u', so the Laplace transform of τ_u' can be estimated by the same means. Then d_{max}, r_{max} and $v_\theta(u)$ can be evaluated by

$$d^*_{max}(u) = d\,\frac{\mathbf{P}(\overline{Y}_{\mathbf{e}_\rho} \leq u)}{\mathbf{P}(\overline{Y}'_{\mathbf{e}_\rho} \leq u)} \qquad r_{max}(u) = c^* - c + d\left(1 - \frac{\mathbf{P}(\overline{Y}_{\mathbf{e}_\rho} \leq u)}{\mathbf{P}(\overline{Y}'_{\mathbf{e}_\rho} \leq u)}\right). \tag{31}$$

and

$$v_\theta(u) := 1 - \frac{\mathbf{P}(\overline{Y}_{\mathbf{e}_\rho} \leq u)}{\mathbf{P}(\overline{Y}'_{\mathbf{e}_\rho} \leq u)}. \tag{32}$$

5.2. Choice of Parameters

Below we report on simulations for some of the derived quantities in the present section. We want to give reasonably realistic simulation scenarios, so we have to make a credible choice of parameter values. There seems to be little guidance in the literature for doing this. In the end, the values we decided on are loosely based on some given in [21,22] together with some pragmatic considerations.

To start with, the initial reserve level u is only determined up to a scale constant. It can be thought of as units of $10 k, or $1 m, etc., as convenient. The mean claim size μis then to be taken relative to u.

The time unit we set to be 0.01 years = 3.65 days, so values of $T = 100, 500, 1000$, as designated in Section 3.3 and in the finite horizon scenarios considered in Section 5.5, correspond to 1 year, 5 years, 10 years. The time value of money is set at $\rho = 0.0005$. Taken together with the time unit specified, this corresponds to a discount rate of 5% p.a. To approximate the infinite time horizon we take $T = 13800$ in (29) so that the error of the asymptotic approximation to (30) is bounded by $e^{-13800\rho} \approx 10^{-3}$.

Safety loadings are taken to be $\theta = 0, 0.025, 0.05, 0.075, 0.1$. The expected claim size $\mu = 2$ and claims rate of $\lambda = 1$ are again as designated in Section 3.3. Thus claims accumulate on average an amount of 2 units per unit time length. This again is taken relative to u. The rate of premium inflow c and the dividend rate d need not be specified because as shown in Section 5.1, only the difference $c - d = (1+\theta)\lambda\mu$ is relevant for the computations in the present section, and this is fixed by our choice of θ, λ and μ.

How to decide on the value of L for the EOL reinsurance is also problematic. Again we could find little guidance in the literature [3]. We want to maintain comparability between the LCR and EOL schemes as far as possible. The values of L used in Tables 4–6 (finite horizon cases) were chosen so

[3] The work of [23] suggests that one common principle in choosing L is to keep it at "a level at which claims become very infrequent".

that the expected claim surpluses were equal at the specified expiration time T of the reinsurance treaties. These were found by solving (17). For the infinite time horizon problem, choosing L by first solving (17) and then letting $T \to \infty$, would render EOL reinsurance equivalent to no reinsurance, as $L \to \infty$ when $T \to \infty$. Hence in order to maintain comparability with LCR, for the simulations in the next section we chose L as a percentile of the claim distribution in such a way that the proportion of the dividend available to support the reinsurance premium was approximately the same between the EOL and LCR schemes.

5.3. *Proportion of Dividend Paid for Reinsurance*

Figure 6 exhibits the graph of $v_\theta(u)$ (see (32)) for each of the LCR and EOL treaties under each of the three claims distributions. For the EOL treaty, L is taken as the 98th percentile of the claims distribution. This percentile was chosen after some experimentation to give similar values for $v_\theta(u)$ in the LCR and EOL cases.

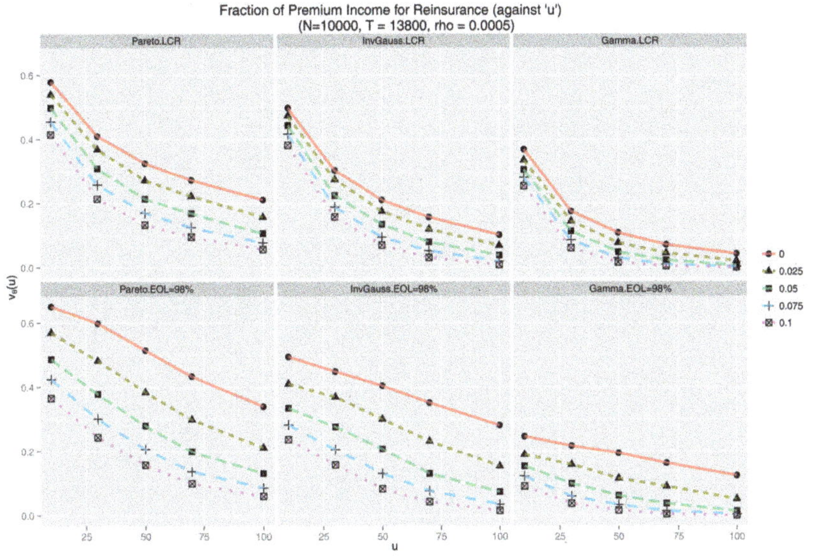

Figure 6. $v_\theta(u)$ (from (32)) is the proportion of the dividend available to pay for reinsurance without reducing the value of the firm. For Pareto, Inverse Gaussian and Gamma claim distributions, initial reserve levels $u = 10, 30, 50, 70, 100$, time value of money $\rho = 0.0005$, and safety loadings $\theta = 0, 0.025, 0.05, 0.075, 0.1$. Top panel: LCR; bottom panel, EOL with L taken as the 98th percentile of the claims distribution. Simulations are done with $N = 10,000$ sample paths.

In both the LCR and EOL frameworks, we observe from Figure 6 that $v_\theta(u)$ varies noticeably across u levels and distributions. As the reserve level increases from $u = 10$ to $u = 100$, the proportion of the dividend the company is willing to pay for reinsurance drops significantly, for each value of θ. The rate of decrease is larger for smaller values of u for LCR but rather uniform across u values for EOL. As the safety loading increases, the insurance company is only willing to apportion a smaller part of the dividend toward reinsurance.

It is interesting to note that $v_\theta(u)$ is bounded by 0.65 in all settings, indicating that the cedant is unwilling to pay more than 65% of the dividend to reinsurance despite the high risk of ruin in cases when θ is low and u is low (e.g., $\theta = 0$ and $u = 10$). In this high risk region, ruin, though being likely (certain when $\theta = 0$), will, with sufficient frequency, occur far enough into the future that the dividend stream lost due to ruin is negligible. Hence the cedant finds it unneccesary to dedicate more than 65% of dividend to reinsurance.

Since we have adopted a "utility indifference" rationale in calculating the premium, the expected values of the company, with and without reinsurance, are forced to be equal. This can also be readily checked: from (21), (23) and (31), we have

$$V_u^* = \frac{d_{max}^*(u)}{\rho}\mathbf{P}(\overline{Y}_{\mathbf{e}_\rho}^* \le u) = \frac{d}{\rho}\mathbf{P}(\overline{Y}_{\mathbf{e}_\rho} \le u) = V_u.$$

5.4. Standard Deviation of Dividend Income

In this section we compare the two reinsurance treaties, and the case with no reinsurance, with respect to the standard deviation of the dividend income. This will provide insight into the stabilising effect, or otherwise, of the reinsurance, which is a primary concern of the cedant company.

To calculate the standard deviation of the dividend income, observe that

$$\sigma(I_u) = \frac{d}{\rho}\sigma(1 - e^{-\rho\tau_u}),$$

while for the reinsured portfolio, by (26),

$$\begin{aligned}
\sigma(I_u^*) &= \frac{d_{max}^*(u)}{\rho}\sigma(1 - e^{-\rho\tau_u'}) \\
&= \frac{d}{\rho}\frac{1 - \mathbf{E}(e^{-\rho\tau_u}; \tau_u < \infty)}{1 - \mathbf{E}(e^{-\rho\tau_u'}; \tau_u' < \infty)}\sigma(1 - e^{-\rho\tau_u'}) \\
&= \frac{1 - \mathbf{E}(e^{-\rho\tau_u}; \tau_u < \infty)}{\sigma(1 - e^{-\rho\tau_u})}\frac{\sigma(1 - e^{-\rho\tau_u'})}{1 - \mathbf{E}(e^{-\rho\tau_u'}; \tau_u' < \infty)}\left(\frac{d}{\rho}\sigma(1 - e^{-\rho\tau_u})\right) \\
&= \frac{c_u^*}{c_u}\sigma(I_u),
\end{aligned} \tag{33}$$

where c_u is the coefficient of variation of $1 - e^{-\rho\tau_u}$ and c_u^* is the coefficient of variation of $1 - e^{-\rho\tau_u'}$. Observe that the change in standard deviation is by a factor

$$s_\theta(u) = \frac{c_u^*}{c_u} \tag{34}$$

which, as for $v_\theta(u)$, depends on u and θ but not on d. Values of $s_\theta(u)$ are summarised in Figure 7, which shows a clear reduction in the standard deviation of the dividend income received, compared with the case of no reinsurance, across all distributions, reserve levels and safety loadings, for both LCR and EOL. The reduction is most significant under the Pareto claim distribution, lessening as the tail of the claim distribution becomes lighter.

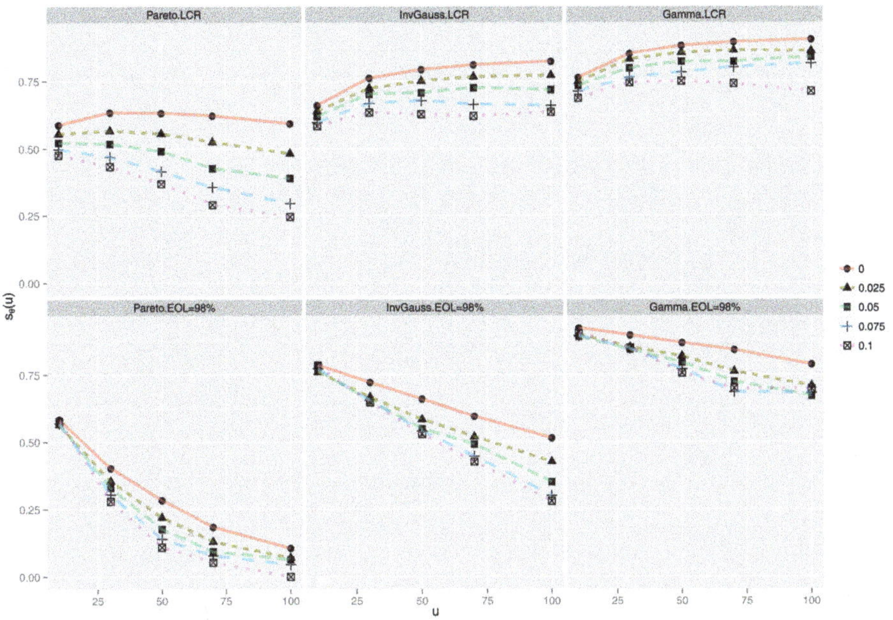

Figure 7. $s_\theta(u)$ (from (34), obtained by approximation at $T = 13,800$) is the ratio of the standard deviation of the dividend income obtained under reinsurance, to that without (infinite horizon case). For Pareto, Inverse Gaussian and Gamma claim distributions, initial reserve levels $u = 10$, 30, 50, 70, 100, time value of money $\rho = 0.0005$, and safety loadings $\theta = 0$, 0.025, 0.05, 0.075, 0.1. Top panel: LCR; bottom panel, EOL, with L taken as the 98th percentile of the claims distribution. Simulations are done with $N = 10,000$ sample paths.

As the safety loading θ increases, in almost all cases, the amount of variance reduction increases. However, looking across u levels, two clearly different trends emerge for LCR and EOL reinsurances. In the EOL setting, $s_\theta(u)$ decreases across all scenarios. In contrast, for LCR, $s_\theta(u)$ increases initially except for larger values θ in the Pareto case. Interestingly, small values of u exhibit the least variance reduction for EOL across all distributions, but, outside of the Pareto case, the most variance reduction for LCR, for the chosen parameters.

Overall, it may be adjudged that reinsurance has a non-trivial stabilising effect on the value of the company, particularly for heavier tailed claims distributions.

5.5. Dividend Adjustment and Reinsurance Premium, Finite Horizon

While it may be useful for planning and evaluation purposes to consider infinite horizon results, in practice a reinsurance treaty is not taken over an infinite time horizon, nor are dividends paid at a constant rate forever. Thus it is also prudent to value the company over a finite time horizon. In this case we should take into account both the value of the dividends paid, $V_{T,u}$, up to the expiration time T of the reinsurance treaty, and also the value of the (liquidated) portfolio, $F_{T,u}$, at time T. Thus, we replace (21) for the uninsured process with

$$V_{T,u} = \frac{d}{\rho}\left(1 - \mathbf{E}e^{-\rho(\tau_u \wedge T)}\right), \quad \text{together with} \quad F_{T,u} = e^{-\rho T}\mathbf{E}(u - Y_T)\mathbf{1}_{\{\tau_u > T\}}. \tag{35}$$

Similarly, for the reinsured process, (23) is replaced by

$$V^*_{T,u} = \frac{d^*}{\rho}\left(1 - \mathbf{E}e^{-\rho(\tau^*_u \wedge T)}\right), \quad \text{together with} \quad F^*_{T,u} = e^{-\rho T}\mathbf{E}(u - Y^*_T)\mathbf{1}_{\{\tau^*_u > T\}}. \tag{36}$$

By analogy with the infinite horizon case, we now wish to find the maximal reinsurance premium the cedant is willing to pay subject to $\tau^*_u \geq \tau_u$ a.s, $V^*_{T,u} \geq V_{T,u}$ and $F^*_{T,u} \geq F_{T,u}$ [4].

Applying the same logic as in Section 5.1, we find that $Y^* = Y'$ is given by (24) and does not depend on d^*. Since $Y'_t \leq Y_t$ for all $t \in [0,T]$, the condition $F^*_{T,u} \geq F_{T,u}$ is automatically satisfied. Thus, arguing as before, the maximizing dividend rate $d^*_{max}(T,u)$ and the corresponding maximal reinsurance premium $r_{max}(T,u)$ (now both depending on T and u) are found by equating $V_{T,u}$ and $V^*_{T,u}$ in (35) and (36). Setting

$$v_\theta(T,u) = \frac{\mathbf{E}\left(e^{-\rho(\tau_u \wedge T)} - e^{-\rho(\tau'_u \wedge T)}\right)}{1 - \mathbf{E}e^{-\rho(\tau'_u \wedge T)}} = 1 - \frac{\mathbf{P}(\overline{Y}_{\mathbf{e}_\rho} \leq u, \mathbf{e}_\rho \leq T)}{\mathbf{P}(\overline{Y}'_{\mathbf{e}_\rho} \leq u, \mathbf{e}_\rho \leq T)}, \tag{37}$$

(where the second equality in (37) follows from (A1) in the Appendix), we find that

$$d^*_{max}(T,u) = d\,[1 - v_\theta(T,u)] \text{ and } r_{max}(T,u) = c^* - c + d v_\theta(T,u). \tag{38}$$

Observe that $0 \leq v_\theta(T,u) \leq 1$, and, as in the infinite horizon case, $v_\theta(T,u)$ depends on u and θ but not on d. Thus, again, only a fixed proportion of the dividend is available to pay for reinsurance if the value of the firm is not to be reduced.

We simulated $v_\theta(T,u)$ with the parameters kept the same as in Tables 1– 3 for LCR reinsurance and Tables 4–6 for EOL reinsurance. As mentioned previously, this is done to maintain comparability between the two reinsurance schemes. In particular L is not the 98-th percentile, as in the infinite horizon case, but is chosen according to (17). The results are summarized in Figure 8, which displays several interesting features.

For both types of reinsurance, the value of $v_\theta(T,u)$ is slightly higher for a Pareto claim distribution than for an Inverse Gaussian, which is greater again than for a Gamma claim distribution. This is consistent with the results for the ruin times in Tables 1–6. It is notable that for $T = 100$, $u = 100$, regardless of θ and the claim distribution, the cedant is essentially unwilling to commit any of the dividend payment to reinsurance. Observe also that when the ruin probabilities under LCR and EOL are comparable in Tables 1–6, the values of $v_\theta(T,u)$ are also comparable, whereas when the ruin probability under LCR is smaller than under EOL, for example when $u = 10$ across all distributions, the cedant is able to contribute a larger portion of the dividend to reinsurance for LCR than EOL.

Considered as a function of u, $v_\theta(T,u)$ is decreasing and apparently convex in the case of the LCR treaty across all values of θ and T and all distributions, and this is also true for the EOL treaty in the $T = 100$ case. For larger T, $v_\theta(T,u)$ is neither decreasing nor convex for EOL. Indeed for small u, $v_\theta(T,u)$ is seen to be increasing. As a function of T, for fixed θ and u, $v_\theta(T,u)$ is increasing for the LCR treaty. For the EOL treaty this is not the case since, for example, $v_\theta(T,u)$ is decreasing for $u = 10$. Finally, for fixed T and u, the influence of the safety loading θ is much less pronounced than in Figure 6.

---

[4] There are other possibilities here, for example requiring $V^*_{T,u} + F^*_{T,u} \geq V_{T,u} + F_{T,u}$, instead of $V^*_{T,u} \geq V_{T,u}$ and $F^*_{T,u} \geq F_{T,u}$. We chose our formulation since it most clearly mirrors the infinite horizon problem. The interested reader may investigate other versions of the optimization problem.

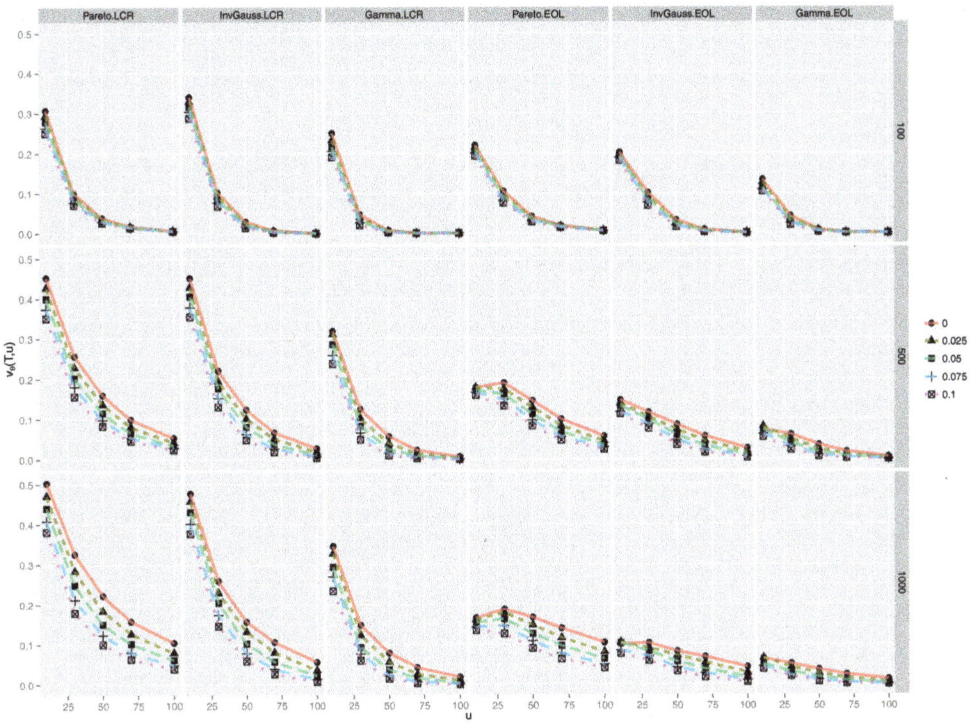

Figure 8. $v_\theta(T,u)$ (from (37)) is the proportion of the dividend available to pay for reinsurance without reduing the value of the firm. For LCR and EOL reinsurance policies, Pareto, Inverse Gaussian and Gamma claim distributions, initial reserve levels $u = 10, 30, 50, 70, 100$, time value of money $\rho = 0.0005$, and safety loadings $\theta = 0, 0.025, 0.05, 0.075, 0.1$. Top panel: $T = 100$; Middle panel: $T = 500$; Bottom panel: $T = 1000$. Retention level L for EOL reinsurance is the solution to (17). For $T = 100$, $L(T) = 5.64, 6.89, 4.49$; for $T = 500$, $L(T) = 12.62, 11.27, 6.10$; for $T = 1000$, $L(T) = 17.84, 13.39, 6.79$ for Pareto, Inverse Guassian and Gamma distributions respectively. Simulations are done with $N = 10,000$ sample paths.

6. Related Literature and Discussion

In this section we mention some related results and propose possibly fruitful areas for future investigation.

6.1. *Beveridge, Dickson and Wu Simulations*

The work of [24] considers a model with a constant dividend barrier. Their insurance risk model incorporates a reinsurance arrangement h that applies to an individual claim, so that if the individual claim amount is x, the reinsurer pays $x - h(x)$, and the primary insurer retains $h(x)$, where $0 \le h(x) \le x$. A dividend barrier, b, is specified such that when the surplus process, net of reinsurance, attains level b, dividends are paid out to shareholders at a specified rate c^* until the next claim occurs. The modified surplus process remains at level b until the next claim occurs, then falls by the (net of reinsurance) amount of that claim. On any subsequent occasion that the net of reinsurance surplus process attains level b, dividends are again payable at rate c^*. Ruin occurs when the surplus process falls below zero, and no dividends are payable after the time of ruin. (See also [25–27].)

Under such a barrier scheme, the cedant's ultimate ruin is certain, and the insurance operation is essentially being used to generate dividend income for the insurance company's shareholders. The work of [24] investigates the effect of the reinsurance for two possible versions of the function h: proportional reinsurance, with $h(x) = ax$, where $0 < a \leq 1$, and excess of loss reinsurance, as we define it.

The emphasis of their study is different to ours, being mainly concerned with the value of net income to shareholders. They find for example that proportional reinsurance does not increase the expected present value of net income to shareholders, at least for the situations they consider, although "it is possible to increase the expected present value of net income to shareholders by effecting (EOL) reinsurance". Other than this their results are mixed and not comparable with ours since in our setup ruin is not certain and we can investigate increases in ruin time with reinsurance and the other effects listed in Section 5.

6.2. *Trimming More Values*

The LCR scheme can be generalised by removing from the claims surplus process, not just the largest claim up to time t, but also the 2nd largest, 3rd largest, etc., up to a total of the r largest claims, $r = 2, 3, 4, \ldots$. In this connection [28] discuss two kinds of reinsurance systems in particular, using the nomenclatures ECOMOR and LCR. ECOMOR stands for *excédent du coû moyen relatif*. In this scheme, the reinsured amount is the sum of the differences between the r largest claims, and the r-th largest, $r = 1, 2, \ldots$, up to a designated time. It was introduced into the actuarial literature by [29]. LCR in [28] is largest claims reinsurance as we define it, in which the reinsured amount is the sum of the r largest claims up to a designated time.

A considerable amount of work has been done on these and related methods; for background we refer to [30], who gives an overview of commonly used forms of reinsurance, and [28] for further literature. The [28] results [5] are concerned with limiting distributions of the reinsured amounts under the ECOMOR and LCR schemes, with subexponential, extremal class or regular variation assumptions on the tail of the claim distribution. They illustrate their results with simulations of the distributions.

Recall the discussion in Section 4.1, where we observed that the Inverse Gaussian case has several sizeable claims apart from the largest one. In order to achieve a similar level of efficiency for the reinsurance policy as in the Pareto case, the cedant can seek covers on the sum of the r largest claims. Then arises the question of an optimal choice of r, etc., which we do not go into here.

Some distributional identities for the r-trimmed version of a Lévy process have been studied in [31]. The continuity properties of various trimming functionals in cádlág space are investigated in [32]. Their formulae could be used to further analyse the first passage time (ruin time) and other path properties of r-trimmed processes.

6.3. *The "Light-Medium-Heavy" Classification*

It is important to stress that our division of claims distributions into "Light", "Medium" and "Heavy"-tailed is not definitive, and the "lightness" of tails is not a uniquely defined concept. For example, if this were to be defined by whether the ratio of tails is asymptotically smaller for one than for the other, the "light-tailed" Gamma(2,1) distribution in (7) is judged "heavier" than the "medium"-tailed Inverse Gaussian in (11) for certain values of the parameters [6] a and b.

---

5 The work of [28] allows a generalised version of the compound Poisson model where the N_t in (1) is replaced by a mixed Poisson process. But their simulations are done with the compound Poisson.

6 But our particular choice of $a = 2$ and $b = 1.5$ makes the Inverse Gaussian heavier-tailed than the Gamma(2,1).

Nevertheless, the classification is a useful way of specifying a range of tail behaviours on which to base simulation investigations.

The work of [33] gives a detailed analysis of the classical Norwegian Fire Claims data set, comparing a number of distributions for goodness of fit and using them to calculate value-at-risk and related measures. Of the six probability models considered some are heavy tailed, such as the GPD (generalised Pareto), others are lighter-tailed (the Weibull-Pareto). They argue "it is certainly tempting to conclude that simpler distributions, such as GPD and FT (folded-t) are preferred for the task of measuring tail risk" but "lead to substantially different risk evaluations". This underlines the value of investigations like ours for understanding the behaviour of the risk process across a variety of tail regimens. The work of [33] further stress the need for formal statistical analysis for measuring and pricing tail risk.

In any case, as we discussed in Section 4.1, the behaviour of ruin probabilities and ruin times for finite u is not necessarily closely correlated with tail heaviness, however defined. These characteristics can be strongly influenced by the distribution of small and medium claim sizes. In this context we refer to discussions in [34,35] where asymptotic analyses of path properties of the process are given for convolution equivalent distributions, and related to the ruin prospects of the company.

On the other hand, of course, in any scenario, reinsurance in either of the ways we have defined it increases the lifetime of the company.

6.4. *Lévy Insurance Risk Models*

The LCR model can be extended in various directions. Insofar as our analysis is restricted to the classical compound Poisson risk process, it can be generalised to a broader class of processes, the "general Lévy insurance risk models". See for example [7–10,36,37] , where these models and some subclasses of them are considered in this context.

7. Summary

We considered two types of reinsurance, EOL and LCR, and investigated the pros and cons of each by simulations. We took as outcomes the extent of increases in ruin times and decreases in ruin probabilities as a result of reinsurance. Using a dividend discount model, we also investigated the amount of the dividend available to pay for reinsurance and the consequent effect on the standard deviation of the company value.

We found in Section 4.2 that the EOL method performs markedly better than no reinsurance in terms of lower ruin probability and longer ruin times mainly when there are heavy tailed claims, whereas the LCR treaty shows consistent improvements over all three classes of claim distributions.

Regarding payment for reinsurance, we saw in Figures 6 and 8 that for a Pareto claim distribution a greater proportion of the dividend is available to pay the reinsurance premium than for Inverse Gaussian, which is greater again than for a Gamma claim distribution. Over a finite time horizon, with equal expected aggregate claims, LCR is at least as effective as EOL in averting ruin (Tables 1–6). When they are equally effective, the proportion of the dividend available to pay for reinsurance is comparable. When LCR is more effective, then the proportion is greater for LCR than for EOL (Figure 5). LCR and EOL both reduce risk considerably as compared with no reinsurance, in a variety of situations, as measured by the standard deviation of the dividend income.

Acknowledgments: This work was partially supported by Simons Foundation Grant #226863, ARC Grant DP1092502, DFG grant SZ/321/2-1 and the ARC Centre of Excellence for Mathematical and Statistical Frontiers (ACEMS).

Author Contributions: All authors contributed equally to the development of the theory and the application in this paper as it evolved. The initial inspiration arose during discussions among Y.F., P.G., R.M., T.W. at a conference on Lévy processes and their applications held at Kioloa in February 2014. Later A.S. initiated the ideas in Section 5 which were then further developed by all parties. Y.F. and T.W. were also responsible for calculations, simulations and figures.

Conflicts of Interest: The authors declare no conflict of interest.

Appendix A. Laplace Transforms

Here we state some useful results concerning Laplace transforms of passage times. We used the formulae in this section for checking the asymptotic values in Section 5.1.

Simulating the Laplace transforms: The Laplace transforms $\mathbf{E}e^{-\rho(\tau_u \wedge T)}$ etc. for finite or infinite times T can be simulated using the following formulae.

Proposition A1. *For any $\rho > 0, T > 0$ and $u \geq 0$,*

$$\mathbf{E}e^{-\rho(\tau_u \wedge T)} = e^{-\rho T} + \mathbf{P}(\overline{Y}_{\mathbf{e}_\rho} > u, \mathbf{e}_\rho \leq T), \tag{A1}$$

while for $\rho > 0$ and $u \geq 0$,

$$\mathbf{E}(e^{-\rho\tau_u}; \tau_u < \infty) = \mathbf{P}(\overline{Y}_{\mathbf{e}_\rho} > u). \tag{A2}$$

The same results hold if Y and τ_u are replaced by Y' and τ'_u.

Proof. For (A1), we have

$$\begin{aligned}
\mathbf{E}e^{-\rho(\tau_u \wedge T)} &= \mathbf{E}(e^{-\rho\tau_u}; \tau_u \leq T) + e^{-\rho T}\mathbf{P}(\tau_u > T) \\
&= \int_{[0,T]} e^{-\rho t}\mathbf{P}(\tau_u \in \mathrm{d}t) + e^{-\rho T}\mathbf{P}(\tau_u > T) \\
&= e^{-\rho T}\mathbf{P}(\tau_u \leq T) + \int_{[0,T]} \rho e^{-\rho t}\mathbf{P}(\tau_u \leq t)\mathrm{d}t + e^{-\rho T}\mathbf{P}(\tau_u > T) \\
&= e^{-\rho T} + \int_{[0,T]} \rho e^{-\rho t}\mathbf{P}(\overline{Y}_t > u)\mathrm{d}t \\
&= e^{-\rho T} + \mathbf{P}(\overline{Y}_{\mathbf{e}_\rho} > u, \mathbf{e}_\rho \leq T).
\end{aligned}$$

A check of the calculation shows this also holds if Y and τ_u are replaced by Y' and τ'_u. Letting $T \to \infty$ then proves (A2) in both cases. □

Although we did not use it in the simulation exercises, the asymptotic dividend d^*_{max} can be estimated similarly using the formula

$$\mathbf{P}(\overline{Y}_{\mathbf{e}_\rho} \leq u, \mathbf{e}_\rho \leq s) \leq \mathbf{P}(\overline{Y}_{\mathbf{e}_\rho} \leq u) \leq \mathbf{P}(\overline{Y}_{\mathbf{e}_\rho} \leq u, \mathbf{e}_\rho \leq s) + e^{-\rho s} \tag{A3}$$

for $\mathbf{P}(\overline{Y}_{\mathbf{e}_\rho} \leq u)$. (Take s large enough that $e^{-\rho s}$ is negligible.)

Explicit Formula for Exponentially Distributed Claims: The Laplace transform of τ_u has been well studied in the literature; see for example [37–41]. Explicit, or even semi-explicit, formulae are rarely available. The simplest instance of an explicit formula is when claims are exponentially distributed with mean $1/\delta$. Then by Proposition 4.1.2 of [6],

$$\mathbf{E}(e^{-\rho\tau_u}; \tau_u < \infty) = e^{-\nu u}\left(1 - \frac{\nu}{\delta}\right),$$

where ν is given by

$$\nu = \frac{(c-d)\delta - \lambda - \rho + \sqrt{((c-d)\delta - \lambda - \rho)^2 + 4(c-d)\rho\delta}}{2(c-d)}.$$

Setting $\rho = 0$ gives the probability of ultimate ruin as

$$\mathbf{P}(\tau_u < \infty) = \frac{\exp(-\theta\delta u(1+\theta)^{-1})}{1+\theta},$$

where $c - d = (1+\theta)\lambda\delta^{-1}$.

An Upper Bound for $P(\tau_u^M < \infty)$*:* With the notation in (13), assume the Cramér case, so that (6) is satisfied for some $\nu_0 > 0$. Assume that C_t is defined on a filtered probability space $(\Omega, \mathcal{F}_t, \mathcal{F}, P)$, and let P^* be the exponentially tilted probability measure given by

$$\mathrm{d}P^* := e^{\nu_0 C_t}\mathrm{d}P \quad \text{on } \mathcal{F}_t.$$

Then

$$\mathrm{d}P = e^{-\nu_0 C_t}\mathrm{d}P^*$$

and

$$\mathrm{d}P = e^{-\nu_0 C_{\tau_u^M}}\mathrm{d}P^*$$

on $\mathcal{F}_t \cap \{\tau_u^M < \infty\}$. It follows from Corollary 3.11 of [37] that

$$\begin{aligned} e^{\nu_0 u} P(\tau_u^M < \infty) &= e^{\nu_0 u} E^* \exp\left(-\nu_0 C_{\tau_u^M}\right) \\ &= E^* \exp\left(-\nu_0 \left(C^M_{\tau_u^M} - u + Z_u^M\right)\right) \end{aligned}$$

where $C^M_{\tau_u^M} - u \geq 0$ is the overshoot for the trimmed process over level u and,

$$Z_u^M = \sup_{0 < s \leq N_{\tau_u^M}} \xi_i \geq 0.$$

So we get

$$e^{\nu_0 u} P(\tau_u^M < \infty) \leq E^* \exp\left(-\nu_0 Z_u^M\right).$$

Assuming ξ_1 has unbounded support, then $Z_u^M \to \infty$ almost surely as $u \to \infty$, so $e^{\nu_0 u} P(\tau_u^M < \infty) \to 0$, whereas $e^{\nu_0 u} P(\tau_u < \infty) \to c > 0$. This shows that the probability of eventual ruin is much smaller when trimming and suggests a way of quantifying this effect via the overshoot of the trimmed process.

References

1. Böcker, K. and Klüppelberg, C. Multivariate models for operational risk. *Quant. Finance* **2010**, *10*, 855–869.
2. Embrechts, P.; Klüppelberg, C.; Mikosch, T. *Modelling Extremal Events for Insurance and Finance*; Applications of Mathematics (New York); Springer: Berlin, Germany, 1997.
3. Embrechts, P.; Samorodnitsky, G. Ruin problem and how fast stochastic processes mix. *Ann. Appl. Probab.* **2003**, *13*, 1–36.
4. Doherty, N.; Smetters, K. Moral hazard in reinsurance markets. *J. Risk Insur.* **2005**, *72*, 375–391.
5. Yan, Z. Testing for moral hazard in reinsurance markets. *Manag. Finance* **2013**, *39*, 696–713.
6. Asmussen, S. *Ruin Probabilities*; Advanced Series on Statistical Science Applied Probability; World Scientific Publishing Co., Inc.: Hackensack, NJ, USA, 2000; Volume 2.

7. Doney, R.A.; Klüppelberg, C.; Maller, R.A. Passage time and fluctuation calculations for subexponential Lévy processes. *Bernoulli* **2016**, *22*, 1491–1519.
8. Klüppelberg, C.; Kyprianou, A.; Maller, R.A. Ruin probabilities and overshoots for general Lévy insurance risk processes. *Ann. Appl. Probab.* **2004**, *14*, 1766–1801.
9. Griffin, P.S.; Maller, R.A.; Roberts, D. Finite time ruin probabilities for tempered stable insurance risk processes. *Insur. Math. Econom.* **2013**, *53*, 478–489.
10. Griffin, P.S.; Maller, R.A.; van Schaik, K. Asymptotic distributions of the overshoot and undershoots for the Lévy insurance risk process in the Cramér and convolution equivalent cases. *Insur. Math. Econom.* **2012**, *51*, 382–392.
11. Chhikara, R.J.; Folks, J.L. *The Inverse Gaussian Distribution: Theory, Methodology, and Applications*; Marcel Dekker: New York, NY, USA, 1989.
12. Asmussen, S.; Binswanger, K. Simulation of ruin probabilities for subexponential claims. *Astin Bull.* **1997**, *27*, 297–318.
13. Gerber, H.U. *An Introduction to Mathematical Risk Theory*; Monograph No. 8; University of Pennsylvania: Philadelphia, PA, USA, 1979; p. 478.
14. Gerber, H.U.; Loisel, S. *Why Ruin Theory Should Be of Interest for Insurance Practitioners and Risk Managers Nowadays*; Actuarial and Financial Mathematics: Bruxelles, Belgium, 2012.
15. Benktander, G. Largest claims reinsurance (LCR). A quick method to calculate LCR-risk rates from excess of loss risk rates. *Astin Bull.* **1978**, *10*, 54–58.
16. Berglund, R.M. A note on the net premium for a generalized largest claims reinsurance cover. *Astin Bull.* **1998**, *28*, 153–162.
17. Kremer, E. Rating of largest claims and ECOMOR reinsurance treaties for large portfolios. *Astin Bull.* **1982**, *13*, 47–56.
18. Kremer, E. Distribution-free upper bounds on the premiums of the LCR and ECOMOR treaties. *Insur. Math. Econom.* **1983**, *2*, 209–213.
19. Kremer, E. The asymptotic efficiency of largest claims reinsurance treaties. *Astin Bull.* **1990**, *20*, 11–22.
20. Kremer, E. Largest claims reinsurance premiums under possible claims dependence. *Astin Bull.* **1998**, *28*, 257–267.
21. Grandell, J. *Aspects of Risk Theory*; Springer Series in Statistics; Springer: New York, NY, USA, 1991.
22. Wikstad, N. Exemplification of ruin probabilities. *Astin Bull.* **1971**, *6*, 147–152.
23. Bradshaw, A.J.; Bride, M.; English, A.B.; Hindley, D.J.; Maher, G.P.M. *Reinsurance and Retentions—A London Market Actuaries' Group Paper*; Casualty Actuarial Society: Arlington, VA, USA, 1991; Volume I.
24. Beveridge, C.J.; Dickson, D.C.M.; Wu, X. Optimal dividends under reinsurance. *Bulletin de l'Association Suisse des Actuaires* **2008**, *2*, 149–166.
25. De Finetti, B. Su un'impostazion alternativa dell teoria collecttiva del rischio. *Trans. Internat. Congr. Actuar.* **1957**, *2*, 433–443.
26. Dickson, D.C.M.; Waters, H.R. Some optimal dividends problems. *Astin Bull.* **2004**, *34*, 49–74.
27. Gerber, H.U.; Shiu, E.S.W. Optimal dividends: Analysis with Brownian motion. *N. Am. Actuar. J.* **2004**, *8*, 1–20.
28. Ladoucette, S.A.; Teugels, J.L. Reinsurance of large claims. *J. Comput. Appl. Math.* **2006**, *186*, 163–190.
29. Thépaut, A. Une nouvelle forme de réassurance: Le traité d'excédent du coût moyen relatif (ECOMOR). *Bull. Trim. Inst. Actu. Fr.* **1950**, *49*, 273–343.
30. Teugels, J.L. *Reinsurance Actuarial Aspects*; EURANDOM Report 2003-006; Technical University of Eindhoven: Eindhoven, The Netherlands, 2003.
31. Buchmann, B.; Fan, Y.; Maller, R.A. Distributional representations and dominance of a Lévy process over its maximal jump processes. *Bernoulli* **2016**, *22*, 2325–2371.
32. Buchmann, B.; Fan, Y.; Maller, R.A. Functional Laws for Trimmed Lévy Processes. Available online: https://arxiv.org/abs/1609.07206 (accessed on 21 November 2016).
33. Brazauskas, V.; Kleefeld, A. Modeling Severity and Measuring Tail Risk of Norwegian Fire Claims. *N. Am. Actuar. J.* **2016**, *20*, 1–16.
34. Griffin, P.S. Convolution equivalent Lévy processes and first passage times. *Ann. Appl. Probab.* **2013**, *23*, 1506–1543

35. Griffin, P.S.; Maller, R.A. Path decomposition of ruinous behaviour for a general Lévy insurance risk process. *Ann. Appl. Probab.* **2012**, *22*, 1411–1449.
36. Garrido, J.; Morales, M. On The expected discounted penalty function for Lévy risk processes. *N. Am. Actuar. J.* **2006**, *10*, 196–216.
37. Kyprianou, A. *Introductory Lectures on Fluctuations of Lévy Processes with Applications*; Springer: Berlin, Germany, 2006.
38. Dickson, D.C.M.; Willmot, G.E. The density of the time to ruin in the classical Poisson risk model. *Astin Bull.* **2005**, *35*, 45–60.
39. Elghribi, M.; Haouala, E. Laplace transform of the time of ruin for a perturbed risk process driven by a subordinator. *IAENG Int. J. Appl. Math.* **2009**, *39*, 221–230.
40. Lima, F.D.P.; Garcia, J.M.A.; Egídio dos Reis, A.D. Fourier/Laplace transforms and ruin probabilities. *Astin Bull.* **2002**, *32*, 91–105.
41. Percheskii, E.A.; Rogozin, B.A. On the joint distribution of random variables associated with fluctuations of a process with independent increments. *Theory Probab. Appl.* **1969**, *14*, 410–423.

risks

MDPI

Article

Mathematical Analysis of Replication by Cash Flow Matching

Jan Natolski and Ralf Werner *

University of Augsburg, Universitätsstraße 14, 86159 Augsburg, Germany; jan.natolski@math.uni-augsburg.de
* Correspondence: ralf.werner@math.uni-augsburg.de; Tel.: +49-821-598-2220

Academic Editor: Luca Regis
Received: 17 August 2016; Accepted: 24 February 2017; Published: 28 February 2017

Abstract: The replicating portfolio approach is a well-established approach carried out by many life insurance companies within their Solvency II framework for the computation of risk capital. In this note, we elaborate on one specific formulation of a replicating portfolio problem. In contrast to the two most popular replication approaches, it does not yield an analytic solution (if, at all, a solution exists and is unique). Further, although convex, the objective function seems to be non-smooth, and hence a numerical solution might thus be much more demanding than for the two most popular formulations. Especially for the second reason, this formulation did not (yet) receive much attention in practical applications, in contrast to the other two formulations. In the following, we will demonstrate that the (potential) non-smoothness can be avoided due to an equivalent reformulation as a linear *second order cone program* (SOCP). This allows for a numerical solution by efficient second order methods like interior point methods or similar. We also show that—under weak assumptions—existence and uniqueness of the optimal solution can be guaranteed. We additionally prove that—under a further similarly weak condition—the fair value of the replicating portfolio equals the fair value of liabilities. Based on these insights, we argue that this unloved stepmother child within the replication problem family indeed represents an equally good formulation for practical purposes.

Keywords: life insurance; replicating portfolio; market consistent valuation; cash flow matching; fair value; stochastic Fermat–Torricelli problem

---

1. Introduction

Market-consistent valuation has gained increasing importance in the risk management of life insurance policies (e.g., Bauer et al. [1]). However, many life insurance contracts have features which are too complicated to undertake analytical analysis. These include participating contracts, surrender options, and guaranteed interest rates, to name a few. They leave only little structure in the payoff profile, thus making analytical risk neutral valuation almost impossible. Therefore, one has to resort to some type of Monte Carlo method for market-consistent valuation of life insurance policies. As a result, Monte Carlo methods of various types have attracted a lot of attention in recent research. Although Monte Carlo methods work quite well for one specific valuation, they prove to be rather inefficient for repeated application in risk capital computation. For instance, the computational inefficiency of nested Monte Carlo methods for risk capital computation (cf. below and Figure 1 for a brief description, or see Bauer et al. [1] for more details) has led to an investigation of alternative methods. Andreatta and Corradin [2], Baione et al. [3], Glasserman and Yu [4], Stentoft [5], and several other authors apply or analyze the well-known least squares Monte Carlo approach, which was originally introduced by Longstaff and Schwartz [6] and Tsitsiklis and van Roy [7] to price American options. Bergmann [8] also mentions the stochastic mesh method of Broadie and Glasserman [9], although no application to life insurance policies is known to our best knowledge.

In hindsight, Pelsser [10] probably first suggested valuation of with-profits guaranteed annuity options—which are typical life insurance products—via *static replicating portfolios*. Although static hedging seems overly simplistic—especially compared to more advanced dynamic hedging—a remarkably good fit of the behaviour of annuity options was obtained by a static portfolio of vanilla swaptions. In general, by constructing such a static replicating portfolio, one tries to form a static portfolio of a finite number of selected financial instruments which are easy to price, such that they generate cash-flows which approximate cash-flows on the liability side at each point in time and in each scenario. If this approximation is accurate, one obtains a good estimate of the market value of liabilities from the fair value of the replicating portfolio. Further, the market consistent embedded value (MCEV) can be obtained accordingly by subtracting this value from the value of the insurer's asset holdings. One could of course determine the value of liabilities directly by Monte Carlo simulations: generate risk-neutral sample paths of liability cash-flows and compute the mean of present values of the discounted cash-flows (e.g., Grosen and Jørgensen [11]). However, as the Solvency II capital requirement demands the computation of the 99.5% value at risk (see EIOPA [12], page 7) of the MCEV distribution in one year under the real world measure, it is not sufficient to compute the MCEV today, but its distribution in the future. This requires the aforementioned nested approach; see Figure 1.

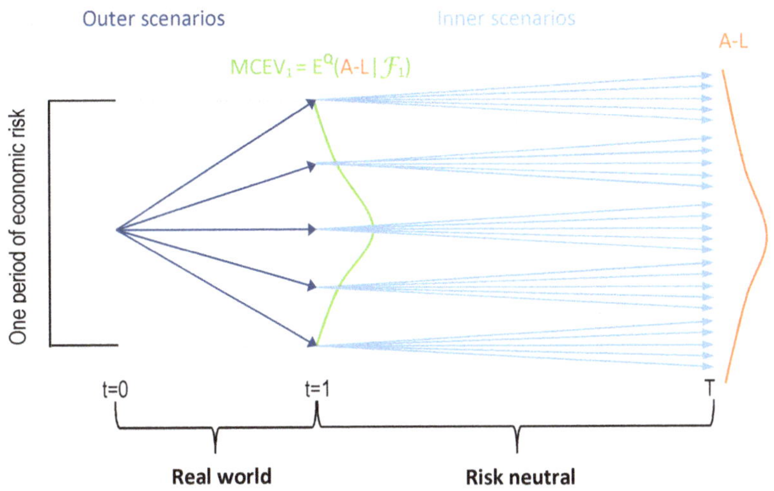

Figure 1. Replicating portfolio approach: Each node at $t = 1$ and $t = T$ represents a state of the portfolio and liabilities. The target is to estimate the 99.5% quantile of the market consistent embedded value (MCEV) distribution at $t = 1$.

As static replication is much more simplistic than dynamic replication, it has been an open question until quite recently, as to whether the approach of replicating portfolio can actually work. Although replication seems to resemble traditional immunization approaches, one major difference stands out: on the one hand, immunization works well in one period (as sensitivities to risk factors have been immunized), but leaves the portfolio un-immunized in the next period, which requires re-immunization (this is the main idea of dynamic delta hedging). On the other hand, replication matches cash flows, so there is hope that although one is not fully immunized in the first period, the immunization is still reasonable in the next period, as future cash flows are still replicated well. Very recent results have shown that replication indeed works under quite general setups, with efficiency comparable to the least squares Monte Carlo approach. The first theoretical foundations for replicating portfolios have been given in a series of papers by Beutner et al. [13], Pelsser and Schweizer [14], and Beutner et al. [15]. They analyze the asymptotic behaviour of matching the terminal value of liabilities (instead of matching cash flows; see below for more details) as the number of scenarios and the number of replicating assets grows at specific relative speeds. Recently, Cambou and Filipovic [16] proved that the matching of terminal values indeed has a mathematical foundation in the sense that a good match of the terminal values is strongly intertwined with a good approximation of the risk measure of the future MCEV (i.e., the resulting risk capital). Simultaneously, Natolski and Werner [17] demonstrated that this foundation holds for any form of matching problem in Natolski and Werner [18] (and many more), especially including all cash flow matching and all terminal value matching problems considered here. In both Cambou and Filipovic [16] and Natolski and Werner [18], it is shown that it is possible to change from the real world measure in the first period to the risk neutral measure while maintaining the strong link between objective function and error in risk capital. These results provide the basis for the practically most relevant replication setup[1] where only the risk neutral measure is considered (see Section 2 for the mathematical setup).

The replicating portfolio approach represents a well-established approach carried out by many life insurance companies within their Solvency II framework for the computation of market risk capital. It is very specific to life insurance companies, and to our best knowledge so far, not used outside life insurance. We note that it could in theory also be used in banks for improving risk figure computation for hard-to-price portfolios[2].

Of course, only considering financial instruments might fall short of matching actuarial risks like mortality or lapse risk. This is one of the well-known weaknesses of replicating portfolios, and usually leads to a remaining mismatch. However, as replicating portfolios are usually only applied within the market risk computation in Solvency II, this only represents a minor issue of replicating portfolios in practice.

As already briefly indicated above, there exist different choices for the specific matching problem. In Natolski and Werner [18], some of these criteria were already investigated in more detail. The focus there was put on the two criteria which are most popular in the insurance industry:

- *Squared cash flow matching*: this was probably the first formulation considered in the context of replicating portfolios. Here, the difference of cash flows at the same time point is measured by the squared L^2-norm, and the sum of these is used as matching criterion. This problem is called (RP_{SCF}) in the following.
- *Terminal value matching*: as an alternative to the cash flow matching criterion, terminal value matching—called (RP_{TV}) below—was introduced by Oechslin et al. [20]. The main idea is that it is expected that a good approximation of the risk capital can already be obtained if the *value* of the cash flows is matched sufficiently well, while the timing of the cash flows should not be of any importance. Usually, cash flows are aggregated to the terminal time point, leading to the consideration of *terminal values*. This point of view was mathematically supported in Natolski and Werner [17].

These two (and other) choices might differ in important properties:

- Depending on the choice of the fitting criterion, similarly good fits of the fitting criterion lead to differing good or even only reasonably good approximations of the risk capital figure. In summary, terminal value matching provides better bounds than cash flow matching. Further, squared cash flow matching provides worse bounds than cash flow matching (to be defined below). Details on the exact relationships are provided in Natolski and Werner [17].

---

1 In Natolski and Werner [18] it is argued that working with the risk neutral measure is feasible, while it is better to keep the mix of measures as indicated in Figure 1.

2 A recent paper by Broadie et al. [19] gives some first arguments in this direction. Although the paper does not explicitly treat replicating portfolio, but focuses on least squares Monte Carlo methods, the idea can also be extended to replicating portfolios. The reason for this is that replication and least squares Monte Carlo are strongly interconnected, as has been shown by Glasserman and Yu [4].

- Depending on the choice of the fitting criterion, the solution of the corresponding optimization problems might pose difficulties. Although all formulations usually lead to convex problems, not all problems might be strictly convex, and thus may have non-unique optimal solutions. Further, non-smooth problems might be much harder to solve than smooth problems. Finally, some fitting criteria (for instance, those based on L^1-norms instead of L^2-norms) lead to an increase of the problem dimension with increasing number of scenarios, while others do not face this issue.
- It is expected by practitioners that the fair value of the replicating portfolio also matches the fair value of the liabilities. This has already been proven for the two most practically relevant criteria, but this question remains open for other criteria.

The analysis of the replication problems in Natolski and Werner [18] focused on the two most popular matching criteria, as these are a) quite easy to analyze and b) are strongly connected. As has been shown in Natolski and Werner [18], the terminal value match can be seen as a squared cash flow match plus an additional dynamic trading strategy moving cash flows optimally in time. From a theoretical perspective, both choices provide a good link between matching criterion and approximation of risk capital (see Natolski and Werner [17]), although terminal value matching dominates squared cash flow matching. Further, both problems lead to strictly convex quadratic optimization problems possessing a unique optimal solution (under rather weak assumptions). From a practical perspective, however, both problems show some unwanted behaviour. Extensive numerical tests (Daul and Vidal [21]) have shown that the out-of-sample performance of terminal value matching is worse than the corresponding performance of (squared) cash flow matching. However, the latter problem reacts more sensitively to the scaling and the conditioning of the data than terminal value matching due to increased dimensions of relevant covariance matrices. The bad out-of-sample performance of terminal value matching can be linked to the property that it actually already includes a dynamic cash flow distribution strategy. This indicates that an unwanted overfitting takes place; i.e., there are too many optimization variables given only a few number of scenarios. As pointed out, it is not feasible to provide more scenarios, as these are computationally quite expensive. Therefore, the consideration of more enhanced replication—for example, by a more dynamic replication strategy—is clearly not advocated.

For the above reasons, it might make sense to look for alternative criteria which have the potential to successfully address these issues. For this purpose, we consider a modified cash flow matching problem—called (RP_{CF})—where the penalization of cash flows does not use the squared $\mathcal{L}^2$-norm, but just the $\mathcal{L}^2$-norm itself. This problem has already been briefly considered in Natolski and Werner [18], but a full analysis was out of the scope of that paper.

Compared to the other two problems (RP_{SCF}) and $(RP_{\widetilde{TV}})$, it has a more complicated objective function, since the objective function cannot be expressed as a convex quadratic function. Thus, it is impossible to obtain an explicit expression for the solution of the problem, and results on the existence and uniqueness of a solution are not straightforward. Further, the objective function of (RP_{CF}) might be non-smooth at certain points. We believe that it is for this reason that problem formulation (RP_{CF}) did not yet get as much attention as the other two formulations, both from practitioners and academics.

In the following, we will argue that on the contrary, there are good reasons to believe that (RP_{CF}) is indeed at least as preferable as (RP_{SCF}) or $(RP_{\widetilde{TV}})$. To be able to do so, we first provide the detailed proofs for the existence and uniqueness of the solution under weak assumptions. Further, we show that despite the similarity to the famous Fermat–Torricelli problem, it matches the fair value of the replicating portfolio and the fair value of liabilities under an additional rather weak assumption. We also prove that the objective function is uniformly convex in practical problem instances (satisfying an additional assumption), a useful feature for optimization and statistical properties. Finally, we demonstrate that (RP_{CF}) can be equivalently cast as a second-order cone problem, which allows its unique solution to be obtained by efficient second-order methods like interior point methods (without the additional assumption satisfied in practical problems). Ultimately, we provide a discussion as to why problem (RP_{CF}) should be preferred over problems (RP_{SCF}) and $(RP_{\widetilde{TV}})$, and why not.

The rest of the paper is organized as follows. In Section 2, we introduce the mathematical setup for the financial market following Natolski and Werner [17], and we recall the cash flow matching problem of the Fermat–Torricelli type. The main Section 3 states and proves the aforementioned properties of the replication problem, and Section 4 concludes.

2. The Mathematical Setup

As mentioned in the introduction, this setup is taken from Natolski and Werner [17]. We fix a finite time horizon $T \in \mathbb{N}$ and set $\mathcal{T} := \{t = 1, 2, \ldots, T\}, \mathcal{T}_0 := \{0\} \cup \mathcal{T}$. Let $\left(\Omega, \mathcal{F}, (\mathcal{F}_t)_{t \in \mathcal{T}_0}, \mathbb{Q}\right)$ be a filtered probability space with risk-neutral[3] measure and numéraire $(N_t)_{t \in \mathcal{T}_0}$, where $\mathcal{F}_0$ is assumed to be complete and trivial and $\mathcal{F}_T = \mathcal{F}$. Denote by

1. $\tilde{\mathbf{C}}_t^F = \left(\tilde{C}_{i,t}^F\right)_{i=1,\ldots,m} \in \mathcal{L}^2(\mathbb{Q})^m$, $t \in \mathcal{T}$, the discounted[4] financial cash flows of all assets at time t, where $1 \le i \le m$ and m denotes the number of available financial assets,
2. $\tilde{\mathbf{A}}^F := \sum_{t \in \mathcal{T}} \tilde{\mathbf{C}}_t^F$ the vector of discounted terminal[5] financial cash flows,
3. $\tilde{C}_t^L \in \mathcal{L}^2(\mathbb{Q})$, $t \in \mathcal{T}$ the discounted liability cash flows, and by
4. $\tilde{A}^L := \sum_{t \in \mathcal{T}} \tilde{C}_t^L$, the discounted terminal value of liability cash flows.

The final cash flow $\tilde{C}_T^F$ is equal to the corresponding asset value. The interpretation is that all assets are sold at the time horizon T. Assets are bought and sold at time t *before* the time t cash flows take place.

The following three replication problems were considered in Natolski and Werner [18], where the first problem (RP_{CF}), cash flow matching, is in the focus of this exposition. In this context, a portfolio α represents the units of the financial instruments which have to be bought or sold.

$$\inf_{\alpha \in \mathbb{R}^m} \sum_{t=1}^{T} \left[\mathbb{E}^{\mathbb{Q}} \left(\left[\tilde{C}_t^L - \alpha^\top \tilde{\mathbf{C}}_t^F \right]^2 \middle| \mathcal{F}_0 \right) \right]^{\frac{1}{2}}. \tag{RP_{CF}}$$

$$\inf_{\alpha \in \mathbb{R}^m} \left[\sum_{t=1}^{T} \mathbb{E}^{\mathbb{Q}} \left(\left[\tilde{C}_t^L - \alpha^\top \tilde{\mathbf{C}}_t^F \right]^2 \middle| \mathcal{F}_0 \right) \right]^{\frac{1}{2}}. \tag{RP_{SCF}}$$

$$\inf_{\alpha \in \mathbb{R}^m} \left[\mathbb{E}^{\mathbb{Q}} \left(\left[\tilde{A}^L - \alpha^\top \tilde{\mathbf{A}}^F \right]^2 \middle| \mathcal{F}_0 \right) \right]^{\frac{1}{2}}. \tag{RP_{TV}}$$

The first formulation penalizes the deviation of cash flows by the $\mathcal{L}^2$-norm, whereas the second formulation penalizes the cash flows by the squared $\mathcal{L}^2$-norm. Otherwise, the formulations are the same. The third formulation (where the sum has moved inside the square inside the expected value) represents the penalized squared deviation of the terminal values.

Remark 1. *It has to be noted that there is no budget constraint in all three optimization problems, as the budget is not restricted, but allowed to vary freely. In Section 3.4, we will characterize the optimal budget, which is equal to the fair value of the replicating portfolio. It is shown there that the optimal budget equals the fair value of the liabilities under rather weak assumptions.*

---

[3] All results of this exposition remain true with one obvious exception: if instead of the risk neutral measure the real world measure is chosen. Naturally, the result on the fair value in Section 3.4 crucially depends on the property that a risk neutral measure is chosen.

[4] We use tilded variables to express the fact that the variable is discounted.

[5] $\tilde{\mathbf{A}}_i^F$ represents the pathwise discounted terminal value of all cash flows of asset i, i.e., the cash flow at time t is invested in the numeraire until time T, and the aggregated value of all these is discounted by the terminal numeraire value to time 0.

Remark 2. *In this context, an open issue concerning the formulation of the optimization problems is the relevance of the particular risk neutral measure chosen. Assuming that the probability space $(\Omega, \mathcal{F}, \mathbb{Q})$ cannot be partitioned into finitely many atoms, the market has to be incomplete, and there are infinitely many risk-neutral measures for each numéraire. Hence, one can choose from a variety of risk neutral measure/numéraire pairs $(\mathbb{Q}, (N_t)_{t=1,\dots,T})$ to construct replicating portfolios. Obviously, for fixed numéraire, the objective function in (RP_{CF}) depends on the specific choice of the risk neutral measure. Thus, the optimal solution (i.e., the replicating portfolio) depends on this risk neutral measure. Similarly, the fair value of both the liability and the replicating portfolio also depend on the choice of the risk neutral measure. Only in the special case of perfect replication (i.e., optimal objective value of 0) is there no dependence on the choice of the measure. As all risk neutral measures for some numéraire are equivalent, the same (unique) replicating portfolio is optimal for all such measures.*

In practice, a natural measure to use in the objective function is the real-world measure. It is well-known (see for example Korn and Schäl [22]) that the real-world measure becomes a martingale measure if the numéraire is chosen as the portfolio process maximizing the logarithmic utility function. Then, the real world measure $\mathbb{P}$ is a martingale measure with numéraire given by the maximizing portfolio process. This way, one can avoid the discussion on the choice of the risk neutral measure and simply use the real world measure together with portfolio process $(\pi_t^*)_{t=1,\dots,T}$ as numéraire.

Unfortunately, this approach is usually not followed in practical settings. The main reason is probably twofold: first, in practice, insurance companies are provided with economic scenario generators (ESG) tools which readily yield risk neutral scenarios for arbitrary numéraires (usually the cash rollup). Second, due to the linear nature of real world scenarios provided by these ESG tools, the utility maximizing portfolio process cannot be calculated due to the missing nested scenario structure.

For further analysis, let us introduce the symmetric matrices

$$Q_t^{\mathrm{SCF}} := \mathbb{E}^{\mathbb{Q}}\left[\left(\tilde{\mathbf{C}}_t^F\right)\left(\tilde{\mathbf{C}}_t^F\right)^\top \middle| \mathcal{F}_0\right],$$

$$Q^{\mathrm{SCF}} := \sum_{t=1}^{T} Q_t^{\mathrm{SCF}}, \text{ and}$$

$$Q^{\mathrm{TV}} := \mathbb{E}^{\mathbb{Q}}\left[\left(\tilde{\mathbf{A}}_i^F \tilde{\mathbf{A}}_j^F\right) \middle| \mathcal{F}_0\right]_{i,j=1,\dots,m}$$

These matrices represent the covariance matrices of the terminal values and the cash flows, respectively. They will play an important role in formulations of (weak) assumptions on the financial market. To obtain existence and uniqueness results (and more), the following few rather weak assumptions will have to be made. These are usually satisfied if financial assets for replication are chosen accordingly. **Assumption 1.** The matrix Q^{SCF} is positive definite or equivalently

$$\nexists u \in \mathbb{R}^m \setminus \{0\} : \forall t = 1, \dots, T : \left(\tilde{\mathbf{C}}_t^F\right)^\top u = 0.$$

Assumption 2. The matrix Q^{TV} is positive definite or equivalently

$$\nexists u \in \mathbb{R}^m \setminus \{0\} : \left(\sum_{t=1}^{T} \tilde{\mathbf{C}}_t^F\right)^\top u = 0.$$

Assumption 3. The numéraire is replicable at any time; that is,

$$\exists u \in \mathbb{R}^m : \forall t = 1, \dots, T : u^\top \tilde{\mathbf{C}}_t^F = 1.$$

Assumption 3 can be easily[6] fulfilled, taking into account that the numéraire is a tradable instrument itself. For any choice of the numéraire, one simply has to provide T financial instruments as follows: for each time t, we add an option on the numéraire to the market with strike 0 and maturity t. Equivalently, this can be seen as an asset which costs N_0 today (today's price of the numéraire) and yields a cash flow of N_t at time t. A proper combination of these options then yields the desired portfolio u as in Assumption 3. Of course, Assumption 3 is only necessary if cash flow matching is considered; for terminal value matching, it is sufficient to include exactly one of these options.

For problems (RP_{SCF}) and (RP_{TV}), the following two properties have been shown in Natolski and Werner [18]:

(1) The solutions to (RP_{SCF}) and (RP_{TV}) exist and under Assumption 1 (Assumption 2 , respectively) they are unique; i.e., there exist unique $\alpha_{\text{opt}}^{\text{SCF}}, \alpha_{\text{opt}}^{\text{TV}} \in \mathbb{R}^m$ such that

$$\alpha_{\text{opt}}^{\text{SCF}} = \underset{\alpha\in\mathbb{R}^m}{\operatorname{argmin}} \left[\sum_{t=1}^{T} \mathbb{E}^{\mathbb{Q}} \left(\left[\tilde{C}_t^L - \alpha^\top \tilde{\mathbf{C}}_t^F \right]^2 \middle| \mathcal{F}_0 \right) \right]^{\frac{1}{2}}$$

$$\alpha_{\text{opt}}^{\text{TV}} = \underset{\alpha\in\mathbb{R}^m}{\operatorname{argmin}} \left[\mathbb{E}^{\mathbb{Q}} \left(\left[\tilde{A}^L - \alpha^\top \tilde{\mathbf{A}}^F \right]^2 \middle| \mathcal{F}_0 \right) \right]^{\frac{1}{2}}.$$

(2) Under Assumption 3 , the fair values of both optimal replicating portfolios equal the fair value of liability cash flows; that is:

$$\mathbb{E}^{\mathbb{Q}} \left(\left(\alpha_{\text{opt}}^{\text{SCF}} \right)^\top \tilde{\mathbf{A}}^F \middle| \mathcal{F}_0 \right) = \mathbb{E}^{\mathbb{Q}} \left(\left(\alpha_{\text{opt}}^{\text{TV}} \right)^\top \tilde{\mathbf{A}}^F \middle| \mathcal{F}_0 \right) = \mathbb{E}^{\mathbb{Q}} \left(\tilde{A}^L \middle| \mathcal{F}_0 \right).$$

For existence and uniqueness, the proofs exploit the convex quadratic structure of the two problems. Both replicating portfolios can be written as solutions to quadratic problems, and under the assumption of no redundant assets, the corresponding quadratic matrices are positive definite. Equality of fair values can then be deduced directly from the corresponding optimality conditions.

So far, problem (RP_{CF}) has not been analyzed on the same level of detail. As pointed out in Natolski and Werner [18], its close connection to the Fermat–Torricelli problem (c.f. Nam [23]) gives strong evidence that on the one hand, existence and uniqueness of a solution is provided, whereas on the other hand, equality of fair values cannot be expected in all cases.

In what follows, we give a detailed proof of the existence and uniqueness of a solution based on the above assumptions. We also show that the optimal replicating portfolio indeed has the same fair value as the liability cash flows under surprisingly weak additional conditions. Further, we prove that for realistic problem instances (i.e., under certain additional assumptions), the numerical solution of (RP_{CF}) can be obtained by efficient standard second-order methods like Newton's method. Going one step further, we provide a reformulation as a linear second order cone program and thus demonstrate that these additional assumptions are actually not necessary to allow for efficient numerical solution by efficient second-order methods. Based on these novel insights, we will argue that (RP_{CF}) ranks at least equal to the two alternative formulations for practical problem instances.

[6] Let us note that in Theorem 4 we will need a somewhat stronger condition; however, this condition can be satisfied exactly along the same lines as Assumption 3 , and can thus also be characterized as rather weak condition.

3. Properties of RP_{CF}

Before we start to provide the results, we need a few technical preparations. Let us define:

$$\varphi(\alpha) := \sum_{t=1}^{T} \varphi_t(\alpha), \text{ with}$$

$$\varphi_t(\alpha) := \left[\mathbb{E}^{\mathbb{Q}}\left(\left[\tilde{C}_t^L - \alpha^\top \tilde{\mathbf{C}}_t^F\right]^2 \middle| \mathcal{F}_0\right)\right]^{\frac{1}{2}} = \left\| \underbrace{\tilde{C}_t^L - \alpha^\top \tilde{\mathbf{C}}_t^F}_{=:\epsilon_t(\alpha)} \right\|_{L^2},$$

so that we may rewrite problem (RP_{CF}) as

$$\inf_{\alpha \in \mathbb{R}^m} \quad \varphi(\alpha).$$

It is easily seen that each φ_t (and thus the objective function φ as well) is convex on the whole $\mathbb{R}^m$. As all φ_t are finite on $\mathbb{R}^m$, they are thus also (locally Lipschitz) continuous. Their directional derivatives in direction d are given by

$$\varphi'(\alpha, d) = \sum_{t=1}^{T} \varphi_t'(\alpha, d), \text{ with}$$

$$\varphi_t'(\alpha, d) = \begin{cases} \|d^\top \tilde{\mathbf{C}}_t^F\|_{L^2}, & \text{if } \varphi_t(\alpha) = 0 \\ \dfrac{\mathbb{E}^{\mathbb{Q}}\left(-\epsilon_t(\alpha) \cdot d^\top \tilde{\mathbf{C}}_t^F \middle| \mathcal{F}_0\right)}{\|\epsilon_t(\alpha)\|_{L^2}} = d^\top \nabla \varphi_t(\alpha), & \text{else.} \end{cases}$$

If φ_t is differentiable, then

$$\nabla \varphi_t(\alpha) = \frac{\mathbb{E}^{\mathbb{Q}}\left(-\epsilon_t(\alpha) \cdot \tilde{\mathbf{C}}_t^F \middle| \mathcal{F}_0\right)}{\|\epsilon_t(\alpha)\|_{L^2}}.$$

Obviously, if φ_t is (continuously) differentiable in a point α, it is also twice continuously differentiable there. Its Hessian is given as

$$\nabla^2 \varphi_t(\alpha) = \frac{\|\epsilon_t(\alpha)\|_{L^2}^2 \, \mathbb{E}^{\mathbb{Q}}\left(\tilde{\mathbf{C}}_t^F \left(\tilde{\mathbf{C}}_t^F\right)^\top\right) - \mathbb{E}^{\mathbb{Q}}\left(\epsilon_t(\alpha) \cdot \tilde{\mathbf{C}}_t^F\right) \left(\mathbb{E}^{\mathbb{Q}}\left(\epsilon_t(\alpha) \cdot \tilde{\mathbf{C}}_t^F\right)\right)^\top}{\|\epsilon_t(\alpha)\|_{L^2}^3}. \tag{1}$$

As φ_t is convex, its Hessian is positive semidefinite. Unfortunately, it cannot be expected that the Hessian is positive definite due to potential rank deficits in $\mathbb{E}^{\mathbb{Q}}\left(\tilde{\mathbf{C}}_t^F \left(\tilde{\mathbf{C}}_t^F\right)^\top\right)$, plus a further rank deficit of at most one (due to the dyadic term in the nominator).

3.1. Existence of Optimal Solution

We begin by showing that a solution to (RP_{CF}) exists in the first place.

Theorem 1. *Under Assumption 1 , problem (RP_{CF}) possesses at least one optimal solution α_{opt}^{CF}.*

Proof. As already observed, φ is convex and continuous. Furthermore, φ is also coercive[7]. To see this, denote by $\lambda_{\min}^{\text{SCF}}$ the smallest eigenvalue of the matrix Q^{SCF}. Due to Assumption 1 , $\lambda_{\min}^{\text{SCF}} > 0$, and we obtain

$$\lambda_{\min}^{\text{SCF}} \|\alpha\|_2 \leq \sqrt{\lambda_{\min}^{\text{SCF}} \cdot \alpha^\top Q^{\text{SCF}} \alpha} = \sqrt{\lambda_{\min}^{\text{SCF}}} \cdot \mathbb{E}^{\mathbb{Q}} \left(\sum_{t=1}^{T} \left[\alpha^\top \tilde{\mathbf{C}}_t^F \right]^2 \middle| \mathcal{F}_0 \right)^{\frac{1}{2}}.$$

By Minkowski's inequality, it follows

$$\begin{aligned} \left[\mathbb{E}^{\mathbb{Q}} \left(\sum_{t=1}^{T} \left[\alpha^\top \tilde{\mathbf{C}}_t^F \right]^2 \middle| \mathcal{F}_0 \right) \right]^{\frac{1}{2}} &\leq \left[\mathbb{E}^{\mathbb{Q}} \left(\sum_{t=1}^{T} \left[\alpha^\top \tilde{\mathbf{C}}_t^F - \tilde{C}_t^L \right]^2 \middle| \mathcal{F}_0 \right) \right]^{\frac{1}{2}} \\ &+ \left[\mathbb{E}^{\mathbb{Q}} \left(\sum_{t=1}^{T} \left[\tilde{C}_t^L \right]^2 \middle| \mathcal{F}_0 \right) \right]^{\frac{1}{2}}. \end{aligned}$$

Finally, it holds

$$\begin{aligned} \left[\mathbb{E}^{\mathbb{Q}} \left(\sum_{t=1}^{T} \left[\alpha^\top \tilde{\mathbf{C}}_t^F - \tilde{C}_t^L \right]^2 \middle| \mathcal{F}_0 \right) \right]^{\frac{1}{2}} &\leq \left[T \cdot \max_{t \in \mathcal{T}} \mathbb{E}^{\mathbb{Q}} \left(\left[\alpha^\top \tilde{\mathbf{C}}_t^F - \tilde{C}_t^L \right]^2 \middle| \mathcal{F}_0 \right) \right]^{\frac{1}{2}} \\ &= \sqrt{T} \cdot \max_{t \in \mathcal{T}} \left[\mathbb{E}^{\mathbb{Q}} \left(\left[\alpha^\top \tilde{\mathbf{C}}_t^F - \tilde{C}_t^L \right]^2 \middle| \mathcal{F}_0 \right) \right]^{\frac{1}{2}} \\ &\leq \sqrt{T} \cdot \sum_{t=1}^{T} \left[\mathbb{E}^{\mathbb{Q}} \left(\left[\alpha^\top \tilde{\mathbf{C}}_t^F - \tilde{C}_t^L \right]^2 \middle| \mathcal{F}_0 \right) \right]^{\frac{1}{2}} \\ &= \sqrt{T} \cdot \varphi(\alpha). \end{aligned}$$

Therefore, in total we have

$$\lambda_{\min}^{\text{SCF}} \|\alpha\|_2 \leq \sqrt{\lambda_{\min}^{\text{SCF}}} \cdot \left(\sqrt{T} \cdot \varphi(\alpha) + \left[\mathbb{E}^{\mathbb{Q}} \left(\sum_{t=1}^{T} \left[\tilde{C}_t^L \right]^2 \middle| \mathcal{F}_0 \right) \right]^{\frac{1}{2}} \right), \tag{2}$$

so that in particular

$$\|\alpha\|_2 \to \infty \Longrightarrow \varphi(\alpha) \to \infty.$$

As a continuous convex and coercive function, φ attains its minimum, and we are finished. □

3.2. Uniqueness of Optimal Solution

Now, let us consider under which conditions we get uniqueness of the optimal replicating portfolio. Let us first consider the rather easy but practically most likely case that no liability cash flow at any time can be replicated:

Assumption 4.

$$\forall \alpha \in \mathbb{R}^m : \min_{t \in \mathcal{T}} \varphi_t(\alpha) > 0\,.$$

---

[7] A function $f : \mathbb{R}^m \mapsto \mathbb{R}$ is called coercive iff $f(x) \to +\infty$ whenever $\|x\| \to \infty$.

Under this assumption, φ is obviously twice continuously differentiable on the whole $\mathbb{R}^m$. In practice, Assumption 4 is usually fulfilled, since liability cash flows are not replicable at any time in the future. If it holds, one can easily show the following strong result.

Theorem 2. *Under Assumptions 1 and 4 , the objective function φ is strictly convex and twice continuously differentiable. Furthermore, it is strongly and uniformly convex on each compact subset of $\mathbb{R}^m$. Especially, the global minimum of φ is unique.*

Proof. Let $\alpha \in \mathbb{R}^m$ be arbitrary. As for each t, φ_t is twice continuously differentiable, and we can consider the Hessian $\nabla^2 \varphi_t(\alpha)$ (cf. (1)). As this Hessian is positive semi-definite, it holds that

$$\begin{aligned}\forall t \in \mathcal{T}, \forall x \in \mathbb{R}^m: \quad & x^\top \mathbb{E}^{\mathbb{Q}}\left(\epsilon_t(\alpha) \cdot \tilde{\mathbf{C}}_t^F\right) \mathbb{E}^{\mathbb{Q}}\left(\tilde{\mathbf{C}}_t^F \cdot \epsilon_t(\alpha)\right)^\top x \\ & \leq \|\epsilon_t(\alpha)\|_2^2 \, x^\top \mathbb{E}^{\mathbb{Q}}\left(\tilde{\mathbf{C}}_t^F \left(\tilde{\mathbf{C}}_t^F\right)^\top\right) x.\end{aligned}$$

As no φ_t vanishes, we have $\epsilon_t(\alpha) \neq 0$ for all t. Then, due to the Cauchy–Schwarz inequality, it holds that this inequality is strict for t if and only if $x^\top \tilde{\mathbf{C}}_t^F \neq 0$ and $\epsilon_t(\alpha)$ is not collinear with $x^\top \tilde{\mathbf{C}}_t^F$. Due to Assumption 1 , for each $x \neq 0$, there is at least one t_0 such that $x^\top \tilde{\mathbf{C}}_{t_0}^F \neq 0$. Now let us assume that $\epsilon_{t_0}(\alpha)$ is collinear to $x^\top \tilde{\mathbf{C}}_{t_0}^F$; i.e., let us assume that

$$\exists \lambda_0 \in \mathbb{R}: \ \lambda_0 x^\top \tilde{\mathbf{C}}_{t_0}^F = \epsilon_{t_0}(\alpha).$$

By definition of ϵ, this is equivalent to

$$\tilde{C}_{t_0}^L = (\lambda_0 x + \alpha)^\top \tilde{\mathbf{C}}_{t_0}^F.$$

However, this means that in t_0, the liability cash flow can be perfectly replicated, which is a contradiction to Assumption 4. Therefore, $\epsilon_{t_0}(\alpha)$ cannot be collinear to $x^\top \tilde{\mathbf{C}}_{t_0}^F$, and the above inequality is strict for each $x \neq 0$. Thus, the Hessian matrix of φ is positive definite, and as α was arbitrary, φ is strictly convex. The remaining claims are straightforward consequences. □

Remark 3. *In Görner and Kanzow [24], it is shown that for uniformly convex φ, Newton's method is globally quadratically convergent on any compact set. From inequality (2), we see that*

$$\{\alpha \in \mathbb{R}^m \mid \varphi(\alpha) \leq \varphi(0)\}$$

is compact and contains the optimal solution. Hence, if we restrict to the optimization on this set we know that Newton's method will be globally quadratically convergent.

Although for practical purposes the following result might not be as important as Theorem 2 (obtained under the stronger Assumption 4), there still remain some cases when Assumption 4 is violated. In particular, this includes all models where liability cash flows are predictable, for example, as in Grosen and Jørgensen [11]. In this more general case, it is still possible to show uniqueness of the optimal replicating portfolio. However, without Assumption 4 , strict convexity and smoothness of the objective function will be lost in general.

Theorem 3. *Under Assumption 1 , the global minimum of φ is unique.*

Proof. Let us assume that φ possesses (at least) two different global minima, called α_1 and α_2. Then, let us consider the midpoint

$$\alpha := \frac{1}{2}(\alpha_1 + \alpha_2),$$

which, due to convexity, has to be optimal as well. Due to the optimality of α, the directional derivative of $\varphi'(\alpha, d)$ has to vanish in all directions d, especially in direction $h := \alpha - \alpha_1$.

As φ is the sum of convex functions φ_t, α can only be optimal if all terms φ_t are linear in direction h (e.g., Nam [23] for the same argument). If $\varphi_t(\alpha) = 0$, this can only be the case if both $\varphi_t(\alpha_1) = 0 = \varphi_t(\alpha_2)$; otherwise, we would have a contradiction to the assumption that both α_1 and α_2 are optimal, and we are done. From $\varphi_t(\alpha_1) = 0 = \varphi_t(\alpha_2)$, it directly follows that h is such that $0 = h^\top \tilde{\mathbf{C}}_t^F$. If, alternatively, $\varphi_t(\alpha) > 0$, then the second derivative in direction h has to vanish for linearity. This can only happen if either $0 = h^\top \tilde{\mathbf{C}}_t^F$ or $h^\top \tilde{\mathbf{C}}_t^F$ is collinear to $\epsilon_t(\alpha)$. In the first case, the directional derivative of φ_t in direction h vanishes, whereas in the second case, we have that

$$\varphi_t'(\alpha, h) = |\lambda_0| \, \|\epsilon_t(\alpha)\|_{L^2} > 0$$

as $h^\top \tilde{\mathbf{C}}_t^F = \lambda_0 \epsilon_t(\alpha)$ for some $\lambda_0 \neq 0$ due to collinearity. So, for all t, we need to have $h^\top \tilde{\mathbf{C}}_t^F = 0$ for optimality. However, due to Assumption 1 , there is at least one t_0 such that $0 \neq h^\top \tilde{\mathbf{C}}_{t_0}^F$; thus, $h^\top \tilde{\mathbf{C}}_{t_0}^F$ has to be collinear to $\epsilon_{t_0}(\alpha)$, which shows that the directional derivative of φ does not vanish in direction h. This is a contradiction to our initial assumption, and we are done. □

In the general case without Assumption 4 , no first- or even second-order method can be used to directly solve the cash flow replication problem (RP_{CF}) due to potential non-smoothness of φ. However, we will show in the following that we can avoid this non-smoothness by an equivalent reformulation as a second-order cone program, which can then be solved by efficient second-order methods.

3.3. Reformulation as Second-Order Cone Program

Let us start with the unconstrained formulation of the cash flow replication problem

$$\min_{\alpha \in \mathbb{R}^m} \varphi(\alpha) = \min_{\alpha \in \mathbb{R}^m} \sum_{t=1}^{T} \varphi_t(\alpha),$$

and let us introduce auxiliary variables $\gamma_t \in \mathbb{R}$ for each term to obtain the obviously equivalent constrained formulation

$$\begin{aligned} &\min_{\substack{\alpha \in \mathbb{R}^m \\ \gamma \in \mathbb{R}^T}} \sum_{t=1}^{T} \gamma_t \\ &\text{subject to} \\ &\varphi_t(\alpha) \leq \gamma_t, \quad t = 1, \ldots, T. \end{aligned}$$

Now, we have

$$\begin{aligned} \varphi_t(\alpha) &= \left\| \tilde{C}_t^L - \alpha^\top \tilde{\mathbf{C}}_t^F \right\|_{L^2} = \left(\left\| \tilde{C}_t^L - \alpha^\top \tilde{\mathbf{C}}_t^F \right\|_{L^2}^2 \right)^{\frac{1}{2}} \\ &= \left(\begin{pmatrix} 1 \\ -\alpha \end{pmatrix}^\top \mathbb{E}^{\mathbb{Q}} \left[\begin{pmatrix} \tilde{C}_t^L \\ \tilde{\mathbf{C}}_t^F \end{pmatrix} \begin{pmatrix} \tilde{C}_t^L \\ \tilde{\mathbf{C}}_t^F \end{pmatrix}^\top \right] \begin{pmatrix} 1 \\ -\alpha \end{pmatrix} \right)^{\frac{1}{2}} \\ &= \left(\begin{pmatrix} 1 \\ -\alpha \end{pmatrix}^\top R_t^{\mathrm{SCF}} \begin{pmatrix} 1 \\ -\alpha \end{pmatrix} \right)^{\frac{1}{2}} \\ &= \left\| H_t^{\mathrm{SCF}} \begin{pmatrix} 1 \\ -\alpha \end{pmatrix} \right\|_2 , \end{aligned}$$

where

$$R_t^{\mathrm{SCF}} := \mathbb{E}^{\mathbb{Q}}\left[\begin{pmatrix}\tilde{C}_t^L \\ \tilde{\mathbf{C}}_t^F\end{pmatrix}\begin{pmatrix}\tilde{C}_t^L \\ \tilde{\mathbf{C}}_t^F\end{pmatrix}^\top\right]$$

and

$$H_t^{\mathrm{SCF}} := (R_t^{\mathrm{SCF}})^{\frac{1}{2}}$$

is the root matrix of the positive semi-definite matrix R_t^{SCF}. In summary, we obtain the linear second order cone program

$$\min_{\substack{\alpha\in\mathbb{R}^m \\ \gamma\in\mathbb{R}^T}} \sum_{t=1}^{T} \gamma_t$$

subject to

$$\left\| H_t^{\mathrm{SCF}} \begin{pmatrix} 1 \\ -\alpha \end{pmatrix} \right\|_2 \leq \gamma_t, \quad t = 1, \ldots, T,$$

which can be solved by efficient numerical methods with superlinear convergence (e.g., Alizadeh and Goldfarb [25]).

3.4. Fair Value of Optimal Solution

Finally, let us consider the equality of fair values. The standard Fermat–Torricelli problem as in Nam [23] is given by

$$\inf_{x\in\mathbb{R}^m} \sum_{t=1}^{T} \|x - a_t\|_2,$$

with $a \in \mathbb{R}^T$ and where $\|.\|_2$ denotes the standard Euclidean norm. In general, this problem does not entail optimality conditions which yield equality of means; i.e., in general,

$$x = \frac{1}{T}\sum_{t=1}^{T} x \neq \frac{1}{T}\sum_{t=1}^{T} a_t.$$

However, although the structure of (RP_{CF}) is very similar, there is a crucial difference. Instead of $x \in \mathbb{R}^m$ being fixed in each t, (RP_{CF}) allows some degree of freedom at each time t in the appearance of the time-dependent random variable $\alpha^\top \tilde{\mathbf{C}}_t^F$. In particular, we may assume that for any t we may trade an option today which has payoff equal to the numéraire at t and no payoff otherwise (i.e., call options on the numéraire with strike price 0 and maturity t). In the context of (RP_{CF}), this corresponds to the freedom of choosing the expectation of $\alpha^\top \tilde{\mathbf{C}}_t^F$ for each t individually. However, since (RP_{CF}) is nothing but a sum of optimization problems in $\mathcal{L}^2$, optimality conditions will yield that it is best to match expectations of $\alpha^\top \tilde{\mathbf{C}}_t^F$ and $\tilde{C}_t^L$. This observation is made precise in the following theorem.

Theorem 4. *Suppose that for any $c \in \mathbb{R}^T$ there exists $\beta \in \mathbb{R}^m$ such that*

$$\forall t \in \mathcal{T} : \beta^\top \tilde{\mathbf{C}}_t^F = c_t. \tag{3}$$

Then, any solution α_{opt}^{CF} to (RP_{CF}) satisfies

$$\mathbb{E}^{\mathbb{Q}}\left(\left(\alpha_{opt}^{CF}\right)^\top \tilde{\mathbf{A}}^F \middle| \mathcal{F}_0\right) = \mathbb{E}^{\mathbb{Q}}\left(\tilde{A}^L \middle| \mathcal{F}_0\right).$$

Proof. Condition (3) implies that for any $\bar{t} \in \mathcal{T}$ there exists $\beta_{\bar{t}} \in \mathbb{R}^m$ such that

$$\beta_{\bar{t}}^\top \tilde{\mathbf{C}}_t^F = \begin{cases} 1, & t = \bar{t} \\ 0, & t \neq \bar{t} \end{cases} .$$

By examining the directional derivatives of the objective function φ in (RP_{CF}) with respect to the direction $\beta_{\bar{t}}$, we see that all but the $\bar{t}$'th summand disappear:

$$\varphi'(\alpha, \beta_{\bar{t}}) = \varphi'_{\bar{t}}(\alpha, \beta_{\bar{t}}).$$

As $\alpha_{\text{opt}}^{\text{CF}}$ is an unconstrained minimum of a convex function, this requires that all directional derivatives are non-negative, especially the ones in directions of $\pm\beta_{\bar{t}}$. If $\varphi_t(\alpha_{\text{opt}}^{\text{CF}}) = 0$ we do not need to inspect the directional derivative, as in this case the cash flow at time $\bar{t}$ is exactly replicated and thus the fair values of these cash flows are equal. Therefore, let us consider the case $\varphi_t(\alpha_{\text{opt}}^{\text{CF}}) \neq 0$. Then, considering both $\pm\beta_{\bar{t}}$, this means that

$$\mathbb{E}^{\mathbb{Q}}\left(- \left[\tilde{C}_{\bar{t}}^L - \alpha^\top \tilde{\mathbf{C}}_{\bar{t}}^F \right] \beta_{\bar{t}}^\top \tilde{\mathbf{C}}_{\bar{t}}^F \middle| \mathcal{F}_0 \right) = 0$$

and thus

$$\mathbb{E}^{\mathbb{Q}}\left(\left[\tilde{C}_{\bar{t}}^L - \alpha^\top \tilde{\mathbf{C}}_{\bar{t}}^F \right] \middle| \mathcal{F}_0 \right) = 0 .$$

As $\bar{t} \in \mathcal{T}$ was chosen arbitrarily, this shows that the fair value of cash flows is in fact equal at any time. In particular, this obviously implies the claim. □

Remark 4. *As a matter of fact, the observation that some degree of freedom becomes available through time dependence of $\alpha^\top \tilde{\mathbf{A}}_t^F$ has already been made in Natolski and Werner [18] in Subsection "Time-separable case". There it was demonstrated that in the case where cash payments are generated at each time separately, (RP_{CF}) and (RP_{SCF}) are equivalent. In particular, fair values of the replicating portfolios are the same and equal to the fair value of liability cash flows. Going one step further, Theorem 4 now illustrates that for matching fair values it is already sufficient if cash payments equal to the numéraire can be generated at each time separately. This can be considered a rather weak condition, which is usually fulfilled in practical settings if the replication instruments are chosen accordingly.*

3.5. Pros and Cons of (RP_{CF}) versus (RP_{SCF}) and $(RP_{\tilde{TV}})$

So far, problem (RP_{CF}) has not received much attention amongst practitioners. The reasons for this are manifold:

1. Problems (RP_{SCF}) and $(RP_{\tilde{TV}})$ possess analytical solutions. Thus, the replicating portfolio can be obtained by simple numerical linear algebra, and no optimization framework is needed.
2. Problems (RP_{SCF}) and $(RP_{\tilde{TV}})$ possess unique solutions with fair values equal to the liability fair value.
3. Problem (RP_{CF}) potentially represents a non-smooth problem, and thus cannot be solved efficiently.

In the above analysis, we have shown that all other reasons besides the first one go up in smoke after a detailed investigation of (RP_{CF}). From a theoretical point of view (see for example Natolski and Werner [17]), terminal value matching should be preferred over cash flow matching, as it yields lower error estimates on the resulting risk capital figure. However, numerous numerical studies have shown that the out-of-sample performance of cash flow matched replicating portfolios is superior to terminal value matched portfolios. Further, if one is interested in matching the cash flow profile (and not only risk capital), then cash flow matching is (almost) inevitable. From this point of view, (RP_{SCF}) should be clearly preferred.

However, due to the long maturity of life insurance contracts (usual models range from 40 to 60 years final maturity), numerical issues cannot be avoided. Usually, the matching error of certain maturities significantly dominates all other maturities. In this case, only the dominating maturities are properly matched. From a statistical point of view (robust statistics, robust least squares), it is well known that this can be partially mitigated if one moves from the square of the L^2-norm to the L^2-norm itself (i.e., if a kind of Fermat–Torricelli structure is chosen). From that perspective, (RP_{CF}) might indeed represent the formulation which leads to the most stable portfolios with satisfying out-of-sample performance. To support such a hypothesis, a thorough numerical analysis is strongly indicated—however, this is clearly beyond the scope of this contribution and is thus left for future research.

4. Conclusions

We picked up on the replication problems presented in Natolski and Werner [18]. Therein, for (RP_{SCF}) and ($RP_{\widetilde{TV}}$), existence and uniqueness results as well as the matching of the fair value of liabilities have been provided. In this contribution, similar results are shown for (RP_{CF}), and we also prove further structural results on this problem. We especially show that it possesses a unique solution under weak assumptions. Furthermore, we supplement Natolski and Werner [18] by showing that the optimal replicating portfolio indeed has the same fair value as liabilities under additional rather weak assumptions. Finally, we also provided a reformulation of (RP_{CF}) as an SOCP for efficient numerical solution. In case an additional assumption holds, (RP_{CF}) can be solved directly by Newton's method, thus rendering the solution of (RP_{CF}) as efficient as for (RP_{SCF}) and ($RP_{\widetilde{TV}}$). Finally we have provided a discussion on the pros and cons of each formulation, which shows that the best formulation still remains to be found.

Author Contributions: The authors, Jan Natolski and RalfWerner, contributed equally to this research paper.

Conflicts of Interest: The authors declare no conflict of interest.

References

1. Bauer, D.; Bergmann, D.; Kiesel, R. On the Risk-Neutral Valuation of Life Insurance Contracts with Numerical Methods in View. *Astin Bull.* **2010**, *40*, 65–95.
2. Andreatta, G.; Corradin, S. *Fair Value of Life Liabilities with Embedded Options: An Application to a Portfolio of Italian Insurance Policies*; Working Paper; 2003.
3. Baione, F.; De Angelis, P.; Fortunati, A. On a Fair Value Model for Participating Life Insurance Policies. *Invest. Manag. Financ. Innov.* **2006**, *3*, 408–421.
4. Glasserman, P.; Yu, B. Simulation for American Options: Regression now or Regression later. In *Monte Carlo and Quasi-Monte Carlo Methods 2002*; Springer: Berlin/Heidelberg, Germany, 2004; pp. 213–226.
5. Stentoft, L. Convergence of the Least Squares Monte Carlo Approach to American Option Valuation. *Manag. Sci.* **2004**, *50*, 1193–1203.
6. Longstaff, F.; Schwartz, E. Valuing American Options By Simulation: A Simple Least-Squares Approach. *Rev. Financ. Stud.* **2001**, *14*, 113–147.
7. Tsitsiklis, J.; van Roy, B. Regression Methods for Pricing Complex American-style Options. *IEEE Trans. Neural Netw.* **2001**, *12*, 694–703.
8. Bergmann, D. *Nested Simulations in Life Insurance*; Institute of Financial Accountants: London, UK, 2011.
9. Broadie, M.; Glasserman, P. A Stochastic Mesh Method for Pricing high-dimensional American Options. *J. Comput. Financ.* **2004**, *7*, 35–72.
10. Pelsser, A. Pricing and Hedging Guaranteed Annuity Options via Static Option Replication. *Insur. Math. Econ.* **2003**, *33*, 283–296.
11. Grosen, A.; Jørgensen, P. Fair Valuation of Life Insurance Liabilities: The Impact of Interest Rate Guarantees, Surrender Options, and Bonus Policies. *Insur. Math. Econ.* **2000**, *26*, 37–57.

12. Europäische Aufsichtsbehörde für das Versicherungswesen und die betriebliche Altersversorgung (EIOPA). *The Underlying Assumptions in the Standard Formula for the Solvency Capital Requirement Calculation*; EIOPA: Frankfurt, Germany, 2014.
13. Beutner, E.; Pelsser, A.; Schweizer, J. *Theory and Validation of Replicating Portfolios in Insurance Risk Management*; Verfügbar auf SSRN 2557368; Social Science Research Network: 2015.
14. Pelsser, A.; Schweizer, J. *The Difference between LSMC and Replicating Portfolio in Insurance Liability Modeling*; Verfügbar auf SSRN 2557383; Social Science Research Network: 2015.
15. Beutner, E.; Pelsser, A.; Schweizer, J. *Fast Convergence of Regress-Later Estimates in Least Squares Monte Carlo*; Verfügbar auf SSRN 2328709; Social Science Research Network: 2013.
16. Cambou, M.; Filipovic, D. *Replicating Portfolio Approach to Capital Calculation*; Verfügbar auf SSRN 2763733; Social Science Research Network: 2016.
17. Natolski, J.; Werner, R. *Mathematical Foundation of the Replicating Portfolio Approach*; Verfügbar auf SSRN 2771254; Social Science Research Network: 2016.
18. Natolski, J.; Werner, R. Mathematical Analysis of different Approaches for Replicating Portfolios. *Eur. Actuar. J.* **2014**, *4*, 411–435.
19. Broadie, M.; Du, Y.; Moallemi, C. Risk Estimation via Regression. *Oper. Res.* **2015**, *63*, 1077–1097.
20. Oechslin, J.; Aubry, O.; Aellig, M.; Kappeli, A.; Bronnimann, D.; Tandonnet, A.; Valois, G. Replicating Embedded Options in Life Insurance Policies. *Life Pensions Risk* **2007**, 47–52.
21. Daul, S.; Vidal, E. Replication of Insurance Liabilities. *RiskMetrics* **2009**, *9*, 79–96.
22. Korn, R.; Schäl, M. On Value Preserving and Growth Optimal Portfolios. *Math. Methods Oper. Res.* **1999**, *50*, 189–218.
23. Nam, M. The Fermat-Torricelli Problem in the Light of Convex Analysis. *arXiv* **2013**, arXiv 1302.5244.
24. Görner, S.; Kanzow, C. On Newoton's Method for the Fermat-Weber Location Problem. *Optim. Theory Appl.* **2016**, *107*, 107–118.
25. Alizadeh, F.; Goldfarb, D. Second-Order Cone Programming. *Math. Program.* **2003**, *95*, 3–51.

MDPI AG
St. Alban-Anlage 66
4052 Basel, Switzerland
Tel. +41 61 683 77 34
Fax +41 61 302 89 18
http://www.mdpi.com

Risks Editorial Office
E-mail: risks@mdpi.com
http://www.mdpi.com/journal/risks

www.ingramcontent.com/pod-product-compliance
Lightning Source LLC
Chambersburg PA
CBHW041218220326
41597CB00033BA/6008